MACROECONOMIC MEDIUM-TERM MODELS
IN THE NORDIC COUNTRIES

CONTRIBUTIONS
TO
ECONOMIC ANALYSIS

164

Honorary Editor:
J. TINBERGEN

Editors:
D. W. JORGENSON
J. WAELBROECK

NORTH-HOLLAND
AMSTERDAM · NEW YORK · OXFORD · TOKYO

MACROECONOMIC MEDIUM-TERM MODELS IN THE NORDIC COUNTRIES

Edited by:

O. BJERKHOLT

Central Bureau of Statistics
Oslo, Norway

and

J. ROSTED

Ministry of Finance
Copenhagen, Denmark

1987

NORTH-HOLLAND
AMSTERDAM · NEW YORK · OXFORD · TOKYO

ISBN: 0 444 70262 8

Publishers:
ELSEVIER SCIENCE PUBLISHERS B.V.
P.O. Box 1991
1000 BZ Amsterdam
The Netherlands

Sole distributors for the U.S.A. and Canada:
ELSEVIER SCIENCE PUBLISHING COMPANY, INC.
52 Vanderbilt Avenue
New York, N.Y. 10017
U.S.A.

PRINTED IN THE NETHERLANDS

Introduction to the Series

This series consists of a number of hitherto unpublished studies, which are introduced by the editors in the belief that they represent fresh contributions to economic science.

The terms 'economic analysis' as used in the title of the series has been adopted because it covers both the activities of the theoretical economist and the research worker.

Although the analytical methods used by the various contributors are not the same, they are nevertheless conditioned by the common origin of their studies, namely theoretical problems encountered in practical research. Since for this reason, business cycle research and national accounting, research work on behalf of economic policy, and problems of planning are the main sources of the subjects dealt with, they necessarily determine the manner of approach adopted by the authors. Their methods tend to be 'practical' in the sense of not being too far remote from application to actual economic conditions. In addition they are quantitative rather than qualitative.

It is the hope of the editors that the publication of these studies will help to stimulate the exchange of scientific information and to reinforce international cooperation in the field of economics.

The Editors

Preface

This book is the first joint presentation of macroeconomic medium-term models of the four Nordic countries: Denmark, Finland, Norway and Sweden. The book is based on papers that were originally presented at the "Seminar on Macroeconomic Modelling in the Nordic Countries" held at Fredriksdal, Lyngby, Denmark in October 1984. The seminar was sponsored by the four Nordic Ministries of Finance whose generous support for editing this book is appreciated.

Two of the papers included have been published earlier in the journal *Economic Modelling*. We are most grateful to the editor of that journal and to Butterworth Scientific Limited for granting us permission to include Juha Tarkka's "Monetary Policy in the BOF3 – A Quarterly Model of the Finnish Economy", originally published in *Economic Modelling*, volume 2, and (in a slightly abbreviated version) Poul Uffe Dam's "The Danish Macroeconomic Model ADAM" published originally in volume 3 of *Economic Modelling*.

Olav Bjerkholt and Jørgen Rosted

Oslo and Copenhagen, 1987

Contents

Macroeconomic Medium-Term Models in the Nordic Countries
O. Bjerkholt and J. Rosted (Editors)
© Elsevier Science Publishers B. V. (North-Holland), 1987

Traditions in Nordic Macroeconomic Modelling

by

Olav Bjerkholt and Jørgen Rosted

Central Bureau of Statistics, Oslo, Norway

and

Ministry of Finance, Copenhagen, Denmark

This book aims at presenting the main models currently in use for government medium-term policy purposes in Denmark, Finland, Norway and Sweden.[1] The models are known as ADAM in Denmark, KESSU in Finland, MODAG in Norway and EMMA in Sweden. The book focuses on the structure of these models and on what they have to say about the function and characteristics of the respective economies in terms of multipliers, dynamic properties, etc. In addition supplementary papers on application of these models, on other models in use and on related issues are also presented. The book does not aim to discuss the full range of model tools used by the Nordic governments, nor does it offer justice to macroeconomic modelling efforts outside government. In the Nordic countries, macroeconomic modelling efforts aimed at establishing operational models for use in forecasting and policy analysis have been dominated by government related projects, although a number of non-governmental and often university based modelling projects — mostly on a small scale — have been launched

---

[1] The Nordic countries comprise Denmark, Finland, Iceland, Norway and Sweden. In the context of this book Iceland has become totally disregarded simply because its small size (250,000 inhabitants), limited resources and special economic structure have led it to give priority to economic research in other directions than towards national macroeconomic model building. Scandinavia — in distinction to the Nordic countries — excludes Finland (and Iceland).

over the years. Comparatively few non-governmental institutions in these countries have established and maintained such models over time.

To the rest of the world the Nordic countries are rather similar small open economies with a high level of income per capita and a well-developed welfare state. The four countries, however, are not quite as similar as it might seem. Their endowments of natural resources are quite different and this fact together with differences in their economic development account for marked differences in economic structure. Sweden, twice the size of the other countries, has by far the most advanced industrial structure with its high quality steel products, machine tools, weapons industry, cars, etc. Denmark is the only country which relies on agricultural exports for a considerable part of foreign earnings, Finland is still in transition towards becoming an advanced industrialized country, while Norway in recent years has had a shrinking industrial sector coupled with expanding raw materials export, foremost crude oil and natural gas.

The four countries have similarities as well as differences with regard to social structure and political system. Despite close political relations over many years the countries have chosen different international economic and military affiliations. Only one of the four countries is a member of the European Community, whereas two of the four are members of the NATO alliance.

In the field of macroeconomic modelling one can also note similarities as well as differences. Differences in political tradition and in the stability of viable parliamentary majorities may partially explain why, for example, Norway introduced large-scale models in economic policy-making many years ahead of Denmark. The presence of strong academic proponents of modelling, such as the late professor Ragnar Frisch, has certainly played a role. The need for models as a tool for government planning may have been experienced differently in different countries. In Norway and Finland this need may have been present in the early post war period to a higher degree than in Denmark and Sweden. In recent years the contact between the modelling environment in the four countries, in particular between the four Ministries of Finance, have certainly led to an increased exchange of ideas and experiences. To what extent these influences have had an impact on the national model building is not easy to assess, but some such influences can be discerned.

One such influence is the Scandinavian model of inflation, originated by Aukrust [1970, 1977]. Known in Norway as the "Aukrust model" and in Sweden as the EFO-model after Edgren et al. [1970]), the Scandinavian model of inflation has been adopted as a convenient paradigm for macroeconomic analysis in all four Nordic countries. While the original Aukrust conception, which the originator traces back to ideas he propounded in the mid-1950s, was based on a clear-cut dichotomy between sheltered and exposed industries, the current version of this idea is more a matter of degree in "exposedness" of industries. Elements of the Scandinavian model of inflation are found in the models of all four countries, and particularly in the Norwegian and Finnish ones.

Another common feature is the reliance upon an input-output structure as the core of the model. Norway pioneered the construction and use of input-output tables in the Nordic countries and is one of the few countries with complete input-output tables for every year since 1949. Frisch was a pioneer in the development of principles of national accounting. By 1930 he had already sketched some conceptual outlines, and this topic became a recurrent theme in his research (see Bjerve [1986]). In the mid-1930s he also developed some ideas of planning systems using methods related to Leontief's input-output tables, tables which had yet to appear. The practical task of establishing the Norwegian national accounting system was to a great extent due to Aukrust.

The influence of Frisch was not limited to national accounts, however. His importance for macroeconomic modelling in Norway can hardly be overestimated. Frisch had been a professor of economics since 1931. He had a strong mathematical and statistical background, which resulted in early econometric work, and he was a founding member of the Econometric Society. Before the war he showed an early interest in macroeconomics and the causes of depression, and he introduced Norwegian politicians to Keynes' ideas of aggregate demand management. After the war Frisch ran the Institute of Economics at the University of Oslo for many years as a laboratory of macroeconomic modelling and he became the father figure for several generations of Norwegian economists.

Frisch grasped at an early stage the importance of the new approach to macroeconomic analysis developed before World War II by J.M. Keynes and others in England and by the Swedish economists and integrated these ideas into his own works. His interest in planning as a remedy to relieve the industrial economy from the misery of depression and unemployment dates from this period. For a long time after World War II his main field of research was macroeconomic models, which he tried to build in an ambitiously large-scale fashion even though data sources were scanty and computers unavailable. His first exercise of this kind was a disequilibrium model developed in 1948 for United Nations' Commission on Employment and Economic Stability, followed by a series of various types of models developed in the 1950s and early 1960s. This work is briefly surveyed in Johansen [1969]. Frisch during this period was far ahead of his time with regard to the actual application of models both in Norway and elsewhere. Some of his simpler models from this period became prototypes of models later developed for practical use in Norway. As noted by Blaug [1985], characteristic of much of Frisch's work is that so much remained unpublished, circulated only as memoranda from the Institute of Economics, University of Oslo, and thus little known outside a limited circle.

Still another common feature of Nordic economic modelling is the use of general equilibrium models of a similar type for long-term macroeconomic analysis. The origin of this tradition is the MSG model, which originated as the doctoral thesis of the late professor Leif Johansen in 1958 (Johansen [1960, 1974]). MSG was put to use by the Ministry of Finance in the late 1960s and has in successive versions been in use ever since. Leif Johansen's model was one of the first examples of models that are now referred to in the international literature as computable general equilibrium (CGE) models and turned out to be a most seminal contribution. In some countries this class of models is referred to as the "Johansen type" model.

The MSG model has been applied in Norway to outline growth perspectives 15–20 years ahead by means of a general equilibrium framework emphasizing the substitution of production factors over time, technological progress and the calculation of equilibrium prices supporting a growth path. MSG has gained increasing importance as long-term issues have become more important in the Norwegian economy. The emergence of Norway as an oil-rich nation has lengthened the horizon of the macroeconomic perspective. Just as the use of the MODIS model has served to integrate short and medium-term policy of different areas, the use of the MSG model has served to coordinate the development and policy issues of different sectors in a long-term perspective.

Models similar to MSG have later been developed in the other Nordic countries, to a considerable extent directly influenced by Leif Johansen's work. In Sweden a model very similar to the original Johansen model has been used by the Ministry of Finance for more than ten years (Restad [1976]). Both in Sweden, Norway and Denmark MSG type models have been of great importance in analysing long-term energy policy issues (see, e.g., Bergman [1978], Bjerkholt et al. [1982]). There is also a similar Finnish model developed by Maenpää. MSG and related models thus play a major role in the Nordic countries, but they are not discussed further in this book. The current status of Johansen's MSG model and a survey of its impact on model development in other countries are presented in Førsund et al. [1985].

With respect to the organisation of model building for government purposes the four countries have found somewhat different solutions. In Norway the model builder for the government is the Central Bureau of Statistics, which has played a role in Norway with regard to model building and econometric work similar to that of INSEE in France but rather different from most central statistical institutions. The model building of the Central Bureau of Statistics started in the 1950s in direct continuation of the national accounting and input-output analyses. While Norway has favoured the Bureau of Statistics as the model building institution for the government, separate and sheltered from the day-to-day tasks of the Ministry of Finance, Sweden and Finland have had most of their model development carried on inside the Ministries of Finance. Denmark, as a latecomer, has followed the Norwegian lead and let the Danish Central Statistical Office be in charge of running the medium-term model.

Among the four Nordic countries Norway has the longest tradition in construction and use of macroeconomic models, stretching back to the early postwar period. The origin of this tradition can be sought in the conscious political efforts to develop a planning system for a mixed economy that could cope with the reconstruction problems and the expected postwar depression, and in a longer perspective lay a secure foundation for full employment and economic growth. The Norwegian government pursued a determined effort to develop a planning system called "national budgeting", a term coined by Frisch, the overall framework of which can be simply explained as budgeting the nation's economy in national accounting terms.

The first operational model put into regular use in Norway by the government administration appeared around 1960 and was named MODIS. This model has survived in successive versions and is still, as MODIS IV, the most important model tool in Norwegian macroeconomic short-term planning (Bjerkholt and Longva [1980]). The MODIS model is an input-output model in prices and quantities with an extremely detailed treatment of the government sector. Apart from private consumption there is little economic behaviour represented in the model. The model is to a great extent designed to operate within a government administration and serves as a tool to collect and organize information as much as to serve as a macroeconomic model in a strict sense. The MODAG model for the Norwegian economy presented in this volume is a successor to the MODIS model. It is less disaggregate (MODIS specifies 200 commodities and 150 industries, MODAG has around 25–30 commodities and industries), but relies as MODIS on an input-output structure as the central core of the model.

This is a characteristic feature of the main models of all four countries.

The Norwegian medium-term model tradition originated in the post-war situation with its emphasis on shortages, rationing, trade restrictions and fear of depression. The political regime in Norway was an uncontested Labour parliamentary majority which lasted from 1945 well into the 1960s. The overall ideology was — and to a considerable extent still is — planned social and economic development with a high profile of government participation, contribution and responsibility in most economic areas. The MODIS model reflected the government ideology in its emphasis on the technical input-output relations as the only real restraints on the development of the economy.

The long-term development of accelerating growth rates of the Norwegian economy culminated in the early 1970s. The ensuing period has been dominated on the one hand by the discovery and exploitation of vast petroleum resources on Norwegian territory and on the other hand by the much more volatile developments of the world economy. The domestic economy was after a long period of high and stable growth rates unprepared for such abrupt changes, and this situation was exacerbated by the opposing influences of an oil bonanza which allowed an unbridled expansion of consumption, and the new austerity in economic policy among the European OECD countries. The long-serving MODIS model was by and large unfit for the task whether the problem was seen as one of incomes policy, as the need for a sectoral reallocation in a small open economy, as the functioning of the labour market or as concerning the interaction between the real and the financial sector. These considerations were all present when the MODAG model was conceived.

The main features of MODAG is set out by Cappelen and Longva who describe in more detail its relation to the MODIS model and the institutional context for which it is designed. The traditional demand driven input-output model of MODIS type has in MODAG been extended with more supply-oriented considerations, particularly in price setting. The Central Bureau of Statistics have also developed a quarterly model, KVARTS, which together with the Danish ADAM model and the Finnish BOF model mentioned below, represent the Nordic countries in Project LINK.

MODAG — or MODAG A as this version is called — is, as the largest of the models presented in this book, a good example of government type modelling in the Nordic countries.

In Finland the use of macroeconomic models for medium-term analysis within the government can be traced back to 1962 and has since then consisted of successive versions of the KESSU model (in the first years of its existence called MEPLAMO). The current version is KESSU III.

The model originated within the Economic Council of Finland in the preparation of a growth programme for 1962–1967. The first version of the model consisted of an input-output framework comprising 41 sectors and consumption and investment equations. Later the model was extended to relative prices and in the late 1960s a full price model was added such that income flows could be calculated. The model was used in assessing the economic prospects for 1965–1970 and for 1969–1973. At this stage the model comprised 220 equations.

The original interest in the model stemmed from considerations of structural problems and growth issues in the Finnish economy. Fiscal budgeting in a medium-term perspective gradually took over as the main concern while at the same time incomes policy emerged as a more important area of economic policy. This led to an increased interest from the Ministry of Finance in taking over the model which was then being run by the Economic Planning Centre, a small body set up to assist the Economic Council, a group which in 1970 was more oriented towards long-term planning and social issues for which the model was less suited. As a result the model was transferred to the Ministry of Finance and has resided there ever since (Leppä and Mannermaa [1984]).

In Finland as in Norway the development of model tools occurred under an overall planning ideology that had broad political support. Towards the end of the period of growth optimism in the 1960s and early 1970s stabilization policy faded somewhat into the background as a major concern and the general ideology favoured welfare issues and social planning. In the mid-1970s the pendulum swang back to emphasize economic planning mainly because of the extended economic problems arising in the aftermath of OPEC I, especially the sharp increase in unemployment from 1975, but partly also as a result of the difficulties in coordinating social policy planning and integration within government decision-making.

The transfer of KESSU to the Ministry of Finance set in motion a new development process for the model. The model was expanded in terms of the number of equations, the solution of the model was made more efficient, and the idea of a model system with KESSU at the centre was born. The model was reconstructed after the adoption of the new System of National Accounts and this improved considerably the treatment of incomes, expenditures and financial balances of the institutional sectors. A need was also felt to pay more attention to coordinate the short and medium-term assessments by better representation of short-term elements of the model.

The development of the KESSU model has followed along lines similar to the transfer from MODIS to MODAG A in Norway. Starting from a conventional disaggregate input-output model, more refined dynamic behavioural relations have been introduced and supply-side factors have been modelled more consistently.

The KESSU model has over time gained a central place in the economic management of the Finnish economy. The current status and development of the model is extensively considered by Leppä and Sourama. The size of the model at present is around 600 equations.

Another long-lasting mode project in Finland is the BOF model of the Research Department of the Bank of Finland. The current version, BOF3, is presented by Tarkka. BOF is a quarterly model rising its own data based on the national accounts definitions and data but developed as part of the modelling effort. The work on the model started in 1970 and the first version was completed in 1972 and BOF has been the Finnish entry in Project LINK since 1973. The BOF is used regularly by the Bank of Finland independent from the government administration and is naturally oriented towards analysing the effects of monetary policy. BOF is basically an income-expenditure model with small open economy assumptions and a quite aggregate input-output structure. In recent years supply-side elements have been much emphasized in the development of the model. The current version has 200 equations.

Another macroeconomic modelling effort not to be mentioned in this book is the model of the Research Institute of the Finnish Economy constructed by Vartia [1974] and others and completed in 1974. Both this model and an earlier model by Koivisto [1972] are mostly oriented towards short-term forecasting rather than economic policy analysis. The size of both of these models is around 40 equations.

Sweden has had medium-term "studies" since immediately after World War II. They are called "studies" rather than "programmes", partly to adhere to the Swedish term "utredning" and partly to express the fact that the Ministry of Finance was less committed to these studies than than counterparts were to the programmes in Norway and Finland. The first one concerned the development of the national income and the fiscal budget in the period 1948–1952/53. These studies have usually covered a period of five years intervals initially, but somewhat more frequently in recent years. Formal models were not applied in these studies until 1970, when the model EMMA was completed. As in Norway ten years earlier the newly developed model was set to work within a well-established institutional and political context of medium-term policy preparation. In Åberg [1971] an attempt is made to make explicit the formal framework for reasoning within these studies prior to 1970. After 1970 the model naturally came to occupy the centre of the stage and after some years it became the centerpiece of a system of models.

The first EMMA version was a quite simple model of 82 equations built around an input-output table with 15 sectors. It included no price relations and, accordingly, a limited range of application. Furthermore, it was a completely static model solved to give a prespecified level of employment. It thus did not include an aggregate consumption function. Exports were scaled to fulfill a prespecified trade balance (in constant prices!). In the ensuing years the model was further developed. The current version is presented by Olofsson.

Shortly after its first use in 1970 the manufacturing industries in the input-output table were split to become 14 instead of the 6 in the original model. The original solution, which residually determined level of private consumption, was later replaced by exogenous private consumption and government consumption became residual instead. The dual price model was developed but not included in EMMA until 1983.

The EMMA model is supplemented by another model called AMMA, presented here by Jansson and Olofsson. This is a more aggregate model with only five sectors and is in most respects rather similar to EMMA but has a more dynamic structure and includes financial flows in a fairly simple way.

The Swedish medium-term modelling seems to have been much less ambitious with regard to model development than in the other countries. This is odd in view of the fact that Swedish governments have generally invested considerable resources into policy studies. Part of the explanation may be that the modelling work occurred inside the Ministry of Finance and not in a more sheltered environment which could have paid more attention to long-term model development goals. Non-government macroeconomic modelling in Sweden includes a number of models developed at universities. Three of which are known as STEP, SNEP and GUESS. None of these seem to have played a role outside the academic environment (Lybeck et al. 1984).

In Denmark macroeconomic model development for use by the government started at a much later stage than in the other Nordic countries. The current model, ADAM (Annual Danish Aggregate Model), is also the first model in regular use by the Danish Ministry of Finance and the first experiments in the use of the model for government purposes started as late as the mid-1970s. The ADAM model original in an academic environment at the University of Copenhagen, mostly as the work of Ellen Andersen. The origin of this project can be traced back to 1966, but even this is much later than the early modelling efforts of Norway and also Finland. The first test version of ADAM was completed in 1971. At that stage cooperation had already started with the Central Statistical Office. After 1971, the Central Statistical Office took over responsibility for the model and it has resided there ever since even though the main user is the Ministry of Finance. This division of labour and responsibility is thus along the same pattern as in Norway and has in Denmark also provided stability, regularity and an impetus for further model development. An advisory committee with members from several institutions influenced the general development of the model from 1970.

The first version of the model from 1971 consisted of 91 equations of which 28 were stochastic relations. The stochastic relations included demand functions for consumption goods (7), investment goods (1), imports (3), price relations for demand categories (9) and sector output (3), employment (2), working hours (2) and wage level. The model was at this stage very much oriented towards cyclical movements and manufacturing and constructions are the only sectors specified. The aim of the project seems to have been to explain and predict the cyclical development of the Danish economy. Dynamic elements are emphasized. The use of the model for policy formulation and analysis does not seem to have been very prominent at this time, but the ensuing development of the model pursued by the Central Statistical Office in close cooperation with the Ministry of Finance has changed the model structure over the years and has turned it into an efficient tool for policy purposes, yet retaining much of the original content. The model was named ADAM in 1974.

The model was revised and reestimated in 1974 and after this followed a period of intensive revisions and extension of the model. The model was extended to comprise the whole economy. Consistency was emphasized in the price relations, the government sector and especially government transfers were dealt with in a more satisfactory way and the model was adapted in various other ways for government use. The 1978 version had 179 equations of which 38 were stochastic. The data base for most estimations included only data from the 1950s and the 1960s due to the fact that the national accounts were under major revisions. Until the late 1970s there existed only two complete input-output tables in Denmark (1953, 1966), while the new system aimed at providing annual input-output tables.

The new national accounts data were taken into use in 1979 and this meant *inter alia* that input-output relations came to play a role in the model. It also led to a major expansion of the size of the model from 1982 when the number of industries was increased from 6 to 19. The subdivisions of industries and the use of input-output relations sharply increased the number of variables which in the 1984 version presented in chapter II amounted to 809 endogenous and 1057 exogenous variables.

Danmarks Statistik [1985] summarizes the general development of the model from an academic forecasting exercise to an administrative tool emphasizing the following elements: firstly, there has been increasing emphasis on consistency, not only formal consistency between different groups of relations, for instance, price, investment and employment relations. Consistency in this sense becomes more important when the length of the horizon of the applications of the model is increased. Secondly, there has been a development away from reduced-form formulations, which reflect the user need to manipulate the model in actual use and thirdly, there has been an increasing amount of detailed specifications of the model reflecting the manifold interests of the user. Disaggregations tend to stretch the available data base to the limit and may have implications which counteract other ambitions in the long-term development of the model. These experiences are well known also from the modelling work in Norway and Finland.

There is one other Danish model which has played a role in the public sphere. This is the SMEC (Short-term Model of the Economic Council), which has been developed under the auspices of the Economic Council, a Danish institution consisting of three economists appointed by the Folketing (Parliament) who give independent advice on economic policy (see Fabritius [1979]. This model originated around the time of the first ADAM version and is a quarterly model based on quarterly national accounts constructed for this purpose. The model seems to have been little used in recent years as ADAM dominates the scene; it played a more important role in the 1970s. SMEC was never used, however, as a government tool.

References

Andersen, Ellen [1975], *En model for Danmark 1949-1965*. København: Akademisk Forlag.

Andersen, Ellen [1985], *Træk av makroøkonometriske modellers historie og udvikling*. København: Akademisk Forlag.

Aukrust, O. [1970], "PRIM I. A Model of the Price and Income Distribution Mechanism of an Open Economy", *The Review of Income and Wealth*, *16*, 51-78.

Aukrust, O. [1977], "Inflation in the Open Economy: A Norwegian Model", in *Worldwide Inflation: Theory and Recent Experience*, ed. Krause and Salant. Washington D.C.: Brookings Institute, 109-166.

Bergman, L. [1978], "Energy policy in a small open economy: The case of Sweden", RR-78-16, IIASA, Luxemburg.

Bjerkholt, O. and S. Longva [1980], *MODIS IV - A model for economic analysis and national planning*. Oslo: Central Bureau of Statistics.

Bjerkholt, O., S. Longva, Ø. Olsen and S. Strøm [1983], *Analysis of supply and demand of electricity in the Norwegian economy*. Oslo: Central Bureau of Statistics.

Bjerve, P.J. [1986], "Ragnar Frisch og Økosirksystemet", *Sosialøkonomen*, *No. 9-10*.

Blaug, M. [1985], *Great economists since Keynes*. London: Harvester Press.

Danmarks Statistik [1979], "ADAM i 1977 og 1978", Rapport fra Modelgruppen, Nr. 4.

Danmarks Statistik [1982], "Det fremtidige arbejde med ADAM", Rapport fra arbejdsudvalget af 23. oktober 1981. Rapport fra Modelgruppen, nr. 5.

Danmarks Statistik [1985], "Input-output systemet i ADAM", Arbejdsnotat, Nr. 19.

Edgreen, G., K.O. Faxén and C.E. Odhner [1970], *Lönebildning och sam-hällsekonomi*. Stockholm: publisher????.

Frabritius, J. [1979], "SMEC III – en simulationsmodel for Danmark", Copenhagen.

Frisch, R.A.K. [1934], "Circulation Planning", *Econometrica, 2*, 258–336 and 422–435.

Førsund, F.R., M. Hoel and S. Longva [1985], *Production, Multi-Sectoral Growth and Planning*. Amsterdam: North-Holland Publishing Company.

Johansen, L. [1960], *A Multi-Sectoral Study of Economic Growth*. Amsterdam: North-Holland Publishing Company.

Johansen, L. [1969], "Ragnar Frisch's contributions to Economics", *Swedish Journal of Economics, 71*, 302–324.

Johansen, L. [1975], *A Multi-Sectoral Study of Economic Growth. Second Enlarged Edition*. Amsterdam: North-Holland Publishing Company.

Koivisto, H. [1972], "A Short-term Forecasting Model for the Finnish Economy", University of Helsinki.

Leppä, A. and K. Mannermää [1984], "The development of the macroeconomic medium-term model", *Finnish Economic Journal, 4*.

Lybeck et al. [1984], "A Comparison of the Dynamic Properties of Five Nordic Macroeconometric Models", *Scandinavian Journal of Economics, 86*, 35–51.

Restad, T. [1976], "Modeller för samhällsekonomisk perspektivplanering", SOU 1976:51. Stockholm: Leberforlag.

Swedish Ministry of Finance [1984], "The 1984 Medium Term Survey of the Swedish Economy. The system of models", Stockholm.

Tarkka, J. [1984], "The BOF3 quarterly model of the Finnish economy", Research Paper, Bank of Finland.

Vartia, P.L.I. [1974], *An Econometric Model for Analyzing and Forecasting Short-term Fluctuations in the Finnish Economy.* Helsinki: Research Institute of the Finnish Economy.

Åberg, C.J. [1971], "Plan och prognos. En studie i de svenska långtids-utredningarnas metodik", 1970 års langtidsutredning, bilaga 9.

Macroeconomic Medium-Term Models in the Nordic Countries
O. Bjerkholt and J. Rosted (Editors)
© *Elsevier Science Publishers B. V. (North-Holland), 1987*

The Danish Macroeconomic Model ADAM*

by

Poul Uffe Dam
Danmarks Statistik,
Copenhagen

1. Introduction

The macroeconomic model ADAM is the core of the macroeconomic model apparatus employed by Danish government agencies. ADAM is in the custody of Danmarks Statistik, the Danish Central Statistical Office, which has been a centre for economic modelling since 1970.

ADAM is an annual model constructed in the modelling tradition of Tinbergen and Klein. The model displays features which are characteristically Keynesian. Gross output is determined by the level of demand, with most groups, in turn, predominantly determined by total income. The model has yet to encompass a financial sector. Accordingly, the interest rates employed in the model enter as exogenous variables. The dynamics of ADAM can in short be described as that of the multiplier-accelerator model. A model structure outline is presented in section 2.

The March, 1984 version of ADAM contains 662 endogenous and 941 exogenous variables. Of the endogenous variables, 72 are determined in stochastic relationships, most of which must be considered behavioural relationships. Many of the remaining equations are identities, but even more

---

* This paper draws heavily on corresponding material prepared in Danish, the latter being the result of the collective effort of the macroeconomic model unit. Able typing and editing assistance has been provided by Bente Henriksen.

belong to the residual groups of quasi-identities, technical relationships, and institutional behavioural relationships.

The latter group of equations is especially to be found in the sections of the model dealing with the government sector. A common problem here is to get tax rules (which change often), etc., represented in the model in a satisfactory way. Of these, a typical equation is specified as the product of an exogenous macro rate and an endogenous base, e.g., income. The rate may be computed so that the equation fits historically, or an adjustment factor may be inserted to pick up the noise. The appropriateness of the specification depends on whether the rate and the adjustment factor can be forecast in an operational way, i.e., linked to changes in tax rules, etc.

The technical relationships are to a large extent related to the input-output system of the model. The input-output model encompassed by ADAM forms the link between gross output and imports on the one hand and the categories of final demand on the other, linking both volumes and prices. The input-output tables used are an integrated part of the national accounts and have been deliberately edited to be very sparse, while still allowing a good part of the input-output coefficients to be modelled.

The parameters of ADAM's stochastic relationships have been estimated, mostly using the ordinary least-squares technique. Non-linear least-squares and iterative procedures have been employed in estimating the parameters of the expenditure system of the model. The lag structures of the two major capital formation relationships have been determined in a linear Almon-lag specification.

The national accounts are the main data source of ADAM. Other important sources are foreign trade statistics, tax statistics and labour market statistics. The data files of the model have in recent years been regularly updated twice a year, following the release dates of the national accounts.

The two main users of the model are the Economic Secretariat of the government and the Ministry of Finance. However, ADAM and related submodels are available to other users both within and outside the government. Since 1981 ADAM has been the Danish link in the international Project LINK, which aims at integrating national and regional macroeconomic models into a world model system.

The needs of the two main users have naturally influenced the development of ADAM. The extraordinarily detailed treatment of government receipts and expenditures is a clear example of that.

The environment of a statistical office has some obvious advantages for economic modelling. The proximity to data, the easy access to interpretations of these data, and the first-hand possibility of getting special data compilations carried out have been factors of the utmost importance in developing the input-output system of ADAM.

On the other hand, the distance, in both physical and institutional terms, from the main users of the model is a disadvantage as the practical use of an economic model is normally a vital source of inspiration for further model development. To overcome this, a pattern of frequent contacts between the handlers of the model unit and the people most actively engaged in the use of the model has been established. Furthermore, a certain level of preparedness in model simulation is maintained at Danmarks Statistik.

After outlining the model structure below, the model will be surveyed in greater detail in sections 3 through 20.[1]

2. Model Structure

The outline of the structure of the model is presented below in 26 equations. This presentation is a considerable simplification of ADAM as it stands today. Thus the dynamic structure of the model, the degree of disaggregation, and the concrete specifications of the relationships have been suppressed.

The variable mnemonics used in the presentation are fairly straightforward and should be clear from the comments below. A bar indicates that the variable is exogenous. It should be noted, though, that some variables are denoted as exogenous in this presentation as a matter of simplification. In actuality, they really are determined predominantly by other exogenous variables.

List of variables

alnar	relative residual increase in *lna*
Enl	balance-of-payments current account surplus
fCo	government consumption expenditure

---

[1] The empirical content of this version of ADAM is presented in the form of multiplier tables in P. Uffe Dam [1986], "The Danish macro-economic Model ADAM – A Survey", *Economic Modelling*, January. A complete list of equations and variables from the latest version of the model — or from the version presented here — will be sent on request to the author.

fCp	private consumption expenditure
fD	final demand
fE	exports
fEe	exports, initial estimate
fIf	gross fixed-capital formation
fIl	change in stocks
fIv	consumption of fixed capital
fM	imports
fX	gross industrial-sector output
$fXmx$	intermediate consumption
H	working hours
$iken$	interest rate on net foreign assets
iko	interest rate on bonds
K^{ϕ}	optimum capital stock
lna	wage rate in manufacturing industries
pco	price of fCo
pcp	price of fCp
pd	price of fD
pe	price of fE
pee	price of fE, initial estimate
pif	price of fIf
pil	price of fIl
pm	price of fM
px	price of fX
Q	employment
Qo	government sector employment
Rpx	relative change in px
Sd	direct taxes
Si	indirect taxes
Te	net non-interest transfers from abroad
$Tien$	net interest receipts from abroad
tsd	summary rate, direct taxes
tsi	summary rate, indirect taxes
Ty	transfers from public sector to households

$Ty_{\phi vr}$ Ty-transfers apart from unemployment benefits

$T_{\phi vr}$ net misc. domestic interest receipts

Ua labor force

Ul unemployment

Y gross domestic product

Yd disposable income

Yf gross domestic product at factor prices

Yr gross operating surplus

Yw compensation of employees

ze price elasticity for fE

Note: prefix f indicates constant prices

List of equations

Commodity Demand:

(1) $fCp = C(Yd, pcp)$

(2) $fCo = C(\overline{Qo})$

(3) $K^{\phi} = K(fX, \overline{iko} - Rpx)$

(4) $fIf = I(K^{\phi})$

(5) $fIl = I(FD)$

(6) $fIv = I(fIf)$

(7) $fE = E(\overline{fEe}, \overline{pee}, pe, \overline{ze})$

(8) $fD = fCp + fCo + fIf + fIl + fE$

Commodity Supply:

(9) $fM + M(fX, fD, \overline{pm}, px)$

(10) $fXmx = X(fX)$

(11) $fX = fD - fM + fXmx$

Labour Market:

(12) $Q = Q(fX, \overline{H}) + \overline{Qo}$

(13) $lna = l(\overline{alnar}, pcp)$

(14) $Yw = Y(Q, lna)$

(15) $Ul = \overline{Ua} - Q$

Prices:

(16) $px = p(px, \overline{pm}, lna)$

(17) $pd = p(px, \overline{pm}, \overline{tsi})$ $d = cp, co, if, il, e$

Transfers and Taxes:

(18) $Ty = T(Ul, lna, \overline{Ty_{\phi vr}})$

(19) $Sd = S(Yw, Ty, Tien, Yr, pif, fIv, \overline{tsd})$

(20) $Si = S(fD, pd, \overline{tsi})$

Balance of Payments:

(21) $Tien = T(\overline{iken}, Enl)$

(22) $Enl = fE \cdot pe - fM \cdot \overline{pm} + Tien + \overline{Te}$

Income:

(23) $Y = pd \cdot fD - \overline{pm} \cdot fM$

(24) $Yf = Y - Si$

(25) $Yd = Yf + Ty + Tien - Sd - pif \cdot ifIv + \overline{T_{\phi vr}}$

(26) $Yr = Yf - Yw$

In equations 1 through 8 total final demand and capital consumption are determined. Private consumption expenditure is determined by disposable income and consumption prices, whereas government consumption expenditure is determined by the employment in the government sector. Gross fixed capital formation is determined by the optimum capital stock, itself a function of gross industrial-sector output and a real interest rate. Changes in stocks are determined by total final demand, and capital consumption follows gross fixed-capital formation. Finally, exports are a function partly of initial estimates of export volumes and prices, and partly of the export prices determined by the model and an exogenous price elasticity.

Equation 9 through 11 describe the determination of total supply. As total supply adapts to total demand in the model, the equations indicate the allocation of the supply to imports and gross domestic industrial-sector output.

The labour market of the model is represented by equations 12 through 15. Employment is determined by domestic output and working hours, whereas the wage rate is determined partly by an exogenous wage component and partly by the price of private consumption expenditure. Having determined employment and the wage rate, compensation of employees follows easily. Unemployment is determined residually from employment and the exogenous specified labour force.

Prices are determined in equations 16 and 17. The price of gross output is a function of domestic and foreign commodity prices and of labour costs. The prices of the final demand components are subsequently determined by output and import prices and by rates of indirect taxes.

Transfers from the public sector to households are determined in equation 18. Evidently, the transfer component most important with respect to model properties is unemployment benefits, it being a function of unemployment and the wage rate. Equations 19 and 20 represent the tax section of the model. Direct taxes are a function of employee compensation, other gross income, transfers and rates of direct taxes. Indirect taxes are a function of final demand, prices thereof and rates of indirect taxes.

Net interest from abroad, described in equation 21, is a function of net foreign assets at the beginning of the year and an interest rate. Equation 22 shows the surplus on the balance-of-payments current account.

Gross domestic product at market prices and at factor prices is compiled in equations 23 and 24, whereas disposable income is established in equation 25 and gross operating surplus in equation 26.

The model structure outlined above is displayed schematically in figure 1. By and large the diagram corresponds to the equations above, but considerable simplifications have been made. For instance, the input-output system of the model is represented, but the balance-of-payments section is omitted.

3. Private consumption expenditure

Private consumption expenditure is represented as a hierarchic system. At the highest level, total consumption expenditure is determined by a

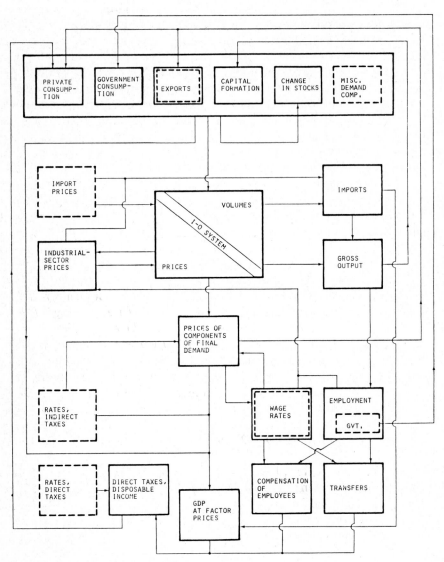

DOTTED LINES INDICATE EXOGENOUS VARIABLES

Figure 1: Model structure outline.

stochastic behavioural relationship. In the next step gross rents are calculated and subsequently, expenditures in the other consumption groups are determined by a dynamic linear expenditure system. Finally, three groups related to transportation, which are treated as one group in the expenditure system, are determined.

The main explanatory variable in the determination of consumption expenditure is disposable income, it being defined as the sum of net operating surplus, compensation of employees, transfers, and net interest receipts less direct taxes. The actual definition of disposable income in the model, $Yd4$, is in some respects rather crude, due to the limited statistical possibilities of delimiting an income variable relevant for consumption decisions.

The relationship for total private consumption expenditure follows the Hendry-specification, of which a basic assumption is that the consumption-income ratio is determined by the steady-state rate of growth of the economy.[2] With variables in fixed prices we obtain the following specification:

$$DLfC = k + b_0 \cdot DLYdd - a \cdot L\big(fC(-1)/Ydd(-1)\big), \qquad (3.1)$$

where D indicates first differences, L logarithms, fC consumption expenditure in constant prices and Ydd disposable income deflated. The specification differs from a simple one by including the lagged consumption-income ratio, which assures the return to the equilibrium level following initial departures.

As the expenditure system encompasses total consumption in current prices, equation (1) is reformulated accordingly. With the variables actually used, the specification is as follows:

$$DLCp4 = k + b_0 \cdot DLYd4 + b_1 \cdot DLpcp4v - a \cdot L\big(Cp4(-1)/Yd4(-1)\big) \quad (3.2)$$

The consumption variable, $Cp4$, differs from the corresponding national account variable by having expenditure on transport equipment transformed to a capital consumption variable. The price variable, $pcp4v$, is derived from the expenditure group prices by using the lagged volumes as weights. In the estimation process the parameter restriction $b_0 + b_1 = 1$ has been employed, implying absence of money illusion.

Private consumption expenditure is divided into the following groups:

---

[2] Cf. Davidson, J.E.H., D.F. Hendry, F. Srba, and S. Yeo [1978], "Econometric modelling of the aggregate time-series relationship between consumers' expenditure and income in the United Kingdom", *The Economic Journal, 88*, p. 661–692.

Consumption sector	Gross output
Food	Cf
Beverages and tobacco	Cn
Other non-durable goods	Ci
Electricity and fuels	Ce
Gasoline and oil for transport equipment	Cg
Personal transport equipment	Cb
Other durable goods	Cv
Gross rents	Ch
Purchased transport and communication	Ck
Other services	Cs
Purchases abroad by resident households	Ct
Purchases in Denmark by non-resident households	Et
Total	Cp

Gross rents are determined separately in a stochastic technical relationship. The explanatory variables of the equation are gross fixed-capital formation in the housing sector, lagged and unlagged.

The allotment of total consumption apart from gross rents to the expenditure groups is determined through the model's dynamic linear expenditure system. A basic assumption underlying the system is that domestic demand per capita for consumption group i, fC, is the outcome of maximizing a dynamic utility function, which has total per capita consumption excluding gross rents as its budget restriction.[3] The relationship for fC follows:

$$fC_i^\star = k_0 + k_1 \cdot fC_i^\star(-1) + k_2 \cdot \frac{1}{kcu \cdot pc_1} + k_3 \cdot \frac{1}{kcu(-1) \cdot pc_i(-1)} \quad (3.3)$$

The variable kcu, is the per capita marginal utility of consumption, which is a function of per capita consumption, lagged expenditure volumes and lagged prices. The occurrence of lagged expenditure groups and the lagged prices in the equation reflects that the utility function is dynamic, allowing for both habit formation and stocks in the decision process.

---

[3] Cf. Philps, L. [1974], *Applied Consumption Analysis*, Amsterdam.

The k-parameters in (3.3) are estimated in an iterative estimation procedure under the *kcu*-restriction mentioned. In the equation for *fCe* a number of frost-days variable is included as an extra explanatory variable. Similarly a term for the expected rate of interest on bank loans enters the *fCv*-equation. The addition of these extra variables to the expenditure system implies non-linear restrictions on the parameters of the two equations, which accordingly, are treated iteratively within the overall estimation procedure.

Consumption expenditure on gasoline and oil and on personal transport equipment is determined by stochastic behavioural relationships with more traditional specifications, the parameters of which are estimated with variables expressed in first differences. The explanatory variables in the *fCg*-relationship are the stock of automobiles and the prices of *Cg* relative to the price of *Ck*. The *fCb*-relationship follows a Stone-Rowe specification, according to which previous expenditures (the stock) lower present expenditure. The explanatory variables of the *fCb*-relationship are disposable income deflated, prices of *Cb* and *Cg* relative to the price of *Ck*, and an interest rate term. The last transport expenditure group, *fCk*, is determined residually.

It should finally be noted that the expenditure system only covers the part of consumption expenditure shared by resident households. Purchases within expenditure groups by non-resident households are determined as constant shares of the total consumption of non-residents, *Et*, which is listed as an export group, cf. section 6.

4. Fixed-capital formation

Gross fixed-capital formation in housing, *fIh*, and in the government sector, *fIob* and *fIom*, and changes in the agricultural breeding stock, *fIt*, constitute separate exogenous variables in the model. The remaining part of capital formation is divided into two groups: on the one hand buildings and civil engineering projects, *fIpb*, and on the other, machinery, transportation equipment, and other equipment, *fIpm*. These two variables are determined in the model by stochastic behavioural relationships, with capital formation in the extraction of crude oil set exogenously.

The two investment equations mentioned are specified according to the flexible accelerator model with adaptations a function of the relative user costs, i.e., the costs of using real capital in the production process relative to product prices. The most important element of the user-cost variable is the real interest rate defined as the bonds rate adjusted for expected price increases and the corporate tax rate. Entrepreneurs are assumed to adjust their capital stock, *Kip*, gradually to the optimum level, *Vkip*:

$$fIp_i = a \cdot \left(Vkip_i - Kip_i(-1) \right) + d \cdot Kip_i(-1) \qquad i = b, m. \tag{4.1}$$

The first term determines net investment, a being the adjustment parameter. The second term determines capital consumption at the depreciation rate d.

The optimum capital stock is assumed to be determined by the expected production level and the expected relative user costs:

$$Vkip_i = b \cdot fXv_i^E + c \cdot ucip_i \cdot fXv_i^E \qquad i = b, m. \tag{4.2}$$

If the expected relative user cost is constant over time, the equilibrium capital-output ratio is implicitly assumed to be constant also. An increase in the relative user costs is assumed to reduce the capital-output ratio ($c < 0$).

The parameters of the two relationships in (4.1) are estimated with the variables specified with first differences. By this procedure the variable $Kip(-1)$ is transformed to the corresponding net investment variable lagged one year. The variable *Vkip* is represented by contemporary and lagged values of a production term (the lag structure being determined in a linear Almon-lag specification) and by contemporary and lagged values of relative user costs multiplied by the production value (the lag structure being chosen from among a few prior selected ones). Both relationships show how expectations adapt slowly to the production level, the lagged production values being rather heavily weighted. The *fIpb*-relationship shows how expectations also adapt slowly to relative user costs.

The production terms *fXvb* and *fXvm* are computed by weighing together gross output from the industrial sectors *a*, *ng*, *ne*, *nf*, *nn*, *nb*, *nm*, *nk*, *ng*, *b*, *qh*, *qs*, *qt*, *qf*, and *qq*, cf. section 7, using as weights capital-output ratios for each of the two types of real capital estimated from the national accounts data for capital formation by industries.

Net fixed-capital formation is derived by subtracting depreciations from gross fixed-capital formation. Depreciation is determined for the housing and the government sectors and for the two categories of private investments treated above. The parameters of the four relationships are estimated with variables specified by first differences, the explanatory variable being the level of net capital formation lagged three quarters of a year.

5.   Changes in stocks

Changes in stocks are divided into 17 groups in the model. Of these groups, changes in agricultural stocks, *fIla*, and in energy stocks, *fIle*, are exogenous variables. Of the remaining 15 groups, 11 are determined by stochastic relations; the rest are determined from the 11 groups using average input-output coefficients.

The 17 change-in-stocks groups are defined either by the stock elements of the input-output table of the model, which stem from either an industry or an import group specified in the rows of the input-output table of the model. The groups *fIla* and *fIle* are defined, however, by aggregating over a few rows.

The stochastic behavioural relationships for changes in stocks are specified according to the flexible accelerator model, cf. section 4. In most relationships the adjustment parameter has been set at unity, corresponding to an assumption of adjustment to the optimum size of stocks without delay. However, for the group *fIlnm*, cf. section 7, a parameter value of less than unity has been found.

The optimum size of stocks is modelled by attaching a stock ratio to expected demand, which is defined as total supply from the relevant industrial sector or import group excluding supply to change in stocks. For the groups *fIlm7* and *fIlm8*, cf. section 7, a real interest term has been added as an explanatory variable.

This leads to some rather simple specifications:

$$fIl_i = k \cdot D(fX_i - fIl_i)^E \tag{5.1}$$

for industrial-sector supplied change in stocks, and similarly for those supplied from imports; D indicates first differences.

6.   Exports

Exports of goods, *Ev*, are divided into nine groups, by and large conforming to the main chapters in SITC, rev. 2. Exports of services are divided into two groups, tourism, *Et*, and other services, *Es*.

Nine of these eleven groups are determined in a rather simple manner from behavioural relationships. The export volumes will react to changes in export prices according to an exogenous elasticity, whereas the underlying pattern of development is given by an initial estimate. The relationships are specified as follows:

$$fE_i = fE_i e \cdot (pe_i v / pe_i ev)^{ze} i, \qquad (6.1)$$

where

$$pe_i ev = (1 - wpe_i 1 - wpe_i 2) \cdot pe_i + wpe_i 1(-1) \cdot pe_i(-1)$$
$$+ \ wpe_i 2(-2) \cdot pe_i(-2) \qquad (6.2)$$
$$pe_i ev = (1 - wpe_i 1 - wpe_i 2) \cdot pe_i e + wpe_i 1(-1) \cdot pe_i e(-1)$$
$$+ \ wpe_i 2(-2) \cdot pe_i e(-2) \, ; \qquad (6.3)$$

$fE_i e$ and $pe_i e$ are initial estimates of the volume and price variables for export group i; the estimates are supposed to be mutually consistent; ze_i is a long-run price elasticity, the first-year elasticity being approximately $(1 - wpe_i 1 - wpe_i 2) ze_i$. The price pe_i is determined as other prices of demand components, cf. section 12. It should be noted that the exogenous weights in (6.2) and (6.3), wpe, are lagged. This implies that the impact of the price in one particular year can be arbitrarily spread to the export volumes of that and the following two years. Another implication of the lags is that the weights in (6.2) and (6.3) do not necessarily add up to unity.

The export volumes for fuels, etc., $fE3$, and other services, fEs, are exogenous.

7.   Gross output and imports

Gross domestic output in ADAM, fX, is disaggregated over 19 industries. The aggregation from the industries of the Danish national accounts to the 19 in ADAM has been determined after extensive analysis. Traditional basic aggregation principles, such as industries having a similar input structure or supplying approximately proportionally to different users, have been considered. In addition the so-called vertical aggregation possibility, i.e., being at hand when the output of one industry is predominantly supplied as input to another one, has been employed. Another guiding principle has been the notion that there ought to be an approximate equality between the number of industrial sectors and the number of final demand components in a model.

Industrial sector	Gross output
Agriculture, etc.	fXa
Extraction of coal, oil and gas	fXe
Petroleum refineries	$fXng$
Electricity, gas and district heating	$fXne$
Food industries	$fXnf$
Beverages and tobacco	$fXnn$
Construction suppliers	$fXnb$
Metal products	$fXnm$
Industrial chemicals, etc.	$fXnk$
Misc. manufacturing industries	$fXnq$
Construction	fXb
Trade	$fXqh$
Ocean and coastal water transport	$fXqs$
Misc. transport, etc.	$fXqt$
Financial institutions	$fXqf$
Misc. services	$fXqq$
Housing sector	fXh
Government sector	fXo
Imputed bank service charges	$fXqi$

Two of the 19 variables in ADAM for gross output in fixed prices are exogenous, i.e., fXe and $fXqi$.[4] The remaining gross output variables in the private industrial sectors are determined from the demand side by input-output relations. Taken together these relationships form a static input-output model, where some of the technical coefficients are endogenous variables in the model.

The basis for determining the technical coefficients is that the per unit of a certain commodity, supplied either from domestic output or from imports, is constant. On the other hand the import share of the total supply of a commodity varies according to an import relation, or in the case of oil, due to the exogeneity of domestic output. The technical coefficients for imports and domestic output will thus vary while their sum is kept

---

[4] The latter is zero by definition; any supply into the industry is to be countered by a corresponding negative value of output originating, $fYfqi$, being exogenous in the model.

constant. In the case of oil, imports adjust to fill total demand and the exogenous domestic output.

Imports are divided into 11 groups, nine of which cover imports of goods, Mv, by and large conforming to the main chapters of SITC (rev. 2). Imports of services are divided into two groups, tourism, Mt, and other services, Ms, the former being identical to private consumption expenditure on tourism.

Each group of imports is determined by two relationships. In the first relationship the share of the import group substituting for domestic output on the home market is determined. The substituting share, denoted by fMz_i, is determined as a rule by a stochastic behavioural relationship. In the second relationship the remaining part of the import group is determined. This non-substituting share, denoted fMu, is determined in an input-output relationship. The fMu-share consists of imports supplied to the government sector, to changes in stocks and to exports, and furthermore of certain special components of imports like oil, cars, ships, aircraft and services.

The stochastic behavioural relationships have the following basic specification:

$$fMz_i = a \cdot fAz_i^E \cdot \left(\frac{fAz_i}{fAz_i^E} \right) \cdot \left(\frac{pm_i(-1/4)}{px_i(-1/4)} \right)^c , \qquad (7.1)$$

with fMz_i the substituting part of import group i, fAz_i the total domestic market for commodity i, fAz_i^E the expected value of fAz_i, pm_i the import price of commodity (import group) i, and px_i being the price of the domestic supply of commodity i. The market for commodity i is determined as follows:

$$fAz_i = \sum_j \left(amidj + \sum_k c_{ijk} \cdot axkdj \right) \cdot fD_j , \qquad (7.2)$$

where c_{ijk} is the share of supply of industry k to use j competing with import group i. The $_{ijk}$-factors, which are inserted as parameters in the model, are compiled from the basic national accounts balances.

The market expectation is modelled to the effect that (fAz_i/fAz_i^E) is equal to one at constant market growth. The term mentioned is included to test the hypothesis that imports are more sensitive to the business cycle than is domestic output, implying b to be greater than one. At $b = 1$ the specification coincides with the traditional logarithmic linear relationship, the scale parameter being unity. The parameters are estimated in first differences of a logarithmic form of (7.1).

For SITC chapters 1, 2 and 4, 6 and 7 the market expectation model has prevailed, the b-values ranging from 1.11 to 1.29. For SITC chapters 5

8 and 9, the traditional log-linear specification has been chosen with the income elasticity held at unity. Having not yet established any stochastic relationship for the remaining import groups, SITC chapters 0 and 3 (ships and aircraft, and other services), these groups are determined by input-output type relationships.

In most of the stochastic relationships the price elasticity has been estimated at the order of magnitude of -1, SITC chapters 1 and 8 and 9 being the most conspicuous — and sensitive — exceptions.

8.　Government sector output

The activities of producers of government services is modelled from the supply side. Gross domestic product at factor cost, $fYfo$, is determined by employment, Qo, and consumption of fixed capital, $fIov$. The supply of commodities to the government sector, $fXov$, is assumed to be proportional to $fYfo$, an assumption which can easily be altered. Gross output, fXo, is by definition made up of the sum of $fYfo$, $fXov$ and taxes linked to production, $fSiqo$, the latter being exogenous.

Government consumption expenditure, fCo, is determined residually by deducting from fXo the supply of government services to other uses. These supplies are determined by input-output coefficients, the most important one being private consumption expenditure on services. The latter supply is determined similarly to $fXov$, cf. above.

The variables Cd, fCd, $Yrod$, and $fYrod$, which are encompassed by the relationships, are normally redundant, but can facilitate the use of special assumptions regarding government activity actually beyond the strict national accounts definition thereof.

9.　Employment

Employment of wage and salary earners is specified for each industrial sector in the model, cf. section 7. In the manufacturing industries and in the construction industry employment is furthermore specified separately for wage and salary earners, respectively. As a matter of definition there is no employment in the qi-sector.

Employment is determined by stochastic behavioural relationships for 13 of the industrial sectors; it is determined exogenously in the remaining ones. These latter industries are smaller or atypical, for example, agriculture, extraction of oil, oil refineries, housing and government. Employment in the large government sector is the dominant variable in the determination of government consumption expenditure, cf. section 8.

Self-employment is specified for agriculture, Qas, and for other industries, Qus, both being exogenous variables. Also exogenous is total labour force, Ua, leaving the amount of unemployment, Ul, to be determined residually.

The outline of the specifications of the employment equations have been unchanged for a number of years. The determination of employment in the industrial sector j, Qj, is specified as follows (denoted in first differences of a logarithmic form):

$$DLQ_j = a + b \cdot DLfXj + c \cdot DLfXv_j + d \cdot DLH_j \,, \tag{9.1}$$

in which $(b + c) = 1$; fX_j and fXv_j are gross output for the year and dynamically weighted gross output for earlier years, respectively; H_j indicates working hours.

An important property of the employment equations is that long-term growth in productivity is given by the numerical value of the parameter a. Accordingly, from a practical point of view long-term productivity growth can be considered to be exogenous in the model. Short-term productivity on the other hand will move cyclically in the model, following changes in gross output.

In the short term the elasticity of employment with respect to gross output is less than unity. The dynamic specification implies that employee productivity and working hours vary together in the short term, cf. next section. As capital stock is not included in the specification in (9.1) the parameter sum $b+c$, which indicates the long term elasticity of employment, does not reflect any specific factor elasticity, but rather that the implicit production function is assumed to be homogeneous of first degree.

The working hours variable in (9.1) is represented partly by a specific variable for normal working hours in the manufacturing industries, $Hhnn$, and partly by contractual working hours, Ha, which is used in most industries outside manufacturing. In all industries the working hours variable is adjusted with the ratio of part-time employed persons. The elasticity parameter d is set *a priori* at -0.65 in all equations with support in older micro-level studies.

A general observation is that the employment equations only to a limited extent capture the changes in employment — this is apparently due to factors other than the ones specified in (9.1). The model is accordingly apt to underestimate changes in productivity.

10. Working hours

Average working hours in manufacturing industry, *Hgn*, are included in the determination of industrial-sector prices in the manufacturing industries and in the construction industry.

The *Hgn* relationship is specified in a form that is closely connected to the one used in the employment relationships, cf. section 9. It follows in logarithmic form:

$$LHgn = a + b \cdot LfXn + c \cdot LfXvn + e \cdot LHnn, \qquad (10.1)$$

where *fXn* is total gross output in the manufacturing industries and *Hnn* is normal working hours therein. It can be noted that neither *Hgn* nor *Hnn* are adjusted by the part-time employment ratio, cf. section 9.

Changes in output are assumed to induce short-term variations in working hours as the elasticity of employment with respect to output is less than unity. In the longer term, however, it is assumed that employment will adjust to the level of output. The parameters *b* and *c* are accordingly expected to be of approximately the same size, *b* being positive and *c* being negative. The estimated parameters, which are very small indeed, conform to this expectation; it is further noted that the parameter *e* is close to unity.

11. Prices of industrial-sector output

Prices of gross output in ADAM's industrial sectors, cf. section 7, are as a rule determined in stochastic behavioural relationships of input-output type specification. The exceptions are agriculture, *a*, and housing, *h*, whose prices are exogenous, the petroleum-related industries, *e* and *ng*, whose prices are attached to the world market energy price due to the heavy impact of imports in these industries, and finally in water transport, *qs*, whose price is attached to the exogenous export price, *pes*, denoting the world market freight rate. Again, as a rule, prices are determined net of indirect taxes on commodities used; the taxes are then subsequently augmented, cf. next section.

The basic specification of the price equations is as follows:

$$pnx_j = a \cdot (\text{costs of commodities used})_j + b \cdot (\text{wage costs})_j, \qquad (11.1)$$

the coefficients a and b assumed to be equal to or somewhat larger than unity. This corresponds to the hypothesis that all costs are fully reflected in the prices, with the addition of a possible mark-up for profits.

The costs of commodities used per unit of output are determined in input-output type relationships similar to the ones used for prices of final demand components, cf. next section. The cost of commodities used are consistently inserted with a lag of one quarter of a year.

The wage costs per unit of output are determined as follows:

$$vl_j = kv_j \cdot lna/(\text{normal output per working hour})_j \,, \qquad (11.2)$$

lna is hourly compensation per wage earner in the manufacturing industry. The wage rate, lna, is inserted without a lag, reflecting the notion that the rate is known at the time of price decisions. Normal productivity is specified in (11.2) as a dynamically weighted average of hourly productivity, it being defined as $fX_j/(Q_j \cdot H_j)$, cf. section 9. A summary correction for differences in industrial wage levels is assured by the factor kv_j, it being inserted as a parameter in most equations.

In the estimation process it turned out that due to multicollinearity it was not possible to determine the parameters a and b in (11.1) in unrestricted estimation. It was consequently necessary to tie one of the free parameters. The practical choice was between assuming $a = 1$ ("constant distribution of income") or $a = b$ ("constant mark-up"). The first hypothesis implies that the costs of commodities used are fully included in prices, without profits being affected. The second hypothesis implies that all costs are fully included in prices, with the result that profits will vary with the costs of commodities used.

The choice between the two hypotheses is of great consequence for model properties, particularly in cases when effects of changes in the competitive position are analysed. The stochastic properties of the equations have been allotted decisive importance in this choice, even if this decision base has sometimes been very flimsy. The true specification may indeed lie somewhere in between the two hypotheses. The outcome has been that the hypothesis of constant mark-up to total costs has been preferred in most cases, the exceptions being industries nn and nb, where the hypothesis of constant distribution of income has been preferred.

Attempts at inserting into the price relationships additional terms representing demand pressure and capacity utilization respectively have been made; so far, however, they have been to no avail.

12. Prices of final demand components

In the model, prices of final demand components, net of indirect taxes, are explained by prices of industry gross output and import prices (inclusive customs duties). The prices are determined by the input-output relationships.

$$pnd_j = \left(\sum_i aidj \cdot px_i + \sum_k amkdj \cdot (pm_k + tm_k) \right) \cdot kpnd_j, \qquad (12.1)$$

aidj being the input-output coefficient for supply for industry i to demand component j, and *amkdj* the corresponding coefficient for supply from import group k. The *kpnd*-factor is computed to the effect that (12.1) fits historically. For the years where final national account figures are available these factors are close to unity, discrepancies being interpreted mainly as aggregation bias.

The purchasers' prices of final demand components are determined by using the appropriate rates of indirect taxes, particularly the rates of specific duties and of VAT, cf. section 17.

$$pd_j = (pnd_j + tp_j)(1 + tg \cdot btg_j) \qquad (12.2)$$

The motor vehicles registration duty, which concerns two components only, is treated similarly to the VAT. This modelling of purchasers' prices reflects the assumption that changes in indirect taxes are fully reflected in the prices.

13. Wage regulating price index

The official wage regulating price index is modelled by a weighted average of ADAM's prices of consumption expenditure groups, cf. section 12, the weights being derived from the official weights of the index. The price index, *pcreg*, which like other prices in the model is on an annual basis, is subsequently expanded into quarterly price indices, *pcr1* through *prc4*.

14. Compensation of employees

The central compensation variable in ADAM is the wage rate *lna*, which is defined as average hourly compensation of wage earners in manufacturing industry. In the compilation of *lna* sickness benefits and vacation benefits are included, whereas a number of other benefits are not. In the modelling *lna* is divided in three components:

$$lna = lnad + lnas + lnar \tag{14.1}$$

Of these variables *lnad* represents the accumulated cost-of-living allowances, and *lnas* the sickness benefits; both components are determined in the model. Wage changes according to labour contracts and wage drift will be reflected in the residual component *lnar*, which is set in the model by the exogenous rate-of-change variable, *alnar*.

By multiplying *lna* by *Ha*, contractual working hours, a contractual annual compensation rate, *lah*, is established. The compensation rate for salary earners in the manufacturing industry, *lnf*, is assumed to follow *lah*, an assumption which can easily be modified though.

Compensation of employees by industrial sectors, Yw_j, is determined as the product of the wage rate and employment, cf. section 9. For the *a*, *e*, *q*, *h*, and *o*-sectors the equations are specified as follows:

$$Yw_j = lnf \cdot Q_j \cdot \frac{1 - bq_j/2}{1 - bqnf/2} \cdot kl_j \, ,$$

where *bq* denotes the ratio of part-time employed persons and *kl* establishes consistency with the national accounts compilation of employee compensation.

In the *n*- and *b*-sectors employment is determined for wage and salary earners separately. For these sectors the compensation equations are specified as follows:

$$Yw_j = (Hgn \cdot lna \cdot Q_j a \cdot \frac{1 - bq_j a/2}{1 - bqn/2} + lnf \cdot Q_j f \cdot \frac{1 - bq_j f/2}{1 - bqnf/2} \cdot kl_j \, , \tag{14.2}$$

where *Hgn* denotes average working hours in the manufacturing industry.

15.   Transfers

Transfers from the public sector to households, *Ty*, are divided into seven groups. These are general pensions, *Typs*, other pensions, *Typr*, unemployment benefits, *Tyd*, other transfers taxable as A-income, *Tysa*, other transfers taxable as B-income, *Tysb*, remaining transfers, *Tyr*, and transfers being repaid, *Tyt*. The groups *Tysa* and *Tyr* are counted net of the repaid transfers. This categorization has been governed predominantly by the mechanisms under which the different kinds of transfers are regulated by their form of taxability.

The two pension groups are determined in the model as one group in an institutional relationship, and subsequently divided using an imputed value of one of them. The determinants in the equation are the number of pensioners, *Upn*, the rate of ordinary old age pensions converted to a base-year level and a price term reflecting the price index regulation of the pensions rate. An adjustment factor secures that the equation fits historically.

The most important group of transfers in a business cycle analysis context is obviously the unemployment benefits. These are determined in a relationship similar to the one used for pensions. The base of the equation is a number of unemployed, *Ulfhk*, counted as full-time insured persons entitled to benefits payments. Other determinants are an average rate of benefits counted in a base-year level and a wage term reflecting the statutory regulation of the rates. The average rate is computed so that the equation fits historically.

The other groups of transfers are treated as either exogenous or imputed variables in the model as it now stands.

16. Direct taxes

Direct taxes are modelled in some detail in ADAM. Apart from a clear intrinsic interest, direct taxes are an important component of disposable income used to explain private consumption expenditure.

Total direct taxes are divided into four main groups in ADAM. These are ordinary personal income and wealth taxes, *Sk*, other personal income taxes, *Sdp*, corporation tax, *Sds*, and motor vehicle weight duty for households, *Sdv*. The main content of ADAM's tax model is the determination of the *k*-group.

The tax model is built as a stylized version of the tax rules. This is however valid to a lesser extent for the two preliminary taxes, *Sba* and *Sbb*, for which the explanatory income variable is a gross figure, than for final taxes, *Ssy*, for which the income variable corresponds to the one actually used in tax assessments. The first preliminary tax, A-tax, *Sba* in the model, is withheld by employers, pension paying institutions, etc., from income classified to that effect, called A-income, *Ya*. The second preliminary tax, B-tax, *Sbb*, is levied explicitly and paid directly.

Each of three taxes mentioned is determined by combining an income term with an average and a marginal tax rate. The marginal tax rate is adjusted in the model from an initial value of zero; the adjustment secures that taxation is regulated for changes in initial estimates of the number of taxpayers and for changes in the price index from which the brackets of the national income tax system are normally regulated. The rates themselves are determined by combining the official tax rates with variables indicating initial estimates of the shares of taxable income in income bracket i, bys_i0, and with variables, bys_i1, indicating the sensitivity of these shares to changes in taxable income. Note that the relationship for determining A-tax includes variables stemming from the advance assessment system, which influences the dynamic properties of the model.

The aforementioned *bys*-variables for income shares are exogenous in ADAM. They are determined in a special model, MISKMASK, developed for this purpose. This model has to be activated only when new income statistics arrive or when new or proposed tax rules are to be inserted into ADAM.

Having determined total final taxes and total preliminary taxes, net tax underpayment is essentially determined also. Combined with total final taxes in a special relationship, this variable, Srn, is expanded into tax underpayment and overpayment, respectively. After proper periodisation and some additional charges, ordinary personal income and wealth taxes, Sk, are determined.

A most important variable in the tax model is taxable income, Ys. This variable is determined in a stochastic relationship having two kinds of income as explanatory variables, A-income and a term for other gross income, respectively. It is believed that some gain in explanatory power, particularly in later years, can be achieved by treating the latter term in a more complex manner than is done now. Note that just as Ys is used for explaining Ssy and Ya for explaining Sba, the last income term mentioned is is used for explaining Sbb. The latter relationship must, however, be regarded as a technical supplement to the former ones, securing an internal consistency of the tax model.

Of the other main groups of direct taxes Sdp and Sds are exogenous, while Sdv is related to the stock of automobiles by an exogenous tax rate.

Some other taxes, classified neither as direct nor indirect taxes, are included in the concept of total taxes. These taxes, which are of minor importance only, are capital taxes, Sak, social security contributions, $Saso$, and compulsory fees, fines and penalties, $Sagb$, all three variables being exogenous.

17. Indirect taxes

Conforming to the treatment in the input-output tables of the national accounts, net total indirect taxes, Si, are categorized into taxes on products and taxes linked to production. The taxes on products are divided into customs duty revenue, Sim, revenue from duties on specific goods and services, net of subsidies, Sip, revenue from VAT, Sig, and revenue from the registration duties on new motor vehicles, Sir. The taxes linked to production, Siq, are divided into taxes on real property, $Siqej$, motor vehicle weight duties from producers, $Siqv$, other production taxes, $Siqr$, and production subsidies, $Siqs$.

Each main group of indirect taxes on products is determined as the sum of a number of groups, each one corresponding to a final demand group, to gross output of an industrial sector or to a group of imports. The revenue of each of these groups of taxes is determined by using a corresponding tax rate. However, the VAT revenue can be summarily adjusted by one rate, tg. Accordingly the revenue from specific duties on consumption expenditure group i, C_i, is determined as follows:

$$Sip_i = fC_i \cdot tp_i, \tag{17.1}$$

and the VAT revenue on the same consumption expenditure group as:

$$Sig_i = C_i \cdot tg \cdot btg_i / (1 + tg \cdot btg_i) \tag{17.2}$$

The btg-variable indicates the specific degree of charging VAT on the group in question. The rates are derived from the input-output tables and adjacent material.

All the main groups of taxes linked to production are exogenous variables in the model.

In addition to determining net indirect taxes, this section of the model also determines indirect taxes, gross and subsidies, respectively. Apart from the determination of a residual group of subsidies the modelling of these variables is done by utilizing model identities.

18. Balance of payments

The modelling of the balance of payments begins with net exports of goods and services, $Envt$, which is derived from the export and import parts of the model, respectively. The surplus on the balance-of-payments current account, $Enlnr$, is established by adding to $Envt$ net transfers relating to the EC, *Tenf*, net compensation from abroad of employees, *Twen*, net unrequited transfers, *Tenu*, and net property and entrepreneurial income (interest) from abroad, *Tien*.

Of these transfers *Tenf* is determined partly from customs duty and VAT revenues, and partly from agricultural exports, while *Tenu*, which includes aid to developing countries, is attached to *GNI*. By combining net foreign assets at the beginning of the year an exogenous interest rate *Tien* is determined.

Net lending of the nation, *Tfen*, is determined by adding to *Enlnr*, net capital transfers from abroad, *Tken*, which is exogenous in the model. The surplus on current account of the official balance-of-payments statistics, which covers the whole of the Danish currency area, that is Denmark including Greenland and the Faroe Islands, is established by further adding net exports from and net transfers to these parts of the country.

19.   Public and private sector balance

With the latest additions and revisions to the list of public sector variables in the model it is possible to determine public sector balances down to net lending, *Tfon*, in accordance with the new national accounts compilation. A good number of the new variables are exogenous so far.

Apart from public sector net lending, the national accounts now show private sector net lending and net lending of the nation. The latter, *Tfen*, is determined in the balance-of-payments section of the model. By using the balance identities, private sector net lending, *Tfpn*, is determined residually, after including an exogenous term, *Tfrn*, from the reconciliation account.

20.   Output originating

For each industrial sector in the model, gross domestic product at factor cost, output originating, is specified in current and fixed prices, Yf_j and fYf_j, respectively. For the government-sector output originating is determined in a special procedure, cf. section 8. For other industries output originating is determined as indicated below, the fixed-price variable for imputed bank service charges being, however, exogenous.

Output originating at the industry level is determined from the supply side. For each industry gross output, Xj (cf. section 7), is reduced by commodities used, Xmx_j, and by indirect taxes, Si_j, cf. section 17.

Using ADAM's input-output model, output originating in fixed prices in industry j is determined as follows:

$$fyf_j = fx_j \cdot \left(1 - \sum_i a_{ij} - \sum_k am_{kj} - asi_j\right). \tag{20.1}$$

Total output originating in fixed prices follows by simple addition.

In principle output originating in current prices is determined by attaching prices to the uses specified in (9,1). The use of commodities in industry j is determined as follows:

$$Xmx_j = fX_j \cdot \left(\sum_i a_{ij} \cdot px_i + \sum_k an_{kj} \cdot (pm_k + tm_k)\right) \cdot kpx_j. \tag{20.2}$$

The adjustment factors kpx_j have the same function as the corresponding kp-factors in the relationships for prices of final demand components, cf. section 12.

Assuring consistency between total output originating, Yf, on the demand and supply side of the model — as we do here — is established by inserting an adjustment factor into the use of commodities, $kxmx$, which is determined in the model for this purpose. The lack of immediate consistency is due to the occurrence of the kp-factors, cf. above; historically, $kxmx$ is unity. In the adjustment procedure five industries are excluded. Output originating in these industries is determined as follows:

$$Yf_j = fX_j \cdot pnx_j - Xmx_j - Siq_j \qquad j = a, e, b, qs, h. \tag{20.3}$$

For the remaining industries output originating is determined as follows:

$$Yf_j = fX_j \cdot pnx_j - Xmx_j \cdot kxmx - Siq_j. \tag{20.4}$$

Macroeconomic Medium-Term Models in the Nordic Countries
O. Bjerkholt and J. Rosted (Editors)
© Elsevier Science Publishers B.V. (North-Holland), 1987

Fiscal Effects and Multipliers
in the
Danish Economy

by

Lars Otto

Institute of Economics
Copenhagen, Denmark

1. The operation of fiscal policy

In this article we will consider all tax and expenditure transactions of government as *fiscal*, irrespective of how they are financed. The reason for this definition, rather than the usual one found in for example Musgrave [1959, p. 528] or Blinder and Solow [1974, p. 4], is ADAM's lack of a money market and endogenous public interest payments to the private sector.

The total effect of changes in the public sector's tax and expenditure is called the *total fiscal effect*. This corresponds to what Hansen [1969, p. 22] called "the effects of total budget changes". With this definition it is possible to discuss the total fiscal effect on the gross domestic product (GDP) and the total fiscal effect on the public sector accounts.

The effect of any direct change in tax rates, pension rates, public employment or purchase of goods is the active part of fiscal policy and is called the *discretionary fiscal effect*. The discretionary effect can thus be seen as a measure of the influence on the economy which comes via public revenue and expenditure from changes in laws and rules, etc.

Any change in private expenditure will via income tax, consumption tax and unemployment benefits have a derived effect on the disposable income of households and on the public sector accounts. This result of fiscal policy is called the *automatic fiscal effect*. The distinction between the discretionary and the automatic part of fiscal policy is to some extent arbitrary, since allowing the automatic effects to work unhindered can be seen as a decision in itself. As an operational definition we have tried to define as discretionary fiscal policy any change in expenditures and taxes that called for a political decision.

2.   Automatic stabilizers

From textbooks on macroeconomic theory it is well known that the GDP-multiplier for a change in public expenditure is reduced by the introduction of taxes that vary with the level of income. We will now analyze the effect of both income and consumption tax on the multipliers in a simple macroeconomic model.

Let $\overline{Y}$ denote income (GDP) at market prices. The income tax T^d is given by

$$T^d = t\overline{Y} + T_0^d, \qquad 0 < t < 1.$$

Let Y and C denote income and consumption in factor prices (market prices net of indirect tax). The consumption tax T^i is given by

$$T^i = sC + T_0^i, \qquad 0 < s < 1.$$

The "real" private consumption depends on the "real" disposal income, i.e.,

$$C = c\left(\frac{\overline{Y} - T^d}{1 + s}\right) + c_0, \qquad 0 < c < 1.$$

Let G be the exogenous government expenditure (there is no tax on G) and using $\overline{Y} = Y + T_i$ the complete model is

$$Y = C + G$$
$$C = c[(Y + T^i - T^d)/(1 + s)] + C_0$$
$$T^d = t(Y + T^i) + T_0^d$$
$$T^i = sC + T_0^i.$$

Solving the model we obtain the multiplier

$$m = \frac{dY}{dG} = \frac{1 + s(1 - c(1 - t))}{(1 + s)(1 - c(1 - t))}.$$

We consider three cases:

(1) The direct tax is independent of income, that is $t = 0$.

$$\left.\frac{dY}{dG}\right|_{t=0} = \frac{1 + s(1 - c)}{(1 + s)(1 - c)} = \frac{1 + s(1 - c)}{(1 + s)(1 - c) - c}$$

(2) The indirect tax is independent of consumption, $s = 0$. The multiplier is then

$$\left.\frac{dY}{dG}\right|_{s=0} = \frac{1}{1 - c(1 - t)}.$$

(3) The indirect tax is independent of income and the indirect of consumption, $t = s = 0$,

$$\left.\frac{dY}{dG}\right|_{\substack{t=0 \\ s=0}} = \frac{1}{1 - c}.$$

We have the standard textbook result that

$$\left.\frac{dY}{dG}\right|_{\substack{t=0 \\ s=0}} > \left.\frac{dY}{dG}\right|_{s=0} > \frac{dY}{dG}.$$

$$\left.\frac{dY}{dG}\right|_{\substack{t=0 \\ s=0}} > \left.\frac{dY}{dG}\right|_{t=0} > \frac{dY}{dG}.$$

That is, both income and consumption taxes are automatic stabilizers,

$$\left.\frac{dY}{dG}\right|_{\substack{t=0 \\ s=0}} - \left.\frac{dY}{dG}\right|_{s=0} > \left.\frac{dY}{dG}\right|_{t=0} - \frac{dY}{dG},$$

implying that the effect of introducing income tax is higher if there is no consumption tax than if there already is a consumption tax. This result can also be seen by considering $\partial^2 m / \partial t\, \partial s$. We find

$$\frac{\partial m}{\partial t} = \frac{-c}{(1 + s)\big(1 - c(1 - t)\big)^2} < 0$$

$$\frac{\partial m}{\partial t} = \frac{-c(1 - t)}{(1 + s)^2\big(1 - c(1 - t)\big)} < 0$$

$$\frac{\partial^2 m}{\partial t\, \partial s} = \frac{c}{(1 + s)^2\big(1 - c(1 - t)\big)^2}$$

and obtain the result that the stabilizing effect of increasing $t(s)$ is lower the higher the value of $s(t)$. One can also show the declining stabilizing efficiency of higher tax rates, i.e,. $\partial^2 m/\partial t^2 > 0$ and $\partial^2 m/\partial s^2 > 0$.

When employment depends upon production, we can consider unemployment benefits as a negative direct tax and the same results hold true.

In table 1, GDP multipliers for government consumption in the ADAM model are given under different assumptions about the automatic stabilizers.

Table 1: GDP Multipliers for government consumption.

	0	1	2	3	123
1st year	1.15	1.26	1.22	1.21	1.57
2nd year	1.57	1.78	1.73	1.74	2.63
3rd year	1.63	1.88	1.84	1.97	3.28

Assumptions:

     0 All automatic effects in force
     1 No income dependent tax
     2 No consumption dependent tax
     3 No unemployment benefits
   123 1, 2 and 3 together

These figures clearly show what our simple model told us: Taxes are automatic stabilizers and more taxes provide more stabilization. Table 2 simply shows the change in the multipliers compared to the situation when all the automatic effects are in force.

Table 2: Change in multipliers due to deleting automatic stabilizers.

	1	2	3	$1+2+3$	123
1st year	.11	.07	.06	.24	.42
2nd year	.21	.16	.17	.54	1.06
3rd year	.25	.21	.28	.74	1.65

Comparing the sum of the effects $(1 + 2 + 3)$ with the combined (123) effect we see, that the latter is twice the size of the former. This theoretically demonstrates the results previously proved above, that the effect of an automatic stabilizer depends on the level of the other automatic stabilizers.

3. The fiscal effect

In the introduction we distinguished between discretionary, automatic and total fiscal effects. We shall study how this distinction works in a simple macroeconomic model such as

$$Y = C + G + I$$
$$C = c(Y - T)$$
$$T = tY + T^{\star}$$

where I is investment and there is no consumption tax. Solving for Y we obtain

$$Y = \frac{I + G - cT^{\star}}{1 - c(1 - t)}$$

and the multipliers are

$$\frac{dY}{dG} = \frac{dY}{dI} = \frac{-1}{c}\frac{dY}{dT^{\star}} = \frac{-1}{cY}\frac{dY}{dt} = \frac{1}{1 - c(1 - t)} \, .$$

If we let subscript 0 denote the base period and 1 the next period, then $DX = X_1 - X_0$ is the change from period 0 to period 1 in the variable X. Later when we need more periods we let $DX_n = X_n - X_{n-1}$.

The discretionary fiscal effect on income DY_D was defined as the effect of any change in public expenditure or tax parameters. In our model we therefore have

$$DY_D = \frac{dY}{dG}(DG - cDT^{\star} - cY_0 Dt) \, .$$

The discretionary effect on income in period n is

$$DY_{Dn} = \frac{dY_n}{dG}DG + \frac{dY_n}{dT^{\star}}DT^{\star} + \frac{dY_n}{dt}Dt \, .$$

The total fiscal effect on income in period 1 is the difference between the actual income in period 1 and the income that would have been generated under unchanged public expenditure and revenue from the base period.

Thus we have

$$DY_T = \frac{G_1 + I_1 - cT_1^\star}{1 - c(1 - t_1)} - \frac{G_0 + I_1 - cT_0}{1 - c}.$$

With a bit of manipulation this can be written as

$$\frac{1}{1 - c(1 - t_1)}(DG - cDT^x - cY_0Dt) + \frac{-ct}{(1 - c)1 - c(1 - t_1)}DI,$$

where we immediately recognize the first term as the discretionary effect. This therefore lead us to suggest that the automatic fiscal effect is

$$DY_A = \frac{-ct_1}{(1 - c)(1 - c(1 - t_1))}DI.$$

One could now ask why there are no automatic effects from G and $T^\star$. It would be tempting to say that the automatic effects from change in G should be

$$\left(\frac{dY}{dG} - \frac{dY}{dG}\bigg|_{t=0}\right)DG = \frac{-ct}{(1 - c)(1 - c(1 - t))}DG,$$

and similar from a change in T^*. If $DT^* = Dt = 0$ then the total effect would be

$$\left(\frac{dY}{dG} - \frac{dY}{dG}\bigg|_{t=0}\right)DG + \left(\frac{dY}{dI} - \frac{dY}{dI}\bigg|_{t=0}\right)DI,$$

which has no simple interpretation. The natural definition of the discretionary effect of a change in G is

$$\frac{1}{1 - c(1 - t_1)}DG.$$

But if G is the only exogenous variable or parameter that has changed, then this is also the total fiscal effect, leaving no room for any automatic fiscal effect. Part of the discretionary effects are due, however, to the existence of automatic stabilizers as explained in section 2.

When we turn to the 2nd period we get the cumulated discretionary fiscal effects of the changes in the 1st period,

$$DY_{D_2} = \left(\frac{dY_2}{dG_1} + \frac{dY_2}{dG_2}\right) DG + \left(\frac{dY_2}{dT_1} + \frac{dY_2}{dT_2}\right) DT + \left(\frac{dY_2}{dt_1} + \frac{dY_2}{dt_2}\right) Dt$$

and similar effects for the later periods.

Note that the discretionary change in period 1 is a permanent change in the policy variables, which means that the changes in the parameters in the following periods are unaffected. It must be emphasized that we consider the changes in the parameters and not the level of the parameters as the discretionary policy.

We want the total fiscal effect for period 2 to show the effect in period 2 of the changes in the budget in period 1, just like the discretionary effect in period 2 shows the effect in period 2 of any discretionary change in period 1. But now things are a little more complicated. The effects should be measured as the difference between the actual income and the income that would have been generated under unchanged level of public expenditure and no endogenous income taxes in period 1. This means for example that the public expenditure in period 2 should be the expenditure that would have occurred if there had been no change in period 1 and the change in period 2 was as before, that is $G_2 - DG_1$ ($= G_0 + DG_2$).

For the endogenous income tax it is a bit more complicated. If there had been endogenous taxes in period 1 the tax revenue would have been $T_1 = t_1 Y_1 + T_1^x$, where Y is income in the "only exogenous tax" model. Thus T_1 is the tax level to be considered also without endogenous taxes. The change in period 1 would be $T_1 - T_0 = Dt_1 Y_0 + t_1 DY_1 + DT_1^*$. Here we can interpret $Dt_1 Y_0 + DT_1^*$ as the direct part of the discretionary change and $t_1 DY_1$ as the automatic part. We want the following periods to show the effects of the total change in period 1. The discretionary part has already been discussed. We want to treat the total and therefore also the automatic effect in a way comparable to the discretionary effect. Thus we want the automatic effect in period 2 to show the effect of the existence of endogenous taxes in period 1. In period 2 and in the following periods we reintroduce endogenous taxes so that we can cumulate the effects of endogenous taxes in period 1. This is just as for the discretionary effect where the change of the instruments in period 2 are the same with or without the discretionary change in period 1. We therefore want a change in taxes in the following periods that stem from the automatic effects in period 1, that is $t_1 DY_1$. But in the following periods we have the automatic stabilizers working and therefore do not obtain the delayed effect of the tax change $t_1 DY_1$ in period 1. We thus treat $t_1 DY_1$ as part of DT_1^*.

4.   Results

We now turn to the results from calculating fiscal effects in the macroeconomic model ADAM (the March, 1981 version). ADAM is particularly suitable to describe income determination in the short run and especially the interplay between public expenditures and taxes and private demand. But ADAM is lacking a description of the intermediate behaviour of the producers and does not describe the wage formation and the interplay between the rate of return and the financial markets.

Standard multipliers

Before we turn to measuring the discretionary fiscal effect we present a selection of some standard multipliers in ADAM.

Table 3: GDP multipliers for government revenue and expenditure.

Elasticities	1st year	2nd year	3rd year
Investment goods	.03	.04	.04
Consumption goods	.09	.12	.13
Employees (full time)	.15	.16	.16
Income tax	−.04	−.07	−.10
Value-added tax	−.04	−.08	−.10

The difference between the expenditure multipliers are mostly due to differences in direct import.

Other multipliers for example of unemployment benefits and pensions looks almost like tax multipliers with a switch of the sign.

Discretionary fiscal effects

Discretionary changes have been defined as

(i)   changes in the number of full-time government employees

(ii) changes in government purchases of goods and service for consumption and investment (in constant prices)

(iii) changes in unemployment benefits and pension rates adjusted for wage and price development, respectively and changes in the real value of other transfer incomes.

(iv) changes in rates for income tax, value added tax and other consumption taxes

(v) changes in the real value of other taxes.

We consider changes in wages and prices as determined by the market and not as discretionary changes.

In table 4 below the discretionary fiscal effects on the gross domestic product measured in 1970-prices are shown. One can see that the fiscal policy in most of the years has had a stimulating effect on growth. After one or two years the effects begin to vanish and there is almost no differences between the 1st and 3rd year effects.

Table 4: Discretionary fiscal effects on GDP. 1970-prices.

Percent	1st year	2nd year	3rd year
1972	1.7	1.7	1.6
1973	0.0	0.2	−0.2
1974	1.1	1.4	1.5
1975[1]	2.4	4.1	4.5
1976	−0.4	−1.5	−2.1
1977	0.7	0.2	0.9
1978	1.2	0.9	0.6
1979	1.2	1.1	0.9
1980	−0.2	−0.9	−1.4
1981	0.6	0.7	0.7
1982	0.6	0.4	0.1
[1] of this tax due to reform	1.5	2.9	3.6

Note: The table shows for every year the percentage difference between GDP with and without discretionary fiscal policy.

The current account of the balance of payments and the level of employment have been the main targets in the use of fiscal instruments. In table 5 we show the discretionary fiscal effects on the current account and employment. Over the years fiscal policy has generally increased employment and in many years also contributed to an improvement of the current account. This was so as a result of the balanced budget effect under increasing government expenditure and because government consumption has higher employment content and less import content than private consumption.

Table 5: Discretionary fiscal effect on the current account of the balance of payments and employment level. Percent of absolute level.

	Employment			Current account		
	1st year	2nd year	3rd year	1st year	2nd year	3rd year
1972	1.9	2.0	2.1	−86.8	−17.4	−10.9
1973	0.5	0.4	0.3	13.5	11.8	22.1
1974	1.3	1.5	1.6	−9.5	−29.2	−8.5
1975[1]	1.4	2.3	2.9	−91.1	−43.2	−58.8
1976	0.1	−0.5	−1.1	13.6	33.9	53.6
1977	0.9	0.6	0.2	−2.6	13.8	15.8
1978	1.4	1.4	1.3	−9.7	−2.9	0.4
1979	1.4	1.5	1.5	−5.7	−4.4	−2.3
1980	0.8	0.3	0.0	15.7	36.7	30.6
1981	0.9	0.9	0.9	−1.4	−2.9	−4.5
1982	0.9	0.9	0.7	0.7	5.3	13.9

Even though the improvement on the balance of payments may seen modest compared with the deficit, there has been a cumulated effect of approximately 15 billion Dkr since 1976 (measured on the third year effects). (The deficit in 1981 was 18 billion Dkr).

In most of the years an increase in employment has only taken place in the public sector, while employment in the private sector has decreased.

As mentioned earlier the total fiscal effect is the total effect of changes in the public sector expenditure and revenue. The total fiscal effect therefore consists of

(i) changes in revenue for direct taxes (income taxes etc.)

(ii) changes in revenue for indirect taxes (consumption taxes etc.)

(iii) changes in the number of full-time government employees

(iv) changes in annual wage for full-time government employees

(v) changes in the government purchases of goods and services for consumption and investment

(vi) changes in prices of goods and services from the private sector

(vii) changes in transfer incomes

Table 6 shows the total fiscal effect on GDP. In every year we notice that the total effect is larger than the discretionary effect. We will come back to this under the automatic effects.

Table 6: Total fiscal effect on GDP, 1970-prices.

Percent	1st year	2nd year	3rd year
1976	−0.2	−0.4	−1.3
1977	1.3	0.4	0.3
1978	1.2	0.8	0.7
1979	1.4	1.2	1.3
1980	0.9	0.6	0.7
1981	2.3	2.2	3.4
1982	1.3	1.0	1.3

Note: The table shows for every year the percentage difference between GDP with and without any change in public expenditure and revenue.

The difference between the total and the discretionary fiscal effect is the automatic fiscal effects. As can be seen in every year the automatic fiscal effects have been positive and contributed to the growth in GDP.

A traditional textbook argument is, that the automatic effects are positive when the economic activity (GDP) is falling and negative when it is rising. There are two main reasons why this pattern does not reveal itself. The textbook argument only takes account of the degressive effect of the automatic rise in income tax. Furthermore, it assumes constant prices and therefore does not consider the expansive effect of public expenditure due to increasing wages and prices, which is the major part of the positive contribution to the automatic effect. Secondly, in all years the automatic effects increase unemployment and therefore also increase disposable incomes by unemployment benefits. There are also other positive automatic effects, such as the adjustment of tax rates due to rising prices and also negative automatic effects, such as increased consumption taxes.

Table 7: Automatic fiscal effects on GDP, 1970-prices.

Percent	1st year	2nd year	3rd year
1976	0.2	1.1	0.8
1977	0.6	0.2	−0.6
1978	0.0	−0.1	0.1
1979	0.2	0.1	0.4
1980	1.1	1.5	2.1
1981	1.7	1.5	2.7
1982	0.7	0.6	1.2

Note: The table shows for every year the percentage difference between GDP with and without any change in public expenditure and revenue.

Before any conclusion is drawn it is important to emphasize the limitations of the model. The lack of producer behaviour in the medium run, the lack of wage determination and the absence of financial markets should be noted. As mentioned earlier these drawbacks may be of less importance in the 1st and 2nd year. The effects in later years can only be interpreted as long-run income determination effects.

The uncertainty of the economic forecasts and the difficulties in a precise measurement of the fiscal effects mean that one must resist engaging in a completely short-run and detailed fiscal management. What has been called fine-tuning of the economy can hardly be realized.

Even though the intermediate results should be used very carefully they seem to imply that a discretionary fiscal policy can affect the intermediate economic development.

References

Blinder, A.S. and R.M. Solow [1974], "Analytical Foundation of Fiscal Policy", in *The Economics of Public Finance*, ed. A.S. Blinder. Washington, D.C.: Brooking Institution.

Hansen, B. [1969], *Fiscal Policy in Seven Countries 1955-65.* Paris: OECD.

Musgrave, R. [1959], *The Theory of Public Finance.* New York: Mc-Graw Hill.

Macroeconomic Medium-Term Models in the Nordic Countries
O. Bjerkholt and J. Rosted (Editors)
© Elsevier Science Publishers B. V. (North-Holland), 1987

Real Wages, Exchange Rates and Employment
in the
Danish Economy

by

Finn Lauritzen
Ministry of Finance
Copenhagen, Denmark

In the Ministry of Finance ADAM has for several years been used to calculate the effects of changes in competitiveness in the short as well as the
medium term. ADAM was originally constructed as a short-term model
with the main emphasis put on analysis of fiscal policy. For the medium-
term auxiliary calculations outside the model may be required.

This paper describes how the model ADAM is used to calculate the
effects of changes in wages and exchange rates. The most important aspect of this is the modelling of imports and exports, which is discussed in
the first section. In the next section multipliers are calculated, and differences between the effects of wage cuts and devaluations are discussed. The
multipliers are summarized in the form of essential elasticities.

1. Determination of imports and exports

Imports in ADAM are determined on a 1-digit SITC level. For each group
imports are calculated as the product of the "market demand" for that
group and the share of imports. Market demand is calculated in an input-
output system in which Danish production is distributed on SITC groups.
The import share depends primarily on the ratio between the import price
and the price of similar Danish production. For each group of imports a

Table 1: Import elasticities.

SITC group	Shares of imports in 1983	Short-run demand elasticity	Price elasticity		
			year 0	year −1	Total
0–Agricultural products	9%	1.00	0.0	0.0	0.0
1–Beverages and tobacco	1	1.73	−1.10	−0.37	−1.47
24–Unprocessed goods	5	1.16	−0.89	−0.30	−1.19
3–Fuels	17	1.00	0.0	0.0	0.0
5–Chemicals	9	1.00	−0.82	−0.28	−1.10
6–Intermediate goods	17	1.18	−0.73	−0.24	−0.97
7–Machineries and other equipment	17	1.25	−0.72	−0.24	−0.96
89–Consumer goods	9	1.00	−1.60	−0.54	−2.14
Y–Ships and aircraft	1	1.00	0.0	0.0	0.0
T–Tourism	7				
S–Services	8	1.00	0.0		0.0
	100%	1.10	−0.55	−0.18	−0.73

demand price elasticity has been estimated, assuming the quantity reaction to lag three months. Furthermore, import shares depend on changes in the growth rates of the import markets. If growth rates rise, import shares will tend to rise also, as domestic producers are unable to expand production quickly in the short run. For four SITC groups a short run "demand elasticity" greater than unity has been estimated. The elasticities of imports are shown in table 1.

This approach to the method of modelling imports is common, but not without problems. It requires separability in the implicit production functions of the sectors and in the utility functions so that the choice between import and domestic production of every single commodity is independent of the choice between inputs or consumption of these commodities. This condition is hardly fulfilled at the chosen level of aggregation, but so far no better approach to the modelling of imports has been found.

Analogous with the determination of imports, exports depend on the demand for Danish exports (i.e., the size of the export market) and the export market shares.

It can be argued that both imports and exports depend on supply-side conditions as well. On the import side, the supply side is mainly determined by external factors, since Danish demand constitutes only a small fraction of the world market. With the export markets, however, supply-side effects must be explicitly taken into account.

On each export market, i.e., the export of a specific good to a specific country, exports depend not only on the relative export price, but also on other parameters of competition such as marketing, quality, design, stability of deliveries, etc. The export price depends on Danish production costs and the prices of competitors. The price also depends on the chosen strategy — whether emphasis is put on price competition or on other parameters. These other parameters of competition may in turn depend on the profitability of the export.

This underlying structure behind the determination of exports can be represented by the following submodel. P_e is the export deflator, F_e the quantity of exports, P_x the world market price (the price of the competition), C the unit production costs, π unit mark-up, Z other parameters of production and Y the size of the market. In (1) and (2) it is assumed that the relation can be log-linearized and in (4) it is assumed that the strategy choice can be represented by a function f_3.

$$P_e = f_1(P_x, C) = P_x^{a_1} \cdot C^{a_2} \tag{1}$$
$$F_e = f_2(P_e, P_x, Z) \cdot Y = P_e^{b_1} \cdot P_x^{b_2} \cdot h(Z) \cdot Y \tag{2}$$
$$\pi = P_e - C \tag{3}$$
$$Z = f_3(\pi) \tag{4}$$

This model can be simplified by assuming that the composite function can be log-linearized around a single point.

$$P_e = P_x^{a_1} \cdot C^{a_2} \tag{5a}$$
$$\begin{aligned} F_e &= P_e^{b_1} \cdot P_x^{b_2} \cdot h\big(f_3(P_e - C)\big) \cdot Y \\ &= P_e^{b_1} \cdot P_x^{b_2} \cdot h\big(f_3(P_e - (P_e \cdot P_x^{-a_1})^{1/a_2})\big) \cdot Y \\ &\approx P_e^{e_1} \cdot P_x^{e_2} \cdot Y \end{aligned} \tag{5b}$$

Alternatively the model can be simplified to

$$\begin{aligned} F_e &= P_x^{a_1 \cdot b_1 + b_2} \cdot C^{a_2 \cdot b_1} \cdot h\big(f_3(P_e - C)\big) \cdot Y \\ &\approx P_x^{c_1} \cdot C^{c_2} \cdot Y \end{aligned} \tag{6}$$

The model (5a–b) is used in ADAM, whereas (6) is incorporated in the present version of the SMEC model of The Economic Council. Both models are, however, deduced from the more complete model (1)–(4) above.

The main advantage of (5) is that export prices and subsequently export values are determined more directly. (Compared to (6), the model (5) is to a higher degree a structural form). On the other hand (5) is valid only when $a_2 = 0$. In the case of perfect competition, where $a_1 = 1$ and $a_2 = 0$, (5) cannot be used.

Another advantage of (5) (as compared to (6)) is that this model corresponds to the classification used in the foreign trade statistics, in which exports are divided into groups of commodities. In (5) both P_e and P_x are vectors of commodity prices, while input-output matrices in (5a) link commodity prices to sectoral prices and production costs. In (6) exports must be distributed by sector (because costs can only be identified by sector), and therefore the existing statistics covering exports are not fully utilized.

Due to these advantages (5) has been preferred to (6). Exports in the model are explained on a 1-digit SITC level. For each group the export is determined as a market demand multiplied by the market share. The market demand depends on the GNPs of our trading partners and the market share in turn depends on the relative export price.

The elasticity for each SITC group has been taken from a study by Gert Åge Nielsen [1983]. Nielsen analyzed 1600 markets for which there is export data available for each year between 1961 and 1980. A market is defined as exports of a 4-digit SITC commodity from Denmark to a specific OECD-country. The price elasticities used in ADAM are aggregates — within each 1-digit SITC group — of the price elasticities of the 4-digit SITC groups in Nielsen's study. These elasticities are shown in table 2.

The true long-run elasticities may be greater than these shown in table 2, partly for the reason that due to statistical errors in the price and quantity data the estimated elasticities may be biased towards -1.

In Nielsens's study the time lags in the reactions of demand to price changes are also investigated. The lags are found to vary from zero to two years with an average of 0.8 years. According to these findings the weights 0.4, 0.4 and 0.2, corresponding to the unlagged price and the price lagged one and two years, respectively, are used in the export functions.

As mentioned above the export model in ADAM is not suited for dealing with exports of goods under perfect competition. Consequently, exports of agricultural products (SITC group 0) are kept exogenous in the model and thus do not change when competitiveness changes. The price of agricultural exports are assumed to follow the ECU. Similarly, exports of ships, aircraft and services are exogenous in the model.

According to (5a) export prices of the "endogenous" SITC groups are determined as a function of domestic costs and world market prices. In the first stage, sectoral prices depend on production costs. Secondly, input-output weights are used to transform sectoral prices to commodity prices.

Table 2: Export elasticities.

SITC group	Shares of exports in 1983	Long-run price elasticity
0–Agricultural products	23%	−1.34
1–Beverages and tobacco	1	−0.97
24–Unprocessed goods	6	−1.11
5–Chemicals	7	−1.13
6–Intermediate goods	10	−1.54
7–Machineries and other equipment	16	−1.39
89–Consumer goods	11	−1.10
Total	74%	−1.32

Thirdly, an elasticity of 0.4 between world market prices and Danish export prices is used. These elasticities are based on investigations of export prices in the study mentioned above (cf. Nielsen [1983]). Nielsen uses the same data material as in the study of demand for Danish exports.

2. Calculated multiplier effects

Using the assumptions stated above the effects of a 5 percent effective devaluation, keeping wages constant, and a wage cut of 5 percent, keeping the exchange rate constant have been calculated. Both changes are calculated with 1984 as the first year. Wages are kept exogenous in the simulations, i.e., wage indexation and Phillips curve effects have been decoupled. Transfers from the public sector are changed in proportion with the change in wages. Receivers of transfers thus face a declining real income. Wages in the public sector are treated similar to wages in the private sector. Import prices of SITC groups 2 and the 4–9 area assumed to decrease by one percent in both simulations.

The reactions of financial markets are very difficult to predict. Generally they depend on the conditions under which the changes take place. Expectations of a repeat in the future of current policy actions will often prove decisive. If, for instance, a devaluation leads to expectations of further devaluation, interest rates will tend to rise.

Table 3: Effects of a 5 percent wage cut.

	1984	1985	1986	1987	1988
Volume changes*					
Private consumption	−0.91	−1.55	−1.23	−0.68	−0.52
Gross investments[1]	0.38	0.57	2.03	3.44	3.45
Imports	−0.81	−1.44	−1.13	−0.68	−0.70
Exports	0.20	0.71	1.29	1.63	1.75
GNP	−0.20	−0.07	0.50	1.04	1.16
Employment	−0.03	0.11	0.49	0.90	1.08
− change in 1,000 persons	−0.73	2.76	12.34	23.24	28.23
Deflators					
Private consumption*	−1.26	−1.90	−2.38	−2.61	−2.72
Imports*	−0.54	−0.51	−0.51	−0.52	−0.52
Exports*	−0.39	−0.93	−1.27	−1.34	−1.61
Real disposable wage*	−2.22	−1.83	−1.68	−1.64	−1.61
Balance of payments**	0.39	0.64	0.67	0.64	0.71
− of which is interest**	0.00	0.03	0.06	0.08	0.11
Government sector surplus**	−0.23	0.30	0.53	0.69	0.81
Central government surplus**	−0.78	1.09	0.70	0.77	0.84

* change in percent of base run
** change in percentage points of GNP
[1] excluding investments in housing and changes in stocks

Due to the uncertain reactions of the financial markets the real rate of interest has been kept constant in both simulations. This assumption makes it easier to compare the multipliers. Moreover, investment in housing has been kept exogenous in the experiments.

Real tax rates are also kept constant. This implies that excise duties as well as income tax brackets follow the consumer price index in the calculations.

The export of tourism is assumed to depend on consumer prices in Denmark relative to consumer prices abroad with an elasticity of −1.2. The multipliers are shown in tables 3 and 4.

The long-run effects of the two changes are similar, but the effects on employment — and subsequently on public finance — are slower in the case of a wage cut than in the case of devaluation. The similarity between the two sets of multipliers can be interpreted as a confirmation of the consistency of the entire model, as relative unit labour costs are changed equally in the two simulations (provided that capital costs and mark-ups

Table 4: Effects of a 5 percent devaluation.

	1984	1985	1986	1987	1988
Volume changes*					
Private consumption	−0.24	−0.05	−0.10	−0.07	−0.20
Gross investments[1]	1.52	4.19	5.22	5.10	4.63
Imports	−0.71	−0.42	−0.03	−0.25	−0.32
Exports	0.88	1.64	1.96	1.87	1.81
GNP	−0.69	−0.19	0.47	1.41	1.33
Employment	0.48	0.97	1.26	1.30	1.24
– change in 1,000 persons	11.63	23.90	31.66	33.47	32.48
Deflators					
Private consumption*	1.42	1.71	1.82	1.97	2.10
Imports*	4.50	4.49	4.46	4.47	4.47
Exports*	3.45	3.61	3.64	3.69	3.73
Real disposable wage*	−1.33	−1.40	−1.30	−1.39	−1.46
Balance of payments**	0.18	0.45	0.48	0.57	0.64
– of which is interest**	−0.15	−0.09	−0.04	−0.01	0.02
Government sector surplus**	1.18	1.08	0.97	0.99	1.11
Central government surplus**	0.41	0.47	0.62	0.81	0.80

* change in percent of base run
** change in percentage points of GNP
[1] excluding investments in housing and changes in stocks

in the long run depend entirely on the wage level and commodity prices).
In other words the implicit price model in the model as a whole has to be
homogeneous of degree 1 (in the long run) with wages and import prices
as the only exogenous variables.

When wages are cut, employment effects are negligible the first two
years. This is due to the time lags in the sectoral price functions and in
the export functions. Contrary to this, the balance of payments improves
immediately because of the rapid decline in real wages and consumption.
The real wage, net of taxes, for an average blue collar worker declines
as much as 2.22 percent the first year, but improves in the course of the
following years. This is also due to the slow response of prices.

In the case of devaluation an immediate difference in prices arises on
the markets for imports and exports. Import shares decline and exports
grow approximately 1 percentage point even the first year. The time lags
in the sectoral price functions imply that real wages decline more gradually.
The balance of payments improves only slightly the first year because of

increasing interest payments on the relatively large Danish foreign debt.

In both experiments, private consumption decreases by only $\frac{1}{2}$ percent, whereas real wages net of tax decreases by $1\frac{1}{2}$ percent. The reason why private consumption is sustained is that the incomes of the unemployed whom find jobs rises, and that net profits in non-corporate firms increases. (It is assumed that the propensity to consume directly out of corporate profits is zero, but to some extent increased corporate profits via wealth effects increase consumption too). Investments grow significantly in order to increase the capital stock in line with the increase in production. The final decline in imports is around $\frac{1}{2}$ percent, while exports grow by almost 2 percent.

The balance of payments and the government sector account improve, both by approximately 1 percent of GNP. Employment increases by 30,000 persons to 1.1 percent of total employment or 2 percent of the number of wage earners in the private sector. Employment in the public sector and the number of self-employed are kept constant in the calculations. The percentage increases in GNP and total employment are almost the same, as the long-run productivity in each sector is exogenous in ADAM.

In figure 1 the effects on the balance of payments and employment in the first 8 years of the simulations are shown. The final effects are almost the same, but the time profile is clearly different.

The slow response of prices plays a crucial role in creating the different time profiles in the two experiments. (One way of interpreting the lags in the price functions is that inflation expectations are implicitly taken into account.) In cases of substantial wage cuts expectations and adaptations might change faster than in these calculations. This will make the time profiles more similar.

To illustrate the effect of changes in total demand, the effects of a tax cut are shown in the diagram. Changes in total demand causes the economy to move downwards to the right or upwards to the left, while an improved competitiveness makes the economy move upwards to the right.

When the multipliers above are compared to other model simulations, differences can stem from different consumption or investment functions, different tax systems or different reactions of public expenditure. A better way of presenting the model simulations is, therefore, to calculate "pure" employment effects, i.e., to combine the changes with expansive fiscal policy in order to maintain an unchanged balance of payments. In table 5 "pure" employment effects are shown.

Another way of presenting the results is to summarize these in the form of elasticities. The multipliers (with endogenous current account) are

Table 5: Employment effects under unchanged balance of payments, 1,000 persons.

	1 year	2 years	3 years	4 years	5 years
5% devaluation	14.7	34.2	46.7	51.0	51.7
5% wage cut	5.9	19.5	34.5	45.7	50.1

Note: 50,000 persons corresponds to 1.91 percent of total employment or to 3.37 percent of the number of wage earners in the private sector.

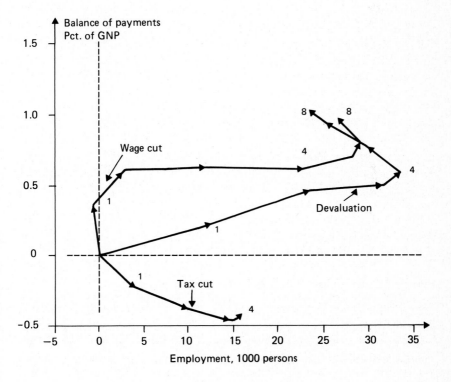

Figure 1: Effects on employment and balance of payments.

Table 6: Overview of elasticities.

Elasticity between	Change	1 year	2 years	3 years	4 years	5 years	6 years
Import shares and	dev.	0.41	0.60	0.64	0.65	0.59	0.56
unit labour costs	wage	0.09	0.27	0.44	0.56	0.65	0.65
Export market shares	dev.	−0.32	−0.66	−0.82	−0.80	−0.77	−0.73
unit labour costs	wage	−0.06	0.22	−0.43	−0.59	−0.67	−0.68
Employment[1] and	dev.	−0.65	−1.07	−1.28	−1.22	−1.09	−0.91
real wage	wage	0.02	−0.06	−0.32	−0.63	−0.78	−0.81
Employment[1] and	dev.	−0.66	−1.25	−1.72	−1.65	−1.49	−1.26
real disposable income	wage	0.03	−0.11	−0.56	−0.97	−1.16	−1.18

Note: Only endogenous employment, i.e., employment of wage earners in the private
sector, is taken into account.

summarized in this way in table 6. The changes in import and export
market shares are related to the changes in relative unit labour costs, and
an elasticity around 2/3 is found for both markets. The elasticity between
employment and real wages is slightly below unity. The elasticities between
employment and real disposable wage is slightly above unity.

If the balance of payments is kept unchanged by fiscal policy, the
elasticity between employment and real wages is −1.5. This can be seen
from table 7, in which the two changes are combined with fiscal policy
to ensure that the balance of payments is unchanged. This combination
does not change the elasticities of import shares and export market shares
significantly. The elasticity between employment and real wages *after tax*
becomes meaningless, since the effect on taxes depends on the kind of fiscal
policy which is used to stimulate demand. The fiscal policy chosen does not
affect real wages, however. The elasticity shown in table 7 should therefore
be a good measure of the flexibility of the economy.

Table 7: Elasticities with unchanged balance of payments.

Elasticity between	Change	1 year	2 years	3 years	4 years	5 years	6 years
Employment and	dev.	−0.82	−1.53	−1.89	−1.85	−1.73	−1.59
real wage	wage	0.12	−0.44	−0.88	−1.23	−1.38	−1.46

3. The uncertainty of the calculations

If the parameters of the import and export price or quantity functions change, the multipliers change too. It is crucial to assess how dependent the results are on the underlying assumptions. Therefore, experiments using alternative parameter values have been carried out. The most influential but uncertain assumptions concern the exporters' pricing behaviour, the demand elasticities with respect to export prices and the sensitivity of import prices to change in Danish production costs.

It is very difficult to evaluate the consequences of a lower or higher elasticity between export prices and production costs. If, for example, producers keep export prices measured in foreign currency constant and thus use the "room for maneuver' solely to increase profits the exported quantity will not change in the model simulations. In reality, however, increasing profits might in the long run be invested in order to consolidate and expand market shares. The calculations depicted in the figures below (in which it is assumed in alternative 1 (and 2) that exporters use 0 (and 80) percent of the "room for maneuver', against 40 percent in the standard calculation), therefore exaggerate the effects of changes in the price behaviour of exporters when the effect on employment is considered, while the effect on the balance of payment perhaps is underestimated (and vice versa).

In alternative 3 it is assumed that import prices are insensitive to Danish production costs. In the standard calculations import prices of the SITC groups 2 and 4–9 decreases by 1 percent in both experiments.

In alternative 4 and 5 it is assumed that the numerical export demand prices elasticities are 0.2 higher or lower for all SITC groups than in the standard calculations.

The results of the calculations are shown in figures 2 and 3 below. The differences are surprisingly small; multipliers can be trusted to be fairly stable against changes in the underlying assumptions. All import, export, employment and price functions used in the simulations are estimated on data for the 1960's and 1970's.

This does not necessarily imply that the model as a whole neither explains the history nor the post-sample data to a sufficient degree. As a test of the entire model ex post simulations of import and export market shares for 1979 to 1983 have been made. Data for the years after 1980 were not used in the estimations.

Great emphasis has been put on investigating whether the elasticities shown in table 6 confirm the recent development in imports and exports. In table 8 import and export market shares, relative unit labour costs and

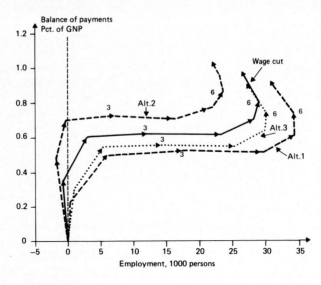

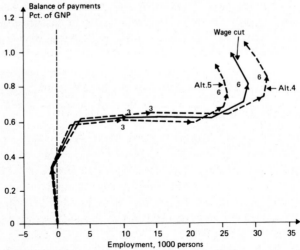

Alternative 1:   Export price increase 0 per cent of «room for manouvre» (standard: 40 pct.)
Alternative 2:   Export price increase 80 per cent of «room for manouvre» (standard: 40 pct.)
Alternative 3:   0 per cent import price decrease (standard: 1 pct.)
Alternative 4:   Export demand price elasticities raisen numerically by 0.2.
Alternative 5:   Export demand price elasticities lowered.

Figure 2: Alternative wage cut calculations.

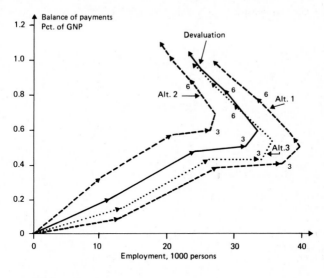

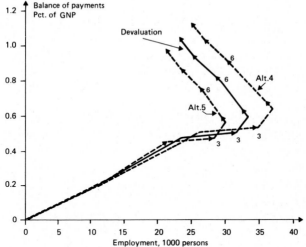

Alternative 1:   Export price increase 0 per cent of «room for manouvre» (standard: 40 pct.)
Alternative 2:   Export price increase 80 per cent of «room for manouvre» (standard: 40 pct.)
Alternative 3:   0 per cent import price decrease (standard: 1 pct.)
Alternative 4:   Export demand price elasticities raised numerically by 0.2.
Alternative 5:   Export demand price elasticities lowered.

Figure 3: Alternative devaluation calculations.

Table 8: Indicators of competitiveness in Denmark 1974–83.

	Import share	Export market share	Relative unit labour costs	Effective exchange rate
1974	1000	1000	1000	1000
1975	999	975	973	1029
1976	1054	919	959	1045
1977	1049	897	962	1037
1978	1043	873	977	1037
1979	1026	898	970	1025
1980	993	934	874	841
1981	987	971	769	877
1982	957	1002	750	836
1983	935	1025	772	844

Sources: Danish national accounts (import shares) and OECD.

the effective exchange rate are shown for the period 1974–83.

The only reason for using unit labour costs in the calculations below is that this is a handy method to test the entire model in a simple way. If, for instance, the capital-output ratio changes, or if aggregate productivity increases when low-effective plants are closed down, unit labour costs will be a bad measure of production costs.

The import share has been calculated as the average — using fixed weights — of import shares for the markets of 117 commodity groups.

Until 1979 relative unit labour costs fluctuated with no clear trend, but since then there has been a sharp decline. As can be seen from the table this improvement of competitiveness is mainly due to a fall in the effective exchange rate.

Many studies have shown that the changes in the total, aggregate import and export shares in the 1970's can to a large degree be explained by different growth rates in markets with varying Danish market shares. The changes in relative unit labour costs in the period after 1979 have, however, been so large that they must be evaluated as explaining most of the changes in imports and exports. The changes since 1979 can therefore be used to test the entire model's ability to explain the effects of changes in competitiveness.

In figure 4 the results of the ex post simulations with 1979 as the base year are shown. The difference between actual and fitted data for the years

1980–83 seems fairly small and this can be interpreted as a confirmation of the model specifications.

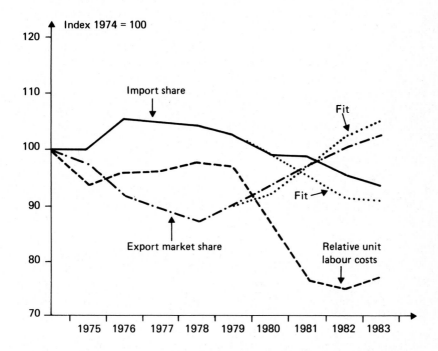

Figure 4: Market shares and relative unit labour costs.

4. The elasticity between real wages and employment

Modigliani and Drèze [1981] discuss the size of the elasticity between real wages and employment in Belgium, when the balance of payments is kept constant. Such calculations of "pure" employment effects have been presented above. In both experiments this elasticity equals −1.5 in the long run. For several reasons this elasticity is a handy and useful way to summarize the wage and devaluation multipliers and to compare them with other multipliers.

The concept of an elasticity between employment and real wages, with the balance of payments kept constant, applies equally well for small open economies (such as the Nordic countries) as for larger, relatively closed economies.

Large economies consist of small, open sub-economies for which the decline in real wage (to take one supposition) can be considered to take place one by one. When the balances of payments are kept constant, the results for the sub-economies can be added up as the result for the entire economy. The reason for this is that the wage cut has smaller employment effects for a big economy than for a small, open economy — on the other hand the accompanying expansive fiscal policy exerts the greatest employment effects on large closed economies. It must therefore be expected that the elasticity for a given economy depends more on the price elasticities of foreign trade than on the size and openness of the economy.

Modigliani and Drèze conclude that in a model which allows for factor substitution and for capacity effects the elasticity mentioned above should be around −2. It is obvious that factor substitution will raise the numerical value of the elasticity, and this may explain why the elasticity in ADAM, with no substitution, is numerically less than 2.

In his thesis Callesen [1984] suggests that the elasticity must be numerically greater (between −1.5 and −2.5) in a regime of classical unemployment than in a regime of keynesian unemployment with an elasticity between −1.0 and −1.5. The reasoning behind this is that the "additional" capacity effects are zero when there is Keynesian unemployment, since capacity utilization in this regime, by definition, is less than unity. In ADAM capacity effects are not taken into account and Callesen's results also seem to corroborate the validity of the model results, given ADAM's present specification.

The elasticity between real wages and employment cannot be expected to be the same (−1.5) in other multiplier experiments. If the terms of trade of an industrialized economy improves — for example, as a consequence of lower oil prices — then both employment and real wages would tend to increase.

One interesting feature of the employment-real wage elasticity is that it measures the trade-off between two of the most crucial economic policy objectives (especially for a given current account). A useful first step in optimal control experiments would be to compare the −1.5 elasticity of with elasticities found in other policy multipliers. The elasticity between employment and real wages, for instance, has been found to be very close to −1 when the number of working hours is reduced. This would seem to make the wage restraint look more advantageous both from a general "government" view and from a wage earners point of view. The example should be interpreted with caution, as a lot of other criteria (welfare considerations, etc.) should be taken into account.

It is our experience from working with ADAM that optimal control experiments require a thoroughly tested and complete model if the results should be reliable. On the other hand, if the model is in complete optimal control experiments will help you to find the model's weak spots. In ADAM, important weak spots are obviously the absence of factor substitution, capacity effects and other supply side effects.

References

Budgetdepartementet [1984], "Beregninger af konsekvenserne af ændringer i løn og valutakurs", Småtryk nr. 37, Copenhagen.

Callesen, Per [1984], "Bæskæftigelse, løn og produktivitet", thesis at Institute of Economics, University of Copenhagen.

Drèze, J.H. and F. Modigliani [1981], "The trade-off between real wages and employment in an open economy (Belgium)", *European Economic Review, 15*, 1–40.

Nielsen, Gert Åge [1983], "En empirisk analyse af dansk eksport", thesis at Institute of Economics, University of Copenhagen.

Macroeconomic Medium-Term Models in the Nordic Countries
O. Bjerkholt and J. Rosted (Editors)
© *Elsevier Science Publishers B. V. (North-Holland), 1987*

Financial Model Building
and Financial Multipliers
of the Danish Economy

by

Jesper Jespersen

Institute of Finance,

Copenhagen School of Business and Administration,

Copenhagen, Denmark

The tradition of integrating real sector and financial sector models is not very well established. In the wake of the "deficit dispute" the necessity of an integration has become more obvious.

Any financial (sub)model should have a firm founding in a double-entry accounting system matching debtors and creditors. The variables of such a balance sheet model are stocks — in contrast to the flow of funds approach. Data are, however, difficult to obtain for many entries. The valuation of financial stocks is also a severe problem hampering financial model building.

The main content of this paper is the presentation of a Danish financial model estimated on quarterly data (1974–1982) with the financial wealth of the private sector and the bond rate as the most important ties to "the real world". The most uncommon feature of the model is the determination of the bond rate as a genuine market clearing price. The properties of the model are analyzed. Multipliers with and without real sector feedback are calculated. The feedback from investments and consumption changes the size of the multipliers considerably and depends on the degree of liquidity sterilization.

1.   The structure of the financial sector model (FINDAN)

The Danish financial model comprises six sectors:

- Private non-bank sector (households and firms)
- Private banks (financial institutions where liabilities are regarded as money)
- Local authorities (holding accounts in private banks)
- Central government (and other authorities holding accounts at the central bank)
- Central bank (Danmarks Nationalbank, Hypotekbanken, Girokontoret and a few minor institutions).
- Foreign sector

There are five different kinds of assets/liabilities:

- Primary liquidity (monetary base)
- Demand (DD) and time (TD) deposits added together
- Loans
- Bonds (including Treasure Bills)
- Foreign exchange.

In principle a 6×6 matrix could be established for each asset/liability; but in practice all sectors do not issue all 5 kinds of liabilities (or hold all 5 assets). For instance, foreign exchange can be issued only by the foreign sector and held only by banks.

With five assets/liabilities and six sectors one could at the most expect 5×25 separate prices. Dependent on the structure of the financial markets, this number is narrowed down. For instance, all bonds, irrespective of the holder issues, are regarded as one homogeneous asset; accordingly, there is only one bond rate.

(a) The price of primary liquidity to firms and households is 1, and the nominal rate of interest is zero. On the other hand for private banks there is a positive price of liquidity often related to the discount rate set by the Central bank. The "money market" where private banks deal in cash does sometimes determine a price different from the discount rate, for example, when money is in short supply during an exchange crisis. This aspect has not yet been integrated into the model, however.

(b) The rate of interest on demand and time deposits is set by the banks more or less by agreement. This means that one finds in these markets an element of monopolistic price setting. The rate of interest on deposits has traditionally been rather closely linked to the discount rate. For "special deposits" — large deposit for a fixed time period — the interest rate is negotiated more freely, but more often than not the outcome is rather closely related to the terms ruling on the money market.

(c) Interest rates for bank loans are set in a similar way as for deposits. When the ceiling on loans was lifted in 1980 the discrepancy between deposit rates and loan rates started to narrow somewhat. Banks accept deposits and grant loans at current rates without much hesitation (except for periods where quantitative restrictions are imposed on them).

(d) A different regime is ruling the bond market. That is a very competitive market with many small demanders and suppliers. The Central Bank, of course, has a dominating role due to its position as the monetary authority and the selling agent of government bonds. The organizations of the daily trading at the bond market requires government bonds to open the market cards, so to speak, from the beginning of the day.

(e) Foreign exchange rates and interest rates are assumed to be determined exogenously.

The framework of the FINDAN model is taken from the textbook portfolio model, as in instance Brainard and Tobin [1968]. The period of estimation is 1/1974–4/1982.[1]

The *private non-bank sector* demands (a) high-powered money, (b) bank deposits and (c) bonds (private and government) and issues (d) bank loans, (e) mortgage bonds and (f) foreign loans. Each asset equation depends on private financial wealth, relative rates of return, income and exchange rate variations. The liability equations also depend upon the development of financial wealth, but only a very weak impact from changes in relative borrowing costs to changes in debt instruments has been estimated. The statistical performance of the foreign loans equation was so poor that it was decided to make the equation an "implicit" one, i.e., derived from the other equations and the balance-sheet requirement.

---

[1] Full details of the model are available from the author

According to the model, the private sector seems more inclined to run down debt than to accumulate further assets when the financial wealth increases. This adjustment pattern might be somewhat overstated due to the lack of a proper consideration of tax rules. Within the Danish tax system gains can be obtained by stretching the balance sheet.

The second sector in the model is the private banks. Due to the price-setting behaviour of the banking sector the balance sheet of the banks is to a large extent quantitatively determined by the behaviour of households and firms with regard to assets and liabilities. Banks are willing, at least in the short run, to accept any amount of deposits offered and grant loans demand (except in periods with quantitative regulations) on the ruling price (and security) conditions. Although banks are free to change the rate of interest on deposits and loans, there has up till now been a close tie between the discount rate and the bank rates.

Private banks' excess reserves during the estimation period have on the average been used to buy bonds (40%) and to pay back loans from the Central bank (60%).

The four remaining sectors (Local authorities, Central government, Central bank and the Foreign sector) are regarded as exogenous to the private one. Accordingly, the only equations holding for these sectors are identities, and institutional relations, and eventually, rules of financing deficits.

The variable that attracts the most interest in the Danish context is without doubt the bond rate. With the market-clearing approach to the bond market the rate of interest is determined as the equilibrating variable of demand and supply. Using a single equation simulation, where the right-hand side variables are given historical values, the bond rate is over the period of estimation tracked within the a boundary of 2 percentage points.

Table 1 illustrates one aspect of the model. The results from a simulation of the entire model through the estimation period give the picture shown in figure 1. Prolonging the simulation period into 1983 creates some difficulties. The pronounced fall in the nominal bond rate from 19.7% in the 4th quarter of 1982 to 13.8% in the 2nd quarter of 1983 is captured by the model only with a somewhat longer time lag.

In order to obtain a picture of how the financial markets interact under the model the following multiplier have been carried out:

Table 1: The effects of an increase in private financial wealth of 10 billion Dkr. in 1962.

Demand for bank deposits	1.6 billion Dkr.
Demand for bonds	0.6 billion Dkr.
Decrease of loans in banks	1.0 billion Dkr.
Decrease of bond debt	5.0 billion Dkr.
Decrease in foreign debt	1.8 billion Dkr.
Total	10.0 billion Dkr.

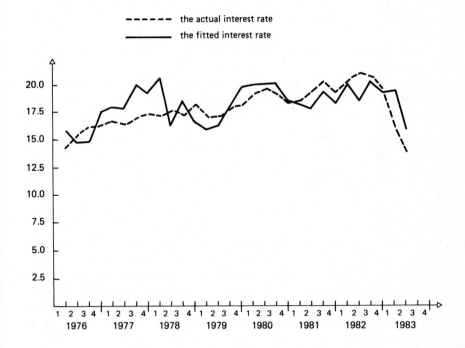

Figure 1: The bond rate, actual and fitted values.

(1) Open Market Operations:

    (a) Sale of 1 billion Dkr. government bond each quarter

    (b) Sale of 1 billion Dkr. government bonds in 1/1978.

(2) Raising the discount rate by 1 percentage point from 1/1978 onwards

(3) A higher interest rate abroad (represented by the Deutschmark-rate).

Multipliers are calculated for the period 1/1978–4/1982. The model seems to be stable, but oscillates around a "moving equilibrium". The latter phenomenon is partly due to the fact that all stocks are measured in nominal terms and nearly doubled over the simulation period.

2.   Effects of open market operations

One billion Dkr. extra government bonds are assumed to be sold each quarter. This adds up to 22 billion kr. higher supply of government bonds at the end of the period. The bond rate reacts by increasing approximately 0.2 of a percentage point every quarter, ending in 4/1982 at about 4 percentage points higher than in the reference path (cf. figure 2).

Had it been a once-only increase in the sale of bonds of 1 billion Dkr. in 1/1978 the picture would have been different. Within the same quarter the interest rate went up by .44 of a percentage point. In the following quarters portfolios adjust, which reduces the rate and in five-year perspective the lasting effect is about .22 of a percentage point.

This rise of the bond rate is, of course, mainly due to the response of the private non-financial sector. This sector ends up with an increased stock of bonds of the magnitude of 32.9 billion Dkr. (far above 22 billion Dkr. in increased government supply. This development is partly due to the reaction of the banking sector where holdings of bonds are reduced when households and firms withdraw their deposits. This reaction of the banks puts of course an extra pressure on the bond rate.

The drastic fall in bond prices due to the increase rate of interest means that the value of the amount of bonds held by the private non-bank sector does not rise much, if at all. The private non-bank sector changes its portfolio partly by running down other assets (deposits in banks and cash) and partly by borrowing — especially abroad, as shown in table 2.

Table 2 also reveals that the effect on the exchange reserves is quite strong, around 40 percent of the purchase of bonds is financed (directly or indirectly) by borrowing abroad.

Table 2: Increased government bond supply. Private non-bank sector reaction.

Reduction of deposits...........................	17.0 billion Dkr.
Reduction of cash...............................	0.9 billion Dkr.
Borrowing abroad	12.2 billion Dkr.
"Borrowing by itself"	0.7 billion Dkr.
Borrowing in banks.............................	2.1 billion Dkr.
Increased resources	32.9 billion Dkr.
Increased bond holdings	32.9 billion Dkr.

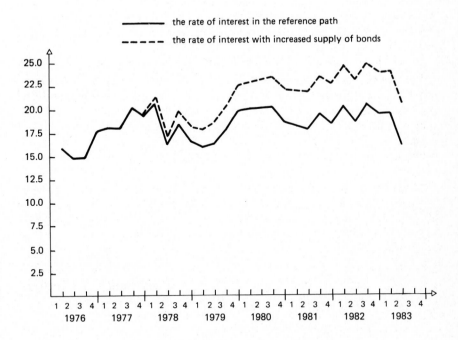

Figure 2: Increasing the supply of bonds by billion Dkr. each quarter
from 1/1978.

Table 3: Increased government bond supply. Private bank sector reactions.

Reduction of deposits	17.0 billion Dkr.
Increased loans	2.1 billion Dkr.
Loss of resources	19.1 billion Dkr.
. . . .	. . . .
Sale of bonds	10.2 billion Dkr.
Reduced cash holdings	0.2 billion Dkr.
Increased borrowing in the central bank	8.7 billion Dkr.
Increase of resources	19.1 billion Dkr.

In table 3 the reaction of the Private bank sector is shown. If banks had not been allowed to increase their borrowing in the central bank they would have been forced to sell even more bonds. This would have resulted in a further rise in the bond rate. But it would also have drawn more foreign exchange to the country.

The amount of money (bank deposit) is reduced considerably due to the increased sale of government bonds. The fall in deposits of 17 billion Dkr. corresponds to a 10 percent fall in the stock of money (4/1982) — at the "price" of 4 percentage points higher bond rate.

3.   Linking FINDAN with the real sector

It follows from the results quoted above that an increased supply of government bonds of ca. 2.5 billion Dkr. in 1/1978 would raise the bond rate by 1 percentage point (with a slightly downward trend). The consequences for the "real world" of such a higher bond rate are calculated by the use of the SMEC III model (see Fabritius [1979], which is summarized below in table 4).

These annual multipliers have been converted into quarterly changes in a crude way. The method used should, however, secure consistency between the nearly and the quarterly effects.

In the simulations with the financial sector model it is of crucial importance how the increased deficit of the public sector is financed. Two alternatives have been studied:

Table 4: "Real" effects of a 1 percentage point higher bond rate, 1978–1982.

Change in (*million Dkr.*):	1978	1979	1980	1981	1982
GDP	+47	− 851	−1202	−1486	−1621
Gross investment	−130	−1150	−1320	−1298	−1111
Housing investment	−3	−592	−524	−439	−369
Current account[1]	−133	−701	−975	−1114	−1094
Public sector	−95	−584	−597	−619	−645
Public sector balance	+228	+1285	+1572	+1733	+1739

[1] A negative sign indicates a reduced deficit on the current account.

(1) money financing (no sterilization)

(2) increased supply of government bonds amounting to the sum of the increased public sector deficit and reduced current account deficit (partial sterilization).

Results are summarized in table 5. If the liquidity effect derived from the reduced balance of payments' deficit and increased public sector deficit is not sterilized then the rate of interest starts to fall from the second quarter onwards. After 12 quarters it is back at the initial level and is still falling. This also implies that the initially positive effect on capital import is reversed, mainly due to the increased liquidity within the private sector.

On the other hand sterilizing the liquidity coming from the current account and public sector (cf. column 2 in table 5) makes the bond rate stay rather unchanged at a level 1 percentage points higher through the entire period.

The exchange reserves go up mainly due to the improved current account. From 1978–82 this adds 4 billion Dkr. to the exchange reserves. Capital import is held back by lower level of private investment. Simulation without any feedback from the real sector give results in between the other two simulations.

Table 5: Simulation results of a 2.5 billion Dkr. increase in the sale of government bonds.

Quarter		Bond rate (%)			Exchange reserves (Million Dkr.)			Money stock (Million Dkr.)		
		1	2	3	1	2	3	1	2	3
1978	1	1.11	1.11	1.11	2169	2169	2169	−735	−735	−735
	2	.91	.91	.91	1639	1664	1642	−1335	−1245	−1350
	3	.98	1.02	1.02	1273	1346	1085	−1883	−1925	−1929
	4	.93	1.02	1.01	1068	1227	1085	−2302	−2421	−2422
1979	1	.78	.97	1.04	1104	1422	988	−2487	−2788	−2790
	2	.73	1.03	1.02	1148	1621	982	−2521	−3079	−3001
	3	.56	.97	.97	1304	1983	1104	−2194	−3030	−2926
	4	.44	.96	.90	1440	2366	1243	−1721	−2801	−2687
1980	1	.32	.92	.83	1577	2757	1344	−1159	−2443	−2417
	2	.22	.92	.80	1604	3033	1391	−721	−2218	−2213
	3	.14	.95	.77	1546	3188	1372	−470	−2253	−2142
	4	.09	1.02	.77	1391	3198	1315	−497	−2682	−2211
1981	1	.01	1.06	.77	1474	3432	1250	−117	−2829	−2336
	2	−.04	1.15	.78	1304	3347	1156	−126	−3521	−2548
	3	−.11	1.14	.73	1322	2712	1246	−67	−3653	−2486
	4	−.16	1.25	.75	1243	3793	1207	150	−4169	−2587
1982	1	−.22	1.18	.68	1284	4267	1319	426	−4025	−2425
	2	−.25	1.28	.69	1151	4174	1230	460	−4655	−2537
	3	−.30	1.22	.63	1152	4514	1287	663	−4748	−2463
	4	−.31	1.24	.60	1076	4658	1293	711	−5074	−2453

1. No sterilization
2. Partial sterilization (the current account and the public sector)
3. No feedback from the real sector

4.   Effects of changes in the discount rate and the foreign rate of interest

Multipliers showing the effects of a change in the discount rate and the foreign rate of interest (represented in the model by the rate on 3 months deposits in Deutschmark) are calculated without any feedback from the real sector.

But knowing that it is only the bond rate among the financial variables that has any significant effect within SMEC III, one can use the results obtained in table 5 to find the combined effects.

When the discount rate is raised, the bond rate follows with some fluctuations approximately half way up. The foreign rate of interest has a somewhat weaker influence (if the discount rate is not raise simultaneously). The bond rate changes only by one-third that of the maximum, and the lasting effect is around 2 percentage points.

The capital import is changing by 1.5 billion Dkr. per percentage point change in the discount rate change and fluctuates between 1/2 and 1 billion Dkr. when foreign rate changes by 1 percentage point.

Also the demand for money seems to be rather volatile in the wake of a change in the short-term rate of interest. Further results are presented in table 6.

5.   Conclusions

This paper has described a model of parts of the financial sector of the Danish economy. No firm empirical results can be derived from this model as the model needs to be fully integrated with the model of the real economy. Combining our model with SMEC III, a model of the real sector of the Danish economy, the results seem to depend quite a lot on the sterilization policy of the monetary authorities. If no sterilization takes place the effect of an increased rate of interest is reversed in the course of a five-year period.

Contrary to the conventional wisdom a higher bond rate did not attract a significant amount of loans in the period up to 1982. Capital imports nearly dried up due to lower activity and thus the demand for credit dwindled.

According to the real sector model (SMEC III) it is mainly the bond rate that influences the demand for investment goods and consumption (via the public sector debt). Therefore, a change in the structure of the interest

Table 6: Multiplier effects of a 1 percentage point increase in the discount rate and the foreign rate of interest.

Quarter		Bond rate (%)		Exchange reserves (Million Dkr.)		Money stock (Million Dkr.)	
		DC	DM	DC	DM	DC	DM
1978	1	.50	.14	1360	−551	1021	−932
	2	.46	.24	1744	−875	1825	−1797
	3	.39	.32	1938	−1054	2552	−2521
	4	.39	.35	2018	−1158	3072	−3907
1979	1	.39	.35	1939	−1079	3272	−3326
	2	.37	.33	1909	−853	3395	−3156
	3	.42	.27	1771	−643	3201	−2800
	4	.43	.23	1746	−505	2856	−2394
1980	1	.48	.19	1496	−426	2487	−2079
	2	.50	.17	1426	−2151	2151	−1868
	3	.52	.16	1459	−475	2020	−1837
	4	.52	.16	1598	−516	2108	−1858
1981	1	.51	.15	1732	−456	2286	−1776
	2	.48	.15	1885	−471	2550	−1756
	3	.47	.14	1971	−453	2719	−1682
	4	.47	.15	2112	−508	2394	−1765
1982	1	.45	.15	2123	−536	3024	−1838
	2	.45	.17	2191	−669	1381	−2095
	3	.42	.18	2295	−747	3349	−2395
	4	.45	.20	2445	−905	3305	−2707

DC – discount rate
DM – foreign rate of interest (Deutschmark 3 months deposits

rate in the direction of relatively lower long-term rates seems to have some advantages regarding activity as well as capital import.

But also in this case it can hardly be stressed too strongly that no empirical results are any better than the underlying model.

References

Brainard, W. and J. Tobin [1968], "Pitfalls in Financial Model Building", *American Economic Review, 58,* 99–122.

Fabritius, J. [1979], "SMEC III – en simulationsmodel for Danmark", Copenhagen.

Macroeconomic Medium-Term Models in the Nordic Countries
O. Bjerkholt and J. Rosted (Editors)
© *Elsevier Science Publishers B. V. (North-Holland), 1987*

KESSU III:
An Econometric Planning Model
for the Finnish Economy

by

August Leppä
The Ministry of Finance,
Helsinki, Finland

1.   Introduction

The current model version KESSU III, developed and used by the Economic
Department of the Ministry of Finance, is the latest link in a chain of models
which started in the 1960's. Over the decades the model has changed in
many ways but it still retains some of its original features. It is based
on an input-output framework and it is used mainly for economic policy
planning in the medium term. The disaggregation, time horizon and policy
orientation are features shared with models of other Nordic Ministries of
Finance, but these properties distinguish KESSU from other Finnish macro
models.

Medium-term fiscal policy planning, the usual time horizon being 3–8
years, is the main purpose of KESSU. The disaggregated and largely exogenous public sector is due to the model's main role. As a planning model
the system is more open than a model used for less conditional forecasting.
Besides fiscal policy planning, the model has been used for several specific
studies including growth scenarios for sectoral plans and evaluation of the
macroeconomic effects of specific projects. The current model version differs from the previous one mainly due to a more refined dynamic structure
of behavioural equations and a more consistent modelling of supply-side
factors.

Throughout the model the dynamic structures of stochastic equations have been specified using the error correction model (ECM) described, for example, by Salmon [1982]. Compared with most alternative dynamic specification hypotheses, ECM has several advantages. It can for instance be derived from the optimizing behaviour of economic agents and it has many desirable statistical properties.

Taking supply-side factors consistently into account in the open sector (i.e., in some manufacturing industries) by using supply determined production in the long run has brought several interesting questions to light. Supply orientation in a few key industries in a disaggregated input-output model is clearly a new feature compared to the former model version KESSU II, with its overall demand orientation. Although the current model version is more suited to structural analysis, new problems have emerged along with the new results.

KESSU III has been developed and used in the Ministry of Finance, but relations with the Central Statistical Office (CSO) are very close. This is evident in the model, whose basis are input-output tables both in production and in prices of which about 80–90 per cent of the time-series of over 800 variables are produced by the CSO. The model is mostly based on data derived from the system of national accounts.

This chapter is intended to give an overall presentation of the model. Empirical results are hardly touched upon. However, certain specifications in the open sector do rely heavily on empirical estimates that in turn affect the model behaviour. Therefore, if this chapter is read together with the chapter by Sourama [in this volume] dealing with policy analysis in KESSU, or with Kaski and Leppä [1986], the character of the model will become clearer.

2.   Main features

The annual dynamic input-output model KESSU III intended for medium-term analysis is of medium size. The model includes approximately 600 equations of which about 200 are truly behavioural stochastic ones. The remaining equations are identities, technical relations and input-output equations. With respect to its use as a disaggregated planning model, KESSU III is fairly closed. Several of the exogenous variables, which in all add up to about 250, are of minor importance. The most influential variable are foreign demand and prices, exchange rates, nominal wages, interest rate, tax rates, public expenditure and some population variables.

The input-output data supplied by the CSO concern the year 1981. Up to now all coefficients have been held constant excluding some occasional corrections on the value-added level. The estimation period for stochastic equations is most often 1961–1982 with yearly data. In some cases, when there has been reason to suspect structural changes in equations, the estimation period has been shortened. The same applies to a few variables for which the time-series from the 1960's are not available. These exceptions refer mainly to foreign trade. In most cases the method used for estimation is OLS.

The most important classifications in the model, the 16 branches of industries, can be seen in table 4. Excluding private consumption most behavioural equations use this classification. Most influential and crucial equations refer to industries. That means, for example, that fixed-capital formation is explained by industries and not by institutional sectors.

The main efforts in the current model version have been directed to developing a well-behaved model for the open sector. Before presenting a more detailed and technical description in the next section, some ideas about this open sector can be discussed. The former model version KESSU II, Mannermaa et al. [1983], was clear-cut Keynesian with demand-determined production and prices following costs. These effects can be found also in KESSU III but only in the short run. Production and prices in the open sector are modelled so that the dynamic specification allows a Keynesian orientation in the short run and supply-determined production with given foreign prices in the long run. The branches in the exposed sector of KESSU III were not selected *a priori*. This was left for empirical studies. Research was restricted to the manufacturing sector but even there some industries were classified only as partially open. Another *a priori* assumption was the form of the production function needed for estimating supply. The chosen function is a combination of the CES and Leontief functions, i.e., the CES value-added function with zero substitution between intermediate inputs and primary factors.

The dynamic properties of the model can be derived both from empirical results and from *a priori* decisions based on the medium-term horizons of the model. In most cases the dynamic specification for single equations includes a long-term restriction, e.g., export volumes are restricted to export supply or prices are tied to costs in the long run. This means that medium-term equilibrium is preferred to short-term forecasting ability. A conflict between behaviour in different time horizons is not a necessary rule but occurs sometimes. The adjustment mechanisms used are intended for adjustment to long-term equilibrium and not for short-term fitting of data.

In a broad sense, there is no automatic equilibrium in the economy imitated by the model. Nominal wages are exogenous, as are exchange rates and rate of interest. Unemployment, current account and public deficit are gaps which are not filled automatically by the model.

3.   Model structure outline

The main emphasis in this presentation is on the open sector, the supply-side effects of which govern the long-run path of the system to a great degree. The sheltered industries with Keynesian orientation can be outlined as a side product by mentioning the important differences compared to the open sector economy. The system is drawn very roughly with only a few central equations in the state of long-run equilibrium and without any dynamic specifications or other details.

The starting point for the exposed sector is the usual assumption about a small open economy in which an exporting firm faces a given world market price and a horizontal demand curve, and which in due course leads to profit-maximizing behaviour and further on to supply determined production. In the model the given world market price implies that in the long run the export prices P_x follows the weighted average of important competing exporters' prices in their exports P_c. Both exports and imports are modelled on the branch level and so it is easy to assume the branch-wise long-term terms of trade as constant, $P_m = P = P_x$. The crucial assumption in this connection is that the domestic price of production P_q follows the export price. Thus according to the general principles of the Scandinavian inflation model (Aukrust [1970]), prices for the domestic market and for exports in the open sector are equal, excluding the effects of costs and adjustment in the short run. The world market price development is transmitted partially also to the sheltered sector through intermediate inputs. Cost pricing with short-term variable mark-up in the sheltered sector together with exogenous wages implies that the co-ordination of foreign prices and domestic wages is of crucial importance to economic policy in this model as it is in reality.

The basic long-run price relations in the open sector can be written as

$$P_x = P_c \tag{1}$$
$$P_m = P_c \tag{2}$$
$$P_q = P_x \tag{3}$$

Both sides of (2) are exogenous and the restriction implied by (2) is imposed in long-term scenarios. With the given classification of industries it was not possible to distinguish industries competing with imports and deriving their prices from import prices, hence P_m does not directly affect P_q.

With exogenous wages there is no equilibrium income distribution in the open sector until a decision concerning incomes policy has been made in policy analysis. Foreign prices are transmitted to the sheltered sector only partially and so the price of intermediate inputs used by the open sector may deviate from P_q, resulting in deviations in the price of value added. The strength of this phenomenon depends on the cost structure in each open industry.

The volume of exports of a profit-maximizing representative firm depends in the long run on the profitable supply potential. Potential output is derived by using a production function, one for each open branch. In practice the theoretical purity of the representative firm cannot be used, one branch in manufacturing may deliver goods abroad and to the domestic market and compete with imports all at the same time. In practice domestic costs can affect also export prices temporarily. They can influence domestic prices of the open sector and import prices are handled only as cost elements because in the long run they coincide with export prices.

On the quantity side the reactions of the representative firm are based on the assumption that the domestic demand is first satisfied and the rest of the potential output Y_p is available for export supply X_s. Thus production for the domestic market is derived from demand and costs are included in prices as long as production prices are not completely determined by foreign competitors. If domestic prices deviate from import prices there is a tendency to change import shares and so production for the domestic market is determined by relative prices and supply to the domestic market is demand determined. Exports to the CMEA countries are handled as production for domestic markets in nature because of their exogenous origin. This results in a relationship where an increase in exports to the East decreases partially the capacity to export to the West.

The export supply X_s, defined on the level of value added, is

$$X_s = Y_p - a_1(Q - a_2 X) \tag{4},$$

where a_1 is the share of value added in total output Q, a_2 is the diagonal element of the respective branch in the Leontief inverse matrix, and X is actual exports.

The assumption that domestic demand is satisfied first is very impor-

tant when evaluating the effects of demand management. In the simplified
world of the model the same product is delivered to both markets but in the
real world the same effect may emerge from resource restrictions. Because
of adjustment dynamics and indirect effects, an increase in domestic demand will not necessarily leave exports unaffected. In practice these effects
are small but noticeable. Assuming the hypothesis of increase returns to
scale leads to the result that an increase in domestic demand has a positive
effect on potential output. In the long-run export behaviour of the open
sector is given as

$$X = a_3 X_s (P_x/P_c)^{b_1} . \tag{5}$$

Using the assumption (1), exports in the open sector depend only on export
supply, and following the logical chain backwards, on potential output,
demand for production factors, their relative prices and profitability. The
final explanation is thus the relation between given world market prices
and domestic costs, which in the model are governed by exogenous nominal
wages. So the explanation is not very far from the equations in KESSU II
based on foreign demand and price competitiveness, because also in KESSU
III changes in foreign demand affect export, although only temporarily
vanishing through the lag structure.

The potential output Y_p or the potential value added of the exporting
industry in the open sector is derived from a CES-Leontief production
function in each branch. In a general form the production function is (6).

$$Q = Q(Y,V) = Q\big(Y(K,N),V\big) \tag{6}$$

$$Y = Y(K,N) = a_4\big((1-f)K^{-g} + f(e^{zt}N)^{-g}\big)^{-1/g} \tag{7}$$

where f is the share of labour costs in value added, z is the rate of Harrod
neutral technical change and g is the substitution parameter.

The set of assumptions behind these equations (6) and (7) might be
treated critically if they are separated from the model but in this connection the important property is the consistency of the production system
with the rest of the model. The value added Y is assumed separable from
intermediate inputs V, which in this model version includes also energy inputs. The separability of value added from V implies that the substitution
between labour N and capital K is not dependant on V. The hypothesis of a separate value-added function $Y(K,N)$ in manufacturing can be
critically discussed, but this procedure suits well the methods in national
accounts.

The question of energy inputs should be discussed in connection with
the main use of the model. For energy analysis the current solution, where

energy is considered as a cost element and not as a production factor, is not sufficient. For medium term structural analysis it can be accepted.

Intermediate inputs are treated with Leontief-technology with constant coefficients. On the dual side this solution leads to residual value-added prices which depend both on export prices and on domestic costs. Thus, the energy input, which is usually nested together with capital inside an enlarged value-added concept, appears here only as a cost factor with fixed-volume coefficients and variable price.

The CES-Leontief formulation enables one to calculate potential output for the branches of the open sector. Elsewhere in manufacturing the demand for production factors can be based on the same function, although there is not necessarily any need for export supply formulation. In other branches, i.e., in typical sheltered industries also the value-added function is of the Leontief form, both in the short and long run. Production is determined by input-output coefficients and the demand for production factors is derived from production. Therefore typical features of each industry in the sheltered sector are not so easily discernible as in the exposed sector.

The constant input coefficients which are used for intermediate inputs imply that the typical firm can affect the volume of intermediate inputs only by changing production or capacity. On the other hand in prices and values the relation between value added and intermediate inputs may change. The chain of reasoning starts from exogenous nominal wages and mark-up prices in the sheltered sector.

$$P_{qs} = a_5 C, \qquad (8)$$

where C is the index of wage costs and intermediate inputs including imports.

Due to this the foreign prices $P_c = P_x = P_m$ are neither in the short run nor the long run completely transferred into domestic production prices in the sheltered sector P_{qs}. Given the production price P with its foreign origin and costs depending at least partially on P_{qs}, the share of value added in value terms may change if the exogenous wages are not adjusted accordingly in the planning process.

Changes in value added can easily be connected with profitability although the formal link in the model, i.e., in manufacturing branches, is through the real price of production factors in which the price of value added is the denominator. Given the CES function with Harrod neutral disembodied technical change, profit-maximizing behaviour implies the following demand function for labour input:

$$N = a_6 Y (Nw/YP_y)^{b_2} e^{zt} . \tag{9}$$

In the short run this labour demand N can be used as an expression for desired labour when the adjustment process is specified. In (9) value added, Y, is a constant share a_1 of total input Q, Nw/Y is labour costs per unit of production and P_y the price of value added.

When the production technology is of the putty-clay form, investment demand becomes

$$I = a_7 Y (c/P_y)^{b_3} . \tag{10}$$

Besides the price of investment goods, the user cost of capital c includes also the rates of interest and depreciation. Functional forms suitable for the demand for factors of production are easily derived from the equilibrium equations. The estimated form for labour is in logarithmic form

$$
\begin{aligned}
\Delta \ln N &= c_0 + c_1 \Delta \ln Y + c_2 \ln(N/Y)_{-1} + c_3 \ln(Nw/YP_y)_{-1} + c_4 t \\
&= c_0 + c_1 \Delta \ln Y + (c_2 + c_3) \ln(N/Y)_{-1} + c_3 \ln(w/P_y)_{-1} + c_4 t
\end{aligned}
\tag{11}
$$

and accordingly $b_2 = c_3/c_2$ and $z = c_4/c_2$. Also investment demand is based on empirical estimates of the coefficients in (11) because the elasticity of substitution b_3, $b_3 = b_2/(1 - b_2) = c_3/(c_2 - c_3)$ and $g = (1 - b_3)/b_3$, is taken as an *a priori* restriction when estimating the actual specification of (10). Estimation of the elasticity of substitution is based on the labour demand equation because the user cost of capital c is likely to be subject to serious measurement errors.

The relation between investments I and capital K is defined by

$$K = I + (1 - d)K_{-1} , \tag{12}$$

where d is the rate of depreciation.

By linking amounts of production factors N and K into the ex post production function (7), an estimate for the potential output Y is obtained. The rate of capacity utilization is the relation between this Y_p and actual Y, which in the short run is determined by demand through the input-output structure. Y is based on (7) only in those two important open branches, i.e., in wood, pulp and paper and the metal industry. In other manufacturing industries the role of capacity utilization is limited and accordingly it is estimated by a simple time trend equation for the capital-output ratio.

The technical possibilities for calculating the potential output Y_p in a macro model was one of the reasons to select this kind of production function. On the other hand CES was preferred to a Cobb-Douglas production function because differences between branches are allowed when the elasticity of substitution is not restricted *a priori*. Cobb-Douglas would have been a more stable framework for medium-term analysis because of the implications regarding income distribution.

Short-term variations in domestic production induced by demand are partially dampened by changing import shares. The static form of a standard import function in each branch leads to a constant import share because of the assumptions (2)–(3). Besides the open sector, also other branches compete with imports and so the effect of relative prices is not completely eliminated from (13).

$$M = a_8(M + Q)(P_m/P_q)^{b_4} . \tag{13}$$

This standard form and its dynamic estimated form doesn't track the development in certain branches where drastic changes in import shares have taken place. Those trendwise changes are outside a standard industry equation and in certain way outside the scope of the model KESSU, too, because supply restrictions or changes in commodity structure have affected the import shares.

In the short-run demand elasticities are usually over unity which restricts the variation in domestic production. Compared to the old model version, KESSU II, this effect may be due to the treatment of imports by branches. The dynamic structure of different demand categories of imports is in the current version hidden behind the single demand elasticity. Demand effects dominate in the short run whereas the price effects are not noticed until later, although these effects are partially offset by the connection of foreign and domestic prices in the open sector.

Since in the long run the open sector firm is facing perfect markets for factors of production and for commodities, production is determined by foreign prices and factor prices. This leads to the possibility of classic unemployment in the open sector, whereas the other side of the economy, the sheltered one, is steered by demand and so mainly by wage incomes. The distinction between these two sectors and time horizons do not coincide completely because potential output is affected also by domestic demand and because foreign demand can temporarily influence production. The empirical properties are more thoroughly discussed in the chapter by Sourama [in this volume].

4.   Central economic blocks

The general assumptions, principles and solutions which were discussed in the former chapter are necessary but not sufficient for a presentation of the model. A complete list of equations has been published separately by Kaski and Leppä [1986]. Simulation properties are discussed in a separate chapter by Sourama. The classification of branches and some parameter estimates can be found in the following tables but still there remain many details which might be of interest. These include questions like the consistency of prices, the treatment of public consumption components or the division of operational surplus in institutional sectors, which are not crucial for the dynamic and causal structure of the model but they ought to be taken into account when analysing policy simulations.

4.1   Exports

The treatment of exports is fairly closed in this kind of disaggregated model. For planning purposes the system can be used in a more exogenous form. Foreign activity and price variables are exogenous because for a small open economy this assumption is easily accepted. Exchange rate or rates for the important exporting branches are exogenous, too. In addition to these, export volumes for certain small industries like agriculture and forestry are exogenous. Trade with the Soviet Union is also exogenous and derived mainly from trade agreements between Finland and USSR. Imports from the East consist mainly of crude oil, and because this commodity is modelled as a separate variable it is possible to balance Soviet trade when using the model. In practical calculations the balance is not achieved every year but over five-year periods. The yearly balance or the temporary imbalance in value terms is determined by the user and not explicitly and automatically in the model. In this connection it is worth remembering that exports to the East are treated as output for domestic markets in nature and therefore their effects on production depend on the shares of manufacturing industries in the eastern trade because of differences in the supply reactions.

There is no standard solution when selecting the appropriate demand variable for foreign activity. The countries in question are selected separately for each exporting industry and the activity variables include, for example, value added, household consumption and production in manufacturing. The same principle is used in competing export prices, the selection of competing exporters depends on the branch in question. The exchange rate for each export industry is treated together or separately from the competing price depending on dynamic reactions. The variables in the model are weighted averages of country data, e.g., in the wood, pulp and paper industry the competing price P_c consists of respective prices in Sweden and Canada.

In estimated form the typical features of different branches are no longer so clear. For example, in export prices of the manufacturing industries the explanations are as follows:

Table 1: Independent variables in export price equation.

Branch	Short-run	P_x	Long-run
Food, beverages		Exogenous	
Textiles	C, P_c		C
Wood, pulp and paper	C, P_c		C, P_c
Metal	C		$P_c{}^*$
Chemicals			C, P_c
Other manufacturing	P_c		C

*The distinction in this table between short and long run effects is made so that variables only in differenced form are classified as having only short-term effects. The effects of level variables also occur instantly.

The shares of long-term influence of domestic costs and competing prices could be determined by data mining but a simple specification has been preferred. The explanation is a mixture only in forest manufacturing and in chemicals.

The estimation of the export volumes by branches is a logical consequence of the principles described earlier and of the empirical results of the price equations. In wood, pulp and paper and metal industries the volume of exports is determined by the export supplies whereas in other manufacturing the explanation is derived from foreign activity and price competitiveness. For instance, the estimated or the final estimated equation for the metal industry is in logarithmic form

$$\Delta \ln X = 0.13 + 0.40 \ln(X_s/X_{-1}) + 0.88 \Delta \ln D - 0.33 \ln(P_x/P_c),$$

where D is production in manufacturing in selected countries and P_c is expressed in Finnish currency. Due to this specification, exports X are tied with unit long-term elasticity to export supply X_s. Because the same reaction holds between P_x and P_c, export supply is also the only important factor in the long run.

4.2   Imports

The import analysis in KESSU III differs from the previous model version, described in detail in Mannermaa et al [1983], in essentially two respects. Firstly, import equations are estimated separately for each industry, i.e., import shares by producing sector, and not for separate demand categories as before. Secondly, the dynamic specification together with the new classification dampens reactions in domestic production to certain simulations. Import prices in Finnish currency are exogenously given in each industry as well as the exchange rate effects on import prices. In general, the assumption (2) is a suitable starting point, but especially in the short run, not a binding restriction.

ECM adjustment was applied to the basic form (13) and as an example in metal manufacturing the estimated import equation took the form

$$\Delta \ln M = -0.60 + 1.39 \Delta \ln Y - 0.55 \ln P - 0.55 \ln(M/Y)_{-1},$$

where Y is now total demand for metal products and P is the relative price P_m/P_q. The equilibrium form (13) used as a desired state in a dynamic adjustment system already includes a long-term restriction of unit elasticity with respect to total demand. In most branches this assumption can be accepted also on the basis of statistical tests. Short-term variation is mainly explained by the differenced activity variable $\Delta \ln Y$, whereas price effects influence the import share more in the long run. In actual scenarios assumptions (1)–(2) imply that in the long run the import share is relatively constant. Constant import share can be justified in medium-term analysis in most branches. In addition typical sources of change in import shares, e.g., changes in commodity structure or supply restrictions, cannot be transformed into variables which are normally used in this model.

The second important point is the classification by industry, excluding some small service items and noncompetitive energy imports. The change in classification can be noticed also in the following table where short (S) and long-term (L) elasticities of estimated equations in manufacturing are given. Formerly the use of aggregate dependant variables, i.e., imports for consumption, capital goods and raw materials, together with aggregate activity variables resulted in a slightly smaller variation in short-term import shares on the branch level. The highest short-term elasticities can be seen in industries delivering goods for final consumption. Metal products and chemicals are delivered to several industries and especially in the case of metal industry for several final-use categories. Phase differences along the business cycle when a certain industry delivers goods for several purposes cannot be explained in this system except with time series tools.

Table 2: Import elasticities in manufacturing industries.

Industry	With respect to demand		With respect to price P_m/P_q	
	S	L	S	L
Food	2.04	1.00		
Textiles	2.12	1.00	−0.73	
Wood, pulp and paper	0.77	1.73	−0.43	−1.31
Metal	1.39	1.00	−0.55	−1.00
Chemicals	1.29	1.00	−0.31	−1.29
Other manufacturing	2.08	2.01	−0.66	−1.10

The relative importance of price and activity variables in short-run behaviour is quite striking and uniform. Activity dominates in the short run, which with these elasticities results in dampening the changes in domestic production.

In most cases the selected equations are estimated using the period of 1970–1982. The changes in parameter values and in specifications compared to the normal estimation period of 1961–1982. The changes in parameter values and in specifications compared to the normal estimation period of 1961–1982 were comparatively large.

Some commodities like crude oil and coal plus a few fruits and coffee are treated as noncompetitive imports using constant coefficients. The missing price parameters of food imports refer to noncompetitiveness, too, but with nonunit elasticity.

4.3   Investment in capital and stocks

Fixed-capital formation in KESSU III is modelled by branches and by functional sectors. The total amount of investment is transformed into estimates by institutional sectors using constant shares in each branch. Investment in stocks is determined in aggregate excluding minor variables for households and central government.

Public investments are easy to consider as policy variables although the exogeneity of public expenditure of the local government is arguable in practice. Energy and agricultural investments are determined by other factors than those which are present in this medium-term model. Housing investment is also exogenous, though this demand component is large and influenced by economic variations. Some simulation results are affected by this lack of a channel between housing investment and household income, but because of recent structural changes in housing investment, reliable behavioural equations with at least some forecasting ability are extremely scarce.

The second type of fixed capital-formation is that in manufacturing industries. Gross investment is derived using partial adjustment for desired investment (10) and one obtained standard investment equation is as follows (this time the example is the textile industry):

$$\Delta \ln I = -1.51 + 1.91 \Delta \ln Y - 0.13 \ln(c/P_y) - 0.52 \ln(I/Y)_{-1}.$$

Similar coefficients of other manufacturing industries can be read in table 3. The most important point which is a result of the chosen CES technology is the overall size of the elasticity of substitution, i.e., the coefficient of real user cost c/P_y. This coefficient is clearly smaller than the value of 1 implied by the the common form for Cobb-Douglas technology.

Table 3: Coefficients in investment functions in manufacturing.

Branch	ΔY	$(I/Y)_{-1}$	c/P_y	long-term elasticity with respect to c/P_y
	S	L	S	L
Food, beverages		−0.69	−0.20	−0.29
Textiles	1.91	−0.52	−0.13	−0.26
Wood, pulp and paper		−0.52	−0.10	−0.19
Metal	1.94	−0.54	−0.16	−0.31
Chemicals		−0.35	−0.09	−0.25

These estimates have been obtained using the *a priori* restriction described in connection with (11) and so these equations are consistent with labour demand equations.

In other branches investment demand is modelled in a bit simpler way, meaning that the user cost c including, e.g., interest rate and price of investment goods, is not used. In some occasions it has not been used because the main problem of finding a consistent solution for both production factors is not solved.

The treatment of investment in stocks is a simple example of error correction adjustment. The desired stocks of industries is tied to the total value added excluding certain branches like agriculture, forestry, financing and insurance ownership of dwellings. This demand component is converted into production using an optimization procedure where the base year structure and changes in production are restrictions. The stock equation is to a certain extent a buffer between demand and supply inducing cyclical movements to the whole model, as well.

4.4 Demand for labour

The operational variable in the form (11) is the number of employees. The differences in reactions with respect to both production factors can be easily noticed when comparing the tables 3 and 4, where the coefficients in manufacturing are derived from analogous estimated functions. The long-term elasticity with respect to real price is *a priori* restricted to be the same in both tables but the speed of adjustment is the relevant factor in this comparison.

The demand for labour in other sectors, i.e., in local and central government, follows by definition the corresponding value added. Because of this the relation between public expenditure and value added is decisive.

Certain specific features can be distinguished already from the values of coefficients although they are more clear in suitable simulations. Labour force can be adjusted relatively quickly in textiles and metal manufacturing although the short-term variations in investment are notable. In other manufacturing branches the labour force adjusts relatively slowly compared to the reactions in capital. These are not very far from self-evident conclusions, e.g., textiles is a relatively labour intensive branch where capital is quite flexible. The metal industry is quite heterogeneous in this respect and so this kind of conclusions should be taken with reservations. Slow reactions, for example, in chemical industry are presumably caused by big inflexible investment plants with vintage type properties in labour demand.

4.5 Consumption

Public consumption is an exogenous demand component in the model sys-

Table 4: Demand for labour, selected coefficients.

Branch	ΔY	$(N/Y)_{-1}$	$w/P_y)$
Agriculture	*		
Forestry	0.39	−0.41	
Food, beverages	0.21	−0.38	−0.11
Textiles	0.73	−0.75	−0.19
Wood, pulp and paper	0.30	−0.26	−0.05
Metal	0.46	−0.73	−0.22
Chemicals	0.28	−0.32	−0.08
Other manufacturing	0.44	−0.51	−0.09
Electricity	**	**	**
House construction	0.89	−0.39	
Other construction	1.01	−0.43	
Trade	0.34	−0.16	
Transport	0.52	−0.20	
Financing	0.86	−0.52	
Housing	*		
Other services	0.49	−0.17	

*   exogenous
** different specification

tem. Central government consumption is one of the main policy variables and although the question of exogenous local government expenditure is a bit more controversial, it is treated as exogenous. The central government consumption is given in components and the only endogenous component, commodities delivered to the households, is of minor importance. Because of this disaggregation employment in this sector can be directly tied to the components of value added.

The consumption of households is based on a classification of 19 categories. The standard equation specification, including a dynamic adjustment with real disposable income and relative price as independent variables, is used in most categories. It is the group of ill-behaving categories like tobacco and housing which deserve individual treatment. The point is that there is no separate function for aggregate consumption, total consumption is a direct sum of the categories. Specific policy proposals may change somewhat the savings rate in the short run (see Sourama [in this volume]). However, in certain categories accumulated savings affect consumption and so a relatively stable savings rate is achieved although it is not *a priori* restricted.

4.6 Prices

The pricing behaviour both in the open and the sheltered sector has already been touched upon but that is not enough. In addition, to the prices of foreign trade, there are two types of prices in KESSU model. Firstly, total output prices are determined on the industry level by dynamic behavioural equations. The resulting functional income distribution, including the effects of foreign prices, is also determined on the industry level. In the next stage prices for final demand components and for intermediate inputs for each industry are calculated using fixed shares of the base year.

In the open sector, prices are influenced by export prices and this influence is extended also to forestry where export prices of wood, pulp and paper dominate in the long run. In other industries the variable mark-up on costs is changed temporarily through the adjustment system and in some cases also by the rate of capacity utilization. The cost variable in (8) includes besides intermediate inputs also wage costs. The estimated form of a dynamic specification in the sheltered economy is the following:

$$\ln P = c_1 P_{-1} + c_2 \ln C + c \ln(C/P)_{-1},$$

where there is no *a priori* restriction with respect to the long-term cost elasticity. If $c_1 = 1 - c_2$ the unit elasticity would be achieved. In practice also the short-term elasticities are very near unity due to the small share of operating surplus in total output. The short-run elasticities, i.e., parameter c_2 in manufacturing are presented in table 5.

Table 5: Short-run cost elasticities of production prices in manufacturing.

Branch	c_2
Food, beverages	1.02
Textiles	0.95
Wood, pulp and paper	0.93
Metal	1.07
Chemicals	0.97

4.7   Compensation for production factors

After the dynamic specifications in the functional part of the model, the equations in the institutional part are quite simple. The list of variables used follows almost in detail, with only a couple of exceptions, the classification and definitions of national accounts. There are three main types of equations or explanations: fixed shares applied to some aggregate variable, variables which are tied to other variables with fixed coefficients or econometric equations. Usually the exogenous information is given in volume form and values are formed using endogenous prices.

The wage and salary income by industries and sectors is obtained by multiplying exogenous average salaries by the number of employees. Social security fees are classified in such a way that each contribution can be directed through the household sector to the corresponding sector: social security funds, financial institutions or central government. Each type of contribution is estimated using exogenous rates, wages and salaries by industry and base-year coefficients with respect to wages. Gross operating surplus by industry is the difference between production price and costs. These estimates are transformed into figures for each institutional sector by using fixed shares for each industry.

4.8   Requited transfers

Entrepreneurial incomes, interest and dividends are the main activities in this group. Exogenous public price policy is reflected in the "profits" of public enterprises. In private sectors entrepreneurial income is tied to the incomes in respective industries. In the same way dividends paid by enterprises follow operating surplus and the total sum of dividends is distributed to receiving sectors by slightly moving shares.

Without other monetary features the treatment of interest in the model is a bit problematic. The interest paid abroad and by the central government can be estimated using the debt system of these sectors, but on other occasions there is a need for exogenous variables such as, e.g., interests received by the central government or interests received from abroad. Another solution is to explain interest items by using saving and investment as a basis. The net interest receipts of financial institutions are estimated as a residual so that paid and received interests in the economy are balanced.

4.9   Unrequited transfers

Under this heading can be handled both direct and indirect taxes, social security contributions and benefits and other transfers.

The direct taxes of enterprises and financial institutions are explained by their taxable income, which is represented by operating surplus. The most important variable, direct taxes of households, is still without an efficient solution. The very simple relation between taxable income and taxes is supplemented by an exogenous variable which can be used to approximate the effects of changes in tax rates. So in dynamic multipliers the effects of these tax rates are biased. Another problem is the concept of taxable income, which in this model version is not completely satisfactory.

Indirect taxes and subsidies in the model are estimated in two stages. Volumes are calculated by constant coefficients in production, consumption or other final demand components. The price components are based on input-output prices and tax rates, or is exogenous. So there is a price variable for each tax type. Besides sales tax there are a full dozen different taxes and half a dozen subsidies.

The reason for this disaggregation is not only to obtain accurate income estimates of the central government but also the need to allocate correctly the cost effects of these taxes.

Social security contributions, which are mainly tied to wages and salaries, and exogenous rates are converted via the household sector to other sectors by type of contribution. Social security benefits are practically all exogenous in volume and the variables are inflated by a corresponding price index which can be derived from the corresponding legislature. Among other transfers, those from the central government to other sectors are exogenous and the system of volumes and prices mentioned above is applied also in this connection. Transfers between other sectors are dealt with by simple technical relations or they are left exogenous. Actual stochastic equations are not used.

4.10   Saving and net lending

The disposable income of each sector can be constructed by the variables mentioned in earlier chapters. In order to determine net lending, only depreciation, investment in capital and stocks, capital transfers and purchases of land are needed. Consumption of fixed capital is obtained by using investment and incomes of the respective sector as an explanation, investment in fixed capital by industry is distributed to institutional sectors by fixed shares and investment in stocks outside industries are exogenous.

Capital transfers are treated as exogenous variables and the net sales of land by the household are distributed to other sectors by constant shares. The current account or balance of payments is treated almost the same way. Small items like factor incomes to and from abroad are exogenous and the same applies also to interest payments to Finland. Interest and redemption payments abroad are estimated with the help of the foreign debt system.

5. Concluding remarks

The presentation of the model KESSU III in this paper cannot be considered comprehensive. The broad ideas given concentrate on the treatment of the exposed sector, which can be considered as a new feature in this model version. The supply-side orientation of the disaggregated input-output model is not yet completely mature and the dynamic behaviour can still be refined but the results, including empirical simulation results, are at least satisfactory.

References

Aukrust, O. [1970], "PRIM 1: A Model of Price and Income Distribution of an Open Economy", *Review of Income and Wealth, 1.*

Kaski, E.-L. and A. Leppä [1986], "KESSU III yhtälöt (Equations in KESSU III)", Helsinki.

Mannermaa, K., E.-L. Kaski, A. Leppä and H. Sourama [1983], "Keskipitkän ajan suunnittelumalli KESSU II (Medium-term planning model KESSU II)", Helsinki.

Salmon, M. [1982], "Error Correction Mechanisms", *The Economic Journal, 92*, 615–629.

Sourama, H. [1987], "KESSU III: the effects of Wage Increases and Fiscal Policy", in this volume.

Macroeconomic Medium-Term Models in the Nordic Countries
O. Bjerkholt and J. Rosted (Editors)
© *Elsevier Science Publishers B.V. (North-Holland), 1987*

KESSU III:
The Effect of Wage Increases
and Fiscal Policy

by

Heikki Sourama

Ministry of Finance,
Helsinki, Finland

1. Introduction

This paper examines the properties of the KESSU III model, by analysing
the effects of wage increases and fiscal policy by means of simulation experiments. The analysis largely proceeds along the lines laid down by Drèze
and Modigliani [1981]. Initially, the effects of a nominal wage increase are
analysed in the case where economic policy will not respond to the deterioration of the current account due to the increase. Following this, the
multiplier effects of fiscal policy on central macroeconomic magnitudes is
reported. Finally, the effects of a wage increase are considered in the case
where the external balance is kept unchanged by means of fiscal policy.

Central assumptions throughout the analysis are a small open economy, accommodating monetary policy and rigid nominal wages once the
wage increase has taken place. As there is no monetary block in the model,
no crowding-out effects through the money market can occur. Since interest rates in Finland have largely been administratively regulated, the
exogenous nominal interest rate in the model is assumed to be unchanged.
The model does not include a wage block either, the nominal average wages
are determined exogenously. Incomes policy Finland has quite often been
based on extensive, centralized settlements.

The assumption of a small open economy means that the exposed
sector is a price-taker in the world market and that, at the given price,

imports are independent of foreign supply and exports of foreign demand. Six of the 16 productive branches in the model at least partly represent the exposed sector. Only two of these six — the forest industries (i.e., wood, pulp and paper) and the metal and engineering industries — fit in with the assumption of a small open economy. Nevertheless, since the bulk of Finland's foreign trade is accounted for by these two branches, the assumption predominates in the model.

The assumption of a small open economy is applied in the model as a long-run relationship by making use of an error correction (EC) mechanism presented by Davidson et al. [1978].[1] The procedure to be used is quite simple in itself. Moreover, the disaggregated assumption of a small open economy is new to the model, so there is not much experience yet with it. The effects of this approach seem to be strongly dependent on the structure of the branch and on the empirical properties of the various equations. Since the results yielded by the model depend crucially on this choice of procedure, in the following we quite extensively examine how the assumption of a small open economy becomes realized through the major branches of the exposed sector.

2.   The effects of a nominal wage increase

Finland has long pursued incomes policies whereby the central labour market organizations have agreed in a comparatively centralized manner on the wage increases to be effective in all sectors. The agreements have been concluded for 1 to 2 years. In addition, the government has endeavoured to promote the establishment of such agreements, although its role has markedly varied.

The centralized incomes policy has also influenced the way in which wages are dealt with in the model. The model has quite often been used to assess the effects of such agreements. On the other hand, in drawing up medium-term target scenarios, one central point has been to determine an incomes policy line which would be compatible with the forecasts made and with the general economic policy lines pursued. Thus, no Phillips-type mechanism, for instance, has been incorporated in the model; instead, the nominal average wages are exogenous variables.

---

[1] For a more recent discussion of the mechanism see, e.g., Salmon [1982] and Nickell [1985].

However, the treatment of wages as exogenous is not unproblematic, since the effect of wage drift on the earnings level has at times been comparatively strong. Modelling wage drift is complicated by the fact that there is no official statistical data on it that corresponds to the productive-branch classification applied in the model. Thus, when the model is used, wage drift must always be estimated outside the model.

No exogenous wage drift estimates have been included in the simulations to be presented below; instead, the nominal average wages have been raised in a centralized and once-and-for-all manner by 1 per cent. Before reporting the results, those central equations of the model through which wages exert their influence are considered. The general properties of the model are more thoroughly discussed in the article by Leppä [1987, in this volume].

2.1   The main channels of influence of wages

In the model a wage increase has two main channels of influence. A rise in nominal wages leads to a rise in real earnings and in consumption, respectively, since costs cannot fully be passed on to prices in the exposed sector. At the same time, however, the rise in labour costs impair profitability in the exposed sector and thus decreases exports, with the result that declining employment also begins to reduce consumption.

Of the productive branches in the model, the textile, clothing, leather product and footwear industries, the forest industries, metal and engineering industries, the chemical industry and other manufacturing industries (excluding food industries), as well as forestry, can be classified within the exposed sector. Exports from the forest industries and from the metal and engineering industries are determined in the long run by supply. In the rest of these branches by contrast, the long-run demand curve is downward sloping and the effects of supply are only partial.

The differences in supply effects are also reflected in the determination of export prices, so that the price-taking and price-making aspects vary from branch to branch. When the long-run demand curve is horizontal, the dynamic specification of export prices is of the form:

$$\Delta \ln P_x = a_0 + a_1 \Delta \ln P_c + a_2 \Delta \ln C + a_3 \ln R + a_4 \ln(P_c/P_x)_{-1} \qquad (1)$$

$$a_1, a_2, a_3, a_4 > 0$$

where

P_x = export price in national currency

P_c = competing export price in competitor countries' currency

C = unit costs due to labour costs, intermediate inputs and net commodity taxes

R = exchange rate.

Because of the error correction mechanism, in the steady state the export price follows only competitors' prices when the exchange rate is fixed. In the short run, efforts are also made to pass costs on to prices; but since costs have been specified only as a difference, effects of changes in the level of unit costs disappear in the course of time, the rate of change depending on the speed of adjustment of the equation.

In another, alternative specification the error correction mechanism works both through the competing price and unit costs:

$$\Delta \ln P_x = a_0 + a_1 \ln\left(P_c/(P_x)_{-1}\right) + a_2 \ln\left(C/(P_c)_{-1}\right) + a_3 \ln R, \qquad (2)$$

in which case the export price is in the long run homogeneous with respect to P_c and C. In a third, extreme case, the EC mechanism is associated only with costs:

$$\Delta \ln P_x = a_0 + a_1 \Delta \ln RP_c + a_2 \Delta \ln C + a_3 \ln\left((C/P_x)_{-1}\right), \qquad (3)$$

in which case the export price responds in the short run to changes in competitors' prices, but only costs are of significance in the steady-state.

The export equations of the model are based on these specifications in such a way that those of the forest industries and the metal and engineering industries are approximately of the form (1), those of the chemical industry are of the form (2) and those for the textile, clothing, leather product and footwear industries and other branches of manufacturing (exclusive the food industry) are of the form (3). The equations (1)–(3) are examples; the accurate form of each equation has been chosen through empirical tests.

In the model the volume of exports is handled separately for trade with the West and trade with the East. In Eastern trade, the Soviet Union is predominant. This trade is based on five-year bilateral trade agreements. By far the largest proportion of imports from the Soviet Union consists of crude oil, which is treated as a noncompeting import in the model, generally through fixed input coefficients. Exports to the East are exogenous in the model.

For the determination of exports to the West, the model includes two basic relationships:

$$\Delta \ln X = a_0 + a_1 \ln(X_s/X_{-1}) + a_2 \ln(P_x/RP_c) + a_3\Delta \ln D \qquad (4)$$
$$a_1, a_3 > 0, \quad a_2 < 0$$
$$\Delta \ln X = a_0 + a_1 \ln(P_x/C) + a_2 \ln(P_x/RP_c) + a_3 \ln D + a_4 \ln X_{-1} \quad (5)$$
$$a_1, a_3 > 0, \quad a_2, a_4 < 0,$$

where

$X =$ volume of exports to the West

$X_s =$ export supply for western markets

$D =$ foreign activity.

The form of (4) is used for the forest industries and the metal and engineering industries and the form of (5) for other branches of manufacturing industry, except the food industry and petroleum refining, whose exports are dealt with as exogenous. The most marked effects of wage increases on export are caused through the form of (4), because of the large size of the branches concerned.

The form of (5) is associated with the export equations (2) or (3) in which costs have permanent effects on the price of exports. Thereby, (5) represents a sort of reduced demand curve, sloping downward with respect to price, into which the effect of the supply side has been incorporated — in a mainly recursive price-quantity chain — via the profitability variable P_x/C. The foreign activity variable D has in (5) also long-run effects because the variable has been specified as level.

In the equation (5), a wage increase immediately affects the volume of exports, both through weakening profitability and a rise in the relative export price. In the long run, however, the effect of P_x/C entirely disappears in cases where price setting is based wholly on costs in accordance with (3). In the case of (2), by contrast, effects through both channels will remain permanent.

According to (4), exports depend in the short run on the relative export price, foreign activity and export supply. In the long run, by contrast, only export supply plays a role, via the EC mechanism, whereas the influence of other terms will disappear. In the steady state the export price depends, according to (1), only on competitors' prices, although the dependence is not wholly complete in the forest industries. Moreover, foreign activity has an influence only as a difference, so that the effects of the changes in the level of activity will disappear with time and the variations in activity will only cause cyclical shocks.

Export supply is obtained simply by deducting from the potential output the production caused by domestic demand and exports to the East. The effects of a wage increase will then depend not only on reactions in potential output and domestic demand but also on changes in imports. Imports are treated within the model according to the producing branch, employing the same classification as in the case of domestic production. Imports affect production via the input-output block of the model, where the import vector is a negative final-product item. Imports and domestic production are then perfect substitutes by definition.

The volume of imports depends on the total demand for the products of the branch concerned and on relative import prices. Dynamic specifications vary. A typical form may be presented, where the market share of imports does not change in the long run if the relative import price is fixed:

$$\Delta \ln M = a_0 + a_1 \Delta \ln D_d + a_2 \ln(D_d/M)_{-1} + a_3 \ln(P_m/P_d), \qquad (6)$$
$$a_1, a_2, a_3 > 0,$$

where

$$M = \text{imports}$$
$$D_d = \text{total demand}$$
$$P_m = \text{import price in national currency}$$
$$P_d = \text{domestic price.}$$

This form is used, for example, for imports of metal and engineering industry products, which form the largest group of imports when broken down by productive branches.

Determination of the potential output is based on the Leontief-function assumption in the case of intermediate inputs and on the CES-function separable from these in the case of labour and capital. Technical change is Harrod-neutral and the production technology is of putty-clay type. The demand equations for labour and capital have been derived from the profit-maximization assumption, whereby the desired levels of production factors have been solved for production and for real input costs. Applying the EC mechanism, the dynamic specifications of the equations are of the form

$$\Delta \ln N = a_0 + a_1 \Delta \ln Y + a_2 \ln(Y/N)_{-1} + a_3 \ln(w/p) + a_4 t \qquad (7)$$
$$\Delta \ln I = b_0 + b_1 \Delta \ln Y + b_2 \ln(Y/I)_{-1} + b_3 \ln(c/p) \qquad (8)$$
$$a_1, a_2, b_1, b_2 > 0, \quad a_3, a_4, b_3 < 0$$

subject to the restriction $a_3/a_2 = b_3/b$, where

N = demand for labour

Y = value added

w = nominal wage, including employers' contributions to social security schemes

t = time

p = price of the value added

I = investments

c = user cost of capital.

The potential output is obtained by substituting N, and I through the capital stock, into the CES function.

A wage increase decreases the potential output according to (7), not only as a result of the nominal wage increase in the productive branch itself, but also because the price of the value added may possibly decline. Particularly in the sheltered sector increased wage costs are passed on to prices, which will also partly raise the intermediate input costs in the exposed sector. At the same time, the price of labour rises in relation to the price of capital, so that through (8) an investment effect, substituting capital for labour, emerges.

The effect of the production variable Y on potential output is positive to the extent that the production meant for the home market will rise as a result of the increase in demand due to increased wages. On the other hand, both production and potential output decrease by a simultaneous fall in export supply and exports as a result of the temporarily increased relative export prices and the crowding-out effect of the increased domestic demand. The resulting net effect due to all these channels depends on the relative strength of the various reactions and the speeds of adjustment.

In branches of manufacturing other than the forest industries and the metal and engineering industries a wage increase will not affect production via potential output; production responds to demand via the input-output system without limitations. The only supply-dependent element is the effect on the volume of exports of the profitability variable P_x/C. Employment and investments are determined, however, by equations of the form (7) and (8), so that a wage increase will give rise to effects bearing on the capital-labour ratio.

In the branches belonging to the sheltered sector, experiments with the CES-function and the cost-minimization principle did not lead to such satisfactory results in estimating employment and investment equations, except in a few cases. The equations are in fact based on equations of the form (7) and (8), without the effects of changes in the relative factor prices. The effect of a wage increase on production and on the demand for the factors of production in the sheltered sector thus exclusively depends on how the increase will cause changes in the demand coming from other sectors.

2.2   Simulation results

The results produced by the model concerning the effects of a once-and-for-all wage increase of 1 per cent can be concisely presented as follows. The effects on households' consumption is positive throughout the eight-year period concerned. As production in the exposed sector declines, however, GDP falls permanently below the control solution level. During the course of time, this will also be reflected in consumption, which tends to return after three years toward its previous level, with weakening employment. The wage increase impairs the external balance of the economy. An increase in domestic demand leads to a rather prolonged rise in imports, while exports decline throughout the period. A drop in employment and a rise in costs also slightly impair the financial position of the general government sector, as fiscal policy is not assumed to respond to the negative effects of the wage increase.

The simulation results are set out in table 1. The control solution, with which the simulation results are compared, is the path for the years 1983–1990 computed from the model.

The exposed sector

On the whole, the reaction of export prices to a wage increase in comparatively slight. The proportion of Finland's merchandise exports accounted for by the forest industries and the metal and engineering industries is of the order of over 70 per cent, so that the aggregate price of exports is determined mainly on the basis of competitors' export prices in accordance with (1). In the case of the forest industries the EC mechanism also works through costs. The effect is so slight, however, that the increase in the export price of this branch will be almost negligible in the long run (see table 2). By contrast, in the short run a distinct tendency for the price-taking branches to also raise their prices when wages are increased is perceptible. This effect disappears in 2 or 3 years. The slight rise in export prices is

Table 1: The effects of a once-and-for all wage increase of 1%.

Year[1]	1	2	3	4	5	6	7	8
Changes at constant prices (%):								
GDP	.00	−.04	−.03	−.03	−.06	−.10	−.13	−.17
Value added, exposed sector[2]	−.13	−.30	−.27	−.26	−.34	−.43	−.50	−.57
Value added, private sheltered sector[2]	.02	.01	.02	.02	.00	−.03	−.05	−.07
Imports	.24	.14	.17	.14	.03	−.06	−.12	−.19
Exports	−.23	−.25	−.29	−.39	−.50	−.61	−.70	−.79
Households' consumption	.20	.24	.30	.29	.27	.25	.23	.21
Gross capital formation, industries	.04	.02	−.04	−.06	−.07	−.10	−.13	−.17
Exposed sector	.12	.03	−.22	−.26	−.28	−.37	−.47	−.55
Private sheltered sector	.01	.02	.02	.02	.00	−.01	−.02	−.03
Real disposable income of households	.31	.27	.27	.27	.25	.23	.21	.19
Changes in price (%):								
Export price	.18	.14	.12	.12	.12	.12	.12	.12
Consumer price	.45	.48	.46	.45	.45	.45	.45	.45
Price of gross capital formation, industries:	.46	.43	.38	.36	.36	.36	.36	.36
Changes in percentage points:								
Surplus on current account in relation to GDP:	−.1	−.1	−.1	−.2	−.2	−.2	−.2	−.3
Foreign debt in relation to GDP:	.0	.1	.2	.3	.5	.7	.9	1.1
Central government debt in relation to GDP	−.1	.0	.0	.0	.1	.1	.2	.2
Changes in employment (%):								
Total	−.01	−.04	−.06	−.07	−.10	−.12	−.15	−.18
Exposed sector	−.06	−.18	−.27	−.33	−.41	−.48	−.55	−.63
Private sheltered sector	.01	.00	.01	.01	.00	−.01	−.02	−.03

[1] The numbers 1–8 refer to the years 1983–1990.
[2] In approximate basic value.

also in part due to the fact that the export prices of agricultural products and foodstuffs are exogenous in the model. It is assumed that they are entirely determined in the world market. In the present calculations, a wage increase will lead to a corresponding increase in export subsidies, when the export quantity of these commodities is assumed to be unchanged.

The decrease in the volume of total exports will be of the order of 0.2–0.3 per cent in the first three years. Following this, the decrease accelerates when the effects of the wage increase begin to be perceptible in the potential output.

A part of the decrease in exports is caused by the fact that, in the calculations, the volume of exports to the East, which is exogenous in the model, has been lowered so that the value equilibrium of bilateral trade will not change in any one year. The need to lower it is caused, according to the input-output system of the model, by a fall in the demand for crude oil beginning with the second year. At the same time the terms of trade slightly improve.[1] From the viewpoint of total exports, however, a decrease in exports to the East determined in this way is not significant.

The responses of exports to western markets will depend principally on exports of forest industry products and metal and engineering industry products through an equation of the form (4). The responses of the two sectors will be clearly different.

The forest industries and the metal and engineering industries

The significance of exports is quite notable in the forest industries. They account for almost 60 per cent of the total output of the branch. If intra-industry linkages are taken into account in addition, output is dependent to the extent of 75 per cent of forest industry product exports. Correspondingly, the role of imports of the products of this branch is slight. The branch is capital-intensive.

The proportion of output accounted for by exports in the metal and engineering industry is of the order of 40 per cent. However, imports of the products of this branch greatly exceed their exports. Variations in total imports depend in fact mainly on imports of crude oil and those of metal and engineering industry products. This branch is distinctly more labour-intensive than the forest industries.

The elasticities of the central equations of the two branches are given in table 2. The forest industries are characterized by a slow adjustment of potential output, due to the capital-intensiveness of the branch, a low substitution elasticity and by sensitivity of the volume of exports to changes

---

[1] An alternative way of dealing with the fall in the consumption of petroleum products due to a wage increase would have been to assume that imports are unchanged, but exports of petroleum products are increased to western markets by a corresponding amount. For this kind of treatment the model includes exogenous variables of its own.

Table 2: Elasticities of some central equations for the forest industries and the metal and engineering industries.

	Forest industries		Metal and engineering industries	
	Short-run[1]	Long-run	Short-run	Long-run
Elasticities of export price with respect to				
P_c	.91	.80	.65	1.00
C	.33	.20	.20	
Elasticities of export quantity with respect to				
X_s	.45	1.00	.40	1.00
P_x/RP_c or P_x/P_c	−1.80	−4.04	−.33	−.84
Elasticities of employment with respect to				
Y	.30	1.00	.46	1.00
W/P	−.05*	−.19	−.22*	−.31
Elasticities of investments with respect to				
Y	.52	1.00	1.93*	1.00
C/P	−.10*	−.19	−.16	−.31
Elasticities of imports with respect to				
D_d	.77	1.73	1.39	1.00
P_m/P_d	−.43	−1.31	−.55	−.99*

[1] The short-run elasticities are those for the first year. In cases where the elasticity is indicated by *, the variable concerned is lagged by one.

in relative export prices. In the metal and engineering industries, by contrast, the reactions of potential output are faster, the substitution elasticity is slightly higher and the short-run import demand elasticity of the products is higher than the corresponding long-run elasticity. In either of the branches, the volume of exports is not immediately adjusted to changes in export supply. The effects will not be felt fully until after 2 or 3 years.

A wage increase affects exports as the potential output decreases in accordance with (7) and (8). If domestic demand stays unchanged, export supply will decrease correspondingly, and the volume of exports adjusts itself toward the decreased supply. The decrease in exports may temporarily be counteracted if the wage increase raises the domestic demand for products and thus reduces export supply.

According to (7) and (8), in the capital-intensive forest industries potential output will be wholly adjusted to changes in relative factor prices only after 5 or 6 years. The supply of exports declines to an extent largely corresponding to the decrease in potential output, since the role of domestic demand is slight in this branch. However, a strong reaction of the volume of exports to a temporary rise in the relative export price in (4) works in such a way that exports distinctly decrease immediately following the wage increase, in spite of the slow reactions of potential output. Production in this branch then decreases throughout the entire period under consideration.

In the metal and engineering industries, the adjustment of potential output takes place more rapidly than in the forest industries. Moreover, the short-run elasticities of investments with respect to production are greater than unity. Because of the structure of the branch, the reactions of potential output then depends primarily on domestic demand and imports.

In the metal and engineering industries the increase in costs will in the short run be passed rather fully on to the price applied in the home market, and the effect will not entirely disappear in the long run either.

This leads to a fall in the relative import price, which in combination with the high demand elasticity of the import equation, means that the rise in domestic demand occasioned by the wage increase will in the short run largely find an outlet in imports of metal and engineering industry products. The domestic production of these products then decreases. On the other hand, a slight increase will be perceptible in export supply, as a result of which the volume of exports will also slightly increase in the first three years, when an effort is made to utilize the freed capacity. This effect is due to the assumption of perfect substitution in the input-output block.

The demand for both foreign and domestic metal products decreases in the long run; the rise in consumption demand slows down, investments decline and the decrease in exports reduces the intermediate input demand for metal products. The potential output will thereby decrease as it is adjusts to decreased production. Exports also decline in the long run, while the price of the production of metal products returns approximately back to its original level from its temporarily risen level, and the real prices of the factors of production thus rise.

In both branches the rise in the capital-labour ratio is slight, since the substitution elasticities are rather low and production technology is of the putty-clay nature. In the short run, however, a distinct rise in investments designed to replace labour is perceptible as the real rate of interest falls. In the metal and engineering branch, however, the resulting rise in the capital-labour ratio is dampened by strong short-run response of investments to changes in production.

The effects of supply, when they are modelled as described above, will thus be strongly dependent on the dynamic properties of the central equations. This is why in estimating the equations particular attention was devoted to the determination of the speeds of adjustment. However, considerable uncertainty is attached to the lag structures, since the model is based on annual data and the samples are thus small. Moreover all equations have been estimated by single-equation methods, despite the system's being fairly simultaneous. The use of simultaneous methods is restricted by the fact that the period for which data on exports is consistent with the classification applied in the model is shorter than those for the other time series. Moreover, the foreign trade series are based on unit values and quantities, and the picture provided by these often differs to a surprising degree from the one offered by the more "genuine" indices used in national accounting.

Other branches of manufacturing

The reactions to wage increases are quicker in the other branches of the exposed sector, since the effects of supply are not transmitted via potential output. The rise in export prices will come to an end in two years and the fall in exports to western markets, correspondingly, in three years.

Output in the industries concerned, however, declines at a slightly accelerating rate throughout the period under consideration. This is due to a fall in the demand for intermediate products in the forest industries and in the metal and engineering industries and to an increase in imports caused by the rise in domestic prices. In addition, the positive effect of households' consumption lessens during the late part of the period.

The substitution elasticities of the factors of production are in these branches of the order of 0.2–0.3 in the long run. The changes in the capital-labour ratio will thus again be comparatively small.

The sheltered sector

Production in the sheltered sector, taken as a whole, stays almost unchanged throughout the period concerned. Partly because of the responses of the exposed sector, reactions within the sheltered sector also vary, however, despite the fact that the wage increase will be passed fully and almost immediately on to prices. The positive effect of the increase in households' consumption does, however, dominate the behaviour of this sector. Since it did not prove possible to apply the cost minimization hypothesis to this sector, at a substitution elasticity different from zero, no changes are perceptible in the capital-labour ratio, except for those due to differences in the speeds of adjustment between the employment and investment equations.

Households' real income and consumption

According to the model, as a result of a wage increase the household sector's real disposable income rises for the whole period under consideration. Since, on account of foreign competition, the wage increase will not be passed on in its entirety to prices, real earnings rise. Pensions also rise in real terms because in Finland they are linked half to consumer prices and half to the index of earnings. Moreover, other transfers from the general government sector to households have been kept unchanged in volume terms.

In accordance with the unchanged fiscal policy assumption, state income tax schedules have been adjusted for the inflation occasioned by the wage increase. In the model the state income tax is determined from a very simple equation, where the yield from the tax is regressed on various types of income. An exogenous term, designed to describe changes in the rates of taxation has been incorporated into the equation, and by manipulating this term, taxation can be altered as desired.

The rates of the proportional local income tax were not varied in the calculations. The volumes of general government sector consumption, investment and current transfers were kept constant. The financial position of the local government sector will then deteriorate when the tax base narrows as a result of decreasing production and employment. In practice this would imply raising the local income tax rates. Since the upwards pressure is comparatively slight, however, the rates have not been changed in the calculations.

On these assumptions, the positive effect of a 1 per cent wage rise on the real disposable income of households is rather steadily of the order of 0.3 per cent for four years. Following this, the effect decreases, as the fall in employment in the exposed sector accelerates once the adjustment process of its potential output begins to gain momentum. Since employment, on the assumptions of the model, is in the last year only 0.2 per cent below the control solution, real income will throughout the period stay higher than in the control solution.

The reactions of real income are reflected in the behaviour of households' consumption expenditure. In the model, there is a separately estimated equation for each of the 19 expenditure categories and total consumption is determined as a sum of these. In most of the categories, consumption depends on real disposable income and the relative price of the expenditure category itself, with dynamic adjustment. The elasticity of the total consumption with respect to real disposable income is initially of the order of 0.7 (as computed from the point 1981), from which it will rise to 0.95 in the long run.

A sort of "wealth variable" has been connected with certain expenditure groups representing mainly durable consumer goods. It was constructed by relating the three-year moving sum of the household sector's net acquisition of financial assets at constant prices to the sector's real disposable income. In combination with the income variable it has such an effect that a permanent change in income will in the long run cause a rise in consumption approximately equal to this change.

The growth of consumption expenditure due to a wage increase is reflected rather strongly in expenditure categories, including metal and engineering industry products. For its part, this affects the reactions described in dealing with the exposed sector. Imports of metal and engineering industry products are then further increased by the fact that, in certain cases, the short-run income elasticities are higher than the long-run elasticities.

It should further be mentioned, as a special feature affecting consumption, that housing investment is exogenous in the model. In estimations, no suitable form that could satisfactorily describe the saturation of the need for dwellings in the years ahead could be found. Consumption expenditure includes as one of its largest subdivisions the imputed dwellings services in accordance with the present SNA. In conformity with the computational procedures of national accounting, the consumption of these services is determined solely on the basis of the dwellings stock. Since a wage increase is not assumed in these calculations to affect housing investment, the consumption of dwellings services will also remain unchanged.

2.3   Conclusions

The negative effects of a wage increase on employment are quite mild during a period of a few years. In the long run, by contrast, there is a distinct trade-off, although it is not particularly strong in that case either. On the level of the whole economy, the elasticity of employment with respect to real wage is of the order of −0.3. The negative effects of a wage increase concentrate, however, almost exclusively in the exposed sector, in which they are noticeable. The corresponding elasticity in this sector is −1.2, and its high value is due to the fact a wage increase leads to a distinct fall in exports. Since imports will at the same time grow for a period of several years and since they do not decline in the long run to the same extent as exports, the external balance of the economy will permanently deteriorate. Unless the current account is in surplus without the wage increase, the economy will before long be compelled to adopt corrective measures, which may further impair employment. After examining effects of fiscal policy, this question is reconsidered in section 4.

3.   The effects of fiscal policy

The general government sector is dealt with in the KESSU model in some detail. One of the most important uses to which the model can be put is medium-term fiscal-policy planning. Since the planning of central government spending is based on a detailed budgetary classification of expenditures by the branches of administration, in particular numerous variables describing current transfers have been incorporated into the model.

However, a classification by the branches of administration or by purpose categories is not used in the model, because a sufficient connection with the data used in fiscal planning can easily be established outside the model. The general government sector's income and outlay and the sector's capital accumulation and its financing are considered in its three major subsectors, namely, central government, local government and social security funds.

Except for subsidies and interest payments, general government expenditures are in the model exogenous in volumes as a general rule. The price indices of expenditures, by contrast, are endogenous in the model, and the same is true of the bulk of incomes.

Direct taxation, as regards both the central government and local government income tax, is dealt with quite simply in the model according to the paying sectors and by means of regression equations in which the yield from taxation is explained by incomes. The average tax rates can be altered by means of exogenous variables. Over ten kinds of commodity taxes are distinguished. Their volumes and prices are determined in the input-output blocks. The changes in the rates of taxation are linked to the price component. Employers' contributions to social security schemes are computed as percentages of the wage bill and, correspondingly, the insured persons' contributions as percentages of an approximation to households' income liable to local income tax.

In the following the dynamic multiplier effects of fiscal policy in the present version of the KESSU model will be discussed. To be considered:

– decreasing central government purchases of goods and services
– decreasing central government employment
– decreasing central government investments
– increasing central government income tax of household.

Each of the cuts and increases is postulated to be constantly equal to FIM 100 million at 1981-prices.[2] None of the other exogenous variables of the model were changed, despite the fact that there are, for instance, legislatively provided linkages to be taken into account exogenously in the normal use of the model.

The measures to be considered are classifiable into two groups differing in nature. Initially, cuts in general government purchases of goods and services and general government investments are considered. A feature common to these measures is that in the first place they reduce the demand for goods and services supplied by the private sector. Also examined are the effects of the reduction of central government employment and the increase of income taxation, both of which primarily decrease the household sector's income. Finally, the efficiency of the measures with regard to various economic policy objectives are compared. The results are set out in tables 3–6.

In considering the results, it should be taken into account that the model does not include a monetary block. The exogenous nominal rate of interest has in the simulations been kept unchanged and the supply of money is assumed to be perfectly elastic. In Finland, the interest rate has largely been determined by the central bank's administrative decisions, so that credit rationing has at least at times been applied in the private money market. The state has satisfied its financing requirements partly by foreign

---

[2] The magnitude of the measures to be dealt with is rather small; FIM 100 million approximately represent 0.7 per cent of central government consumption in 1983.

Table 3: The multiplier effects of a reduction of central government purchases of goods and services, purchases cut by FIM 100 million at 1981-prices.

Year[1]	1	2	3	4	5	6	7	8
Changes at constant prices (millions of FIM):								
GDP	−87	−99	−94	−95	−97	−97	−98	−98
Value added, exposed sector[2]	−22	−29	−20	−20	−23	−24	−24	−25
Value added, private sheltered sector[2]	−42	−48	−49	−49	−50	−50	−50	−50
Imports	−39	−47	−37	−37	−41	−42	−43	−45
Exports	3	9	−9	7	5	5	4	3
Households' consumption	−22	−32	−39	−40	−38	−38	−39	−40
Gross capital formation, industries	−5	−9	−11	−10	−10	−11	−11	−11
Exposed sector	−1	−4	−5	−4	−3	−4	−4	−4
Private sheltered sector	−4	−5	−6	−6	−7	−7	−7	−7
Real disposable income of households	−34	−40	−39	−39	39	40	40	40
Changes at current prices (millions of FIM):								
Net lending, central government	105	122	137	157	181	208	237	271
Net lending, local government	−10	−13	−14	−15	−16	−17	−18	−19
Surplus on current account	49	74	70	77	91	103	117	133
Changes in employment (1,000 persons)								
Total	−.6	−.7	−.8	−.9	−.9	−.9	−1.0	−1.0
Exposed sector	−.1	−.2	−.2	−.2	−.2	−.2	−.2	−.2
Private sheltered sector	−.3	−.3	−.4	−.4	−.4	−.4	−.4	−.4

[1] The numbers 1–8 refer to the years 1983–1990.
[2] In approximate basic value.

loans. Domestic bond issues have been agreed on by the state together with financial institutions, so that this form of financing has been only partly available. During the past few years, the significance of the administratively unregulated money market has greatly increased. Variation in interest rates has also thereby increased and credit rationing has simultaneously decreased. In such circumstances the linking of the effects coming from the money market to the model will before long become increasingly necessary.

Table 4: The multiplier effects of a reduction of central government investments cut by FIM 100 million at 1981-prices.

Year[1]	1	2	3	4	5	6	7	8
Changes at constant prices *(millions of FIM)*								
GDP	−98	−111	−103	−103	−105	−105	−104	−104
Value added, exposed sector[2]	−25	−31	−19	−20	−23	−23	−23	−23
Value added, private sheltered sector[2]	−60	−66	−65	−64	−64	−64	−63	−63
Imports	−38	−48	−35	−36	−40	−40	−41	−42
Exports	7	14	13	11	10	11	11	12
Households' consumption	−22	−34	−43	−44	−41	−40	−41	−41
Gross capital formation, industries	−6	−11	−13	−12	−12	−13	−13	−13
Exposed sector	−1	−5	−6	−4	−3	−4	−4	−4
Private sheltered sector	−5	−6	−7	−8	−9	−9	−9	−9
Real disposable income of households	−38	−44	−42	−42	−42	−42	−42	−42
Changes at current prices *(millions of FIM):*								
Net lending, central government	94	108	117	134	155	178	202	230
Net lending, local government	−8	−11	−11	−12	−13	−14	−14	−15
Surplus on current account	52	80	72	80	96	110	125	142
Changes in employment *(1,000 persons):*								
Total	−.6	−.8	−.8	−.9	−.9	−.9	−1.0	−1.0
Exposed sector	.0	−.1	−.1	−.1	−.1	−.1	−.1	−.1
Private sheltered sector	−.5	−.7	−.7	−.8	−.8	−.8	−.9	−.9

[1] The numbers 1–8 refer to the years 1983–1990.
[2] In approximate basic value.

Table 5: The multiplier effects of decreasing central government employment, the state's labour costs cut by FIM 100 million at 1981-prices.

Year[1]	1	2	3	4	5	6	7	8
Changes at constant prices (millions of FIM):								
GDP	−124	−136	−144	−146	−144	−144	−146	−147
Value added, exposed sector[2]	−3	−8	−2	−2	−1	0	0	0
Value added, private sheltered sector[2]	−13	−20	−25	−26	−26	−26	−27	−28
Imports	−8	−16	−18	−17	−16	−16	−18	−19
Exports	0	1	2	2	1	0	0	0
Households' consumption	−31	−44	−57	−60	−58	−57	−59	−60
Gross capital formation, industries	−2	−3	−5	−5	−6	−6	−6	−6
Exposed sector	0	−1	−2	−1	−1	−1	−1	−1
Private sheltered sector	−1	−2	−3	−4	−4	−5	−5	−5
Real disposable income of households	−50	−55	−58	−59	−58	−59	−60	−61
Changes at current prices (millions of FIM):								
Net lending, central government	53	62	67	76	87	100	114	129
Net lending, local government	−13	−15	−17	−18	−19	−20	−21	−22
Surplus on current account	9	22	29	31	32	36	43	50
Changes in employment (1,000 persons)								
Total	−1.2	−1.3	−1.5	−1.6	−1.6	−1.6	−1.7	−1.7
Exposed sector	.0	.0	−.1	−.1	−.1	−.1	−.1	−.1
Private sheltered sector	−.1	−.1	−.1	−.2	−.2	−.2	−.2	−.2
Central government	−1.2	−1.2	−1.2	−1.2	−1.2	−1.2	−1.2	−1.2

[1] The numbers 1–8 refer to the years 1983–1990.
[2] In approximate basic value.

Table 6: The multiplier effects of increasing the state income taxation of households, the income tax increased by FIM 100 million at 1981-prices.

Year[1]	1	2	3	4	5	6	7	8
Changes at constant prices (millions of FIM):								
GDP	−53	−78	−96	−98	−94	93	−95	−97
Value added, exposed sector[2]	−9	−18	−19	−19	−17	−17	−18	−19
Value added, private sheltered sector[2]	−29	−42	−52	−53	−51	−51	−52	−52
Imports	−21	−35	−40	−39	−36	−36	−39	−41
Exports	0	3	4	4	2	1	1	0
Households' consumption	−70	−98	−129	−132	−126	−124	−125	−127
Gross capital formation, industries	−4	−7	−11	−12	−12	−12	−13	−13
Exposed sector	0	−2	−4	−3	−3	−2	−2	−3
Private sheltered sector	−4	−5	−7	−9	−9	−10	−11	−10
Real disposable income of households	−115	−124	−128	−129	−128	−127	−128	−128
Changes at current prices (millions of FIM):								
Net lending, central government	98	111	117	131	151	172	195	221
Net lending, local government	−3	−6	−8	−9	−10	−10	−11	−12
Surplus on current account	26	50	64	71	73	82	96	111
Changes in employment *(1,000 persons):*								
Total	−.2	−.3	−.5	−.6	−.6	−.7	−.7	−.7
Exposed sector	.0	.0	−.2	−.2	−.2	−.2	−.1	−.1
Private sheltered sector	−.2	−.3	−.3	−.4	−.4	−.5	−.6	−.6

[1] The numbers 1–8 refer to the years 1983–1990.
[2] In approximate basic value.

3.1 Decreasing central government purchases of goods and services and central government investments

The effects of central government purchases of goods and services and those of central government investments depend, initially, on their commodity composition. In the model the breakdown according to the producing sector is based on the 1981 input-output table, and in the normal use of the model this breakdown is, as a rule, kept more or less unchanged, just as has been done here.

The measures initially affect the various branches in distinctly different ways. Of central government investments, 85 per cent consists of products of the sheltered sector, almost exclusively of construction. On the other hand, the purchases of goods and services are distributed more evenly between various branches. The share of the exposed sector is about 30 per cent and that of the sheltered sector is 50 per cent, the rest consisting of purchases of non-market goods and services from the local government sector and on commodity taxes.

Despite their differences in commodity structure, the multiplier effects of both measures on GDP are quite similar. For two years, the effects of investments are slightly stronger than those of the purchases of goods and services. Following this, both multipliers become stabilized and equal about unity. The effects on value added in the exposed sector are also virtually identical. By contrast, a cut in the purchases of goods and services will decrease the value added in the private sheltered sector less; part of the effect then directed via non-market goods and services to the local government sector.

That the effects become increasingly similar is of course because construction uses, as its inputs, products of the exposed sector to a significant extent. Since, in addition, the reactions of households' consumption and gross capital formation by industries are fairly equal in both cases, the differences in the initial incidence of demand will be narrowed as a result of the indirect effects.

In both cases the reduction of central government demand leads to a slight increase in exports due to freed capacity. In the case of central government investments, the multiplier effect on exports is stronger (of the order of 0.1), since in that case the products of the supply-determined branches of the model will be of greater significance. On the whole, however, the effect is slight, since by far the largest part of the effects of general government demand is directed to the demand-determined branches of the model. Moreover, the reduction of general government investments primarily affects the demand for metal and engineering industry products, and the effects of changes in this demand is largely offset as a result of quick and strong reactions registered by this branch's imports and potential output. Because of increased exports, however, the current account will improve slightly more in the case of investment.

A reduction of general government demand in the model has little effect on prices. A very mild price rise is perceptible in the short run, as a result of a decline in labour productivity. In the long run, the assumption of constant returns to scale and the Harrod-neutral technical change signify that the unit costs will not change. The relative fall in employment and in investments in industries will be equal to the fall in production. As production drops in both cases by about as much, the choice of measure has no significance in this respect. The same conclusion applies to household consumption, since the negative effects are due to a decline in employment.

The state's financial position will improve slightly more when purchases of goods and services are cut. This is due, according to the model, to the yield from indirect taxes and the differences caused by this regarding central government debt and the debt service expenditures.

In both cases, however, the improvement in the state's financial position becomes slightly overestimated. A fall in employment will reduce the social security funds' income, which should be compensated for, in principle, by increasing transfers from the central government to these funds. The fall in employment will also impair the municipalities' finances, which implies either cuts in local government spending or increased local income taxation. Changes like this are not, however, made in the exogenous variables of the model.

3.2 Decreasing central government employment and increasing the income taxation of households

Both a reduction of central government employment and the increasing of the income taxation of households will immediately decrease the household sector's income. These measures differ, however, in that a reduction of employment reduces simultaneously and to the same extent the value added in the central government sector and, thus, the entire GDP. Increased taxation, on the other hand, reduces the purchasing power of all households with incomes liable to taxation, so that the effects on GDP are transmitted through the private sector.

The size of the reduction of employment is determined in the calculations in such a way that the state's labour costs drop by FIM 100 million, at constant prices. Households' real disposable income will, however, drop in that case by considerably less. A part of the decrease consists of non-wage labour costs. Moreover, a decrease in the wage bill reduces the yield from direct taxation.

On the other hand, an increase of FIM 100 million decreases real income to the same extent. This effect is further reinforced by the decrease in employment caused by a fall in consumption demand. When taxes are increased, the impact on the private sector is thus considerably more pronounced. Correspondingly, the state's financial position improves more markedly, since the employment reactions in the private sector are slow.

The multiplier effects on GDP are considerably stronger, however, when central government employment is cut. This is of course because central government production drops entirely to the same extent. The effect is further supplemented by the decrease in production in the private sector, due to a fall in household consumption. Since households' real income falls less than in the tax increase case, the effects on household consumption and on production in the private sector are correspondingly smaller.

When income taxes are increased, output in the central government sector stays unchanged and the effect is felt only in the private sector. Despite a more notable drop in households' real income, the multiplier effect on GDP is less, since a part of the decrease in consumption demand directly affects imports. The increasing of income taxation will then strengthen the current account more notably, at the same time as the losses in employment will be smaller.

In both cases the state's financial position improves, but the effect has also in this case been partly overestimated, since other relevant exogenous variables of the model have not been changed. The overestimation is greater in the case where central government employment is decreased. The financial position of the social security funds will then deteriorate more sharply. The position of the local government sector in this case weakens slightly more notably.

3.3   Conclusions

According to the model, all the fiscal policy measures considered will have permanent effects on production also in the long run. The differences between the measures can therefore be concisely described by examining the results for the last year of the period under consideration. The central objectives when fiscal policy is used are to increase employment, strengthen the external balance of the economy or reduce central government debt. The results yielded by the model regarding these objectives are set out in table 7.

Generally speaking, the differences between the effects of the different measures are not particularly large. Regarding the employment objective, however, definitely the most effective measure is to increase employment through the general government sector. In that case the negative effects on the current account and on the state's financial position will be least. The effects of the other measures on central government debt are, on the other hand, much the same. The current account deficit can most easily

Table 7: The effects of the fiscal policy measures in the last year of the simulation period.

	Employment	Foreign debt in relation to GDP	Central government debt in relation to GDP
	1000 persons	Percentage points	
Decreasing central government purchases of goods and services	−1.0	−0.1	−0.3
Decreasing central government investments	−1.0	−0.2	−0.3
Decreasing central government employment	−1.7	−0.05	−0.16
Increasing state income taxation	−0.7	−0.1	−0.3

be reduced by cutting central government investment. This is also the measure that decreases employment least if the aim is to reduce central government debt simultaneously. Otherwise, the most advantageous measure for strengthening the external balance is to increase the state income tax.

4. Wage increase and unchanged current account

Section 2 considered the effects of a once-and-for-all kind of wage increase, proceeding on the assumption that economic policies will not respond to the negative effects of this increase. A wage increase will then lead to a permanent weakening in the current account, to which economic policies have to respond before long. The present section will examine what are the effects of a wage increase if the deterioration of the external balance is eliminated by resorting to the fiscal policy measures dealt with in section 3.

As was noted above, the employment losses are largest if domestic demand is decreased by reducing employment in the general government sector. The losses will be smallest, on the other hand, if public investments are used as the fiscal policy instrument. The instruments for the simulation experiments were chosen between these two extremes. Total central government consumption expenditure was reduced first, and following this, an increase of central government income tax was tried.

The measures have to be quite sizable. They must eliminate the growth of imports caused by the rise in domestic demand, in addition to which, imports have to be further reduced to an extent corresponding to the decreased exports. Since no more than one-third of central government consumption is accounted for by purchases of goods and services, its effects on the current account are not strong. Equilibrium can be gained in the long run only when central government consumption has been cut by over 10 per cent compared with the control solution. The elasticity of employment with respect to real wage will then definitely exceed −2. In the case of the state income tax, the elasticity will not exceed −1. The results are thus comparable to those presented by Drèze and Modigliani [1981].

Either of the measures will improve the state's financial position. The scope for manoeuvre thus produced could in principle be used to improve employment, provided that this could be done in a way which would not strain the current account. If a balance budget, for instance, were used to balance the current account, in such a way that public employment were increased at the same time as income taxation were raised, the elasticity of employment with respect to real wage would become lower in the model. Correspondingly, the increase in taxation would be greater, so that the assumption of rigid nominal wages would become increasingly critical.

Table 8: The effects of a once-and-for-all increase of 1% in nominal wages in the last year of the simulation period.

	Without constraints	Unchanged current account	
		Central government consumption	Central government income tax
Changes in quantities (%):			
GDP	−.17	−1.12	−.58
Value added, exposed sector	−.57	−1.00	−.87
Value added, private sheltered sector	−.07	−.65	−.55
Household consumption	.21	−.62	−.78
Consumption of central government		−11.35	
Gross capital formation, industries	−.17	−.48	−.45
Employment, private and public sector	−.18	−1.22	−.51
Exposed sector	−.63	−1.06	−.96
Private sheltered sector	−.03	−.46	−.44
Debt of central government in relation to GDP, percentage points.	−.20	−2.0	−2.2
Elasticities of employment with respect to real wage:			
Total, private and public sector	−.3	−2.3	−1.0
Exposed sector	−1.2	−2.1	−1.8
Private sheltered sector	−0.1	−1.3	−1.1

Appendix

Table 9: The GDP multipliers of fiscal policy in KESSU III.

Year	1	2	3
Central government investment	.98	1.11	1.03
Central government purchases of goods and services	.87	.99	.94
Central government employment	1.24	1.36	1.44
Central government income tax	−.53	−.78	−.96

References

Davidson, J., D.F. Henry, F. Srba, and S. Yeo [1978], "Econometric modelling of the aggregate time series relationship between consumers' expenditure and income in the U.K.", *Economic Journal, 88,* 661–692.

Drèze, J.H. and F. Modigliani [1981], "The trade-off between real wages and employment in an open economy (Belgium)", *European Economic Review, 15,* 1–40.

Leppä, A. [1987], "KESSU III - An econometric planning model for the Finnish Economy", in this volume.

Nickell, S. [1985], "Error correction, partial adjustment and all that: an expository note", *Oxford Bulletin of Economics and Statistics, 47,* 119–129.

Salmon, M. [1982], "Error correction mechanisms", *Economic Journal, 92,* 615–629.

Macroeconomic Medium-Term Models in the Nordic Countries
O. Bjerkholt and J. Rosted (Editors)
© Elsevier Science Publishers B. V. (North-Holland), 1987

Monetary Policy in BOF3,
A Quarterly Model of the
Finnish Economy

by

Juha Tarkka

Bank of Finland
Helsinki

1. Introduction

This paper describes the structure of the monetary-financial block in the BOF3 quarterly econometric model of the Finnish economy. The effects of monetary policy are discussed in the light of simulation experiments performed with the model. These experiments include a shock to the money supply interest rate; in addition, the financial repercussions of fiscal policy are evaluated by comparing the government consumption multipliers under various assumptions for monetary accommodation.

BOF3 is an econometric model of the Finnish economy developed and operated by the Research Department of the Bank of Finland. The present version is based on earlier generations of BOF models, the first of which was completed in 1972.[1] The model is used regularly as a tool in forecasting and policy analysis. In addition to the Bank, BOF3 is also run at the coordination centre of Project LINK at the University of Pennsylvania as

---

[1] A recent account of the equations in BOF3 is "The BOF3 Quarterly Model of the Finnish Economy: Equations and Overview" (Bank of Finland [1984] Research Department TU 14/84). For earlier versions, see Bank of Finland [1972], "A Quarterly Model of the Finnish Economy", series D:29 and J. Waelbroeck (ed.) [1976], *The Models of Project LINK*, North-Holland.

a part of the LINK world econometric model. A predecessor of the present version was linked to the world model in 1974.

BOF3 is a medium-sized, quarterly model. At present the standard version consists of 198 equations, of which some 88 may be considered to be behavioural. The model is basically in the "Keynesian" income-expenditure tradition, and the detailed modelling of the components of aggregate demand is thus emphasized. Aggregate demand less imports is converted into value added of four production sectors by means of a compact input-output system. The sectors are: (i) agriculture, (ii) services and government, (iii) forestry, and (iv) mining and manufacturing. Pricing, employment and incomes are also analyzed on this level of aggregation.

The basic Keynesian structure has been amended to take into account the supply side supply side effects, a small open economy and monetary effects. The goal has been to have a model which in the short run displays the demand-determined Keynesian effects but which in the long run tends to a "Classical" equilibrium growth path. On this path, unemployment is at its "normal" or "natural" level and prices are in parity with world market prices. The assumptions on the supply side include a Cobb-Douglas production function for the value-added in each sector. This has been used to derive employment, investment and pricing equations.

The wage-price block resembles the Scandinavian model of inflation. The open sectors — manufacturing and forestry — are assumed to be price takers in the long run, with domestic costs having only temporary effects on open sector prices. By contrast, the closed sectors are assumed to fix their prices according to their costs. Manufacturing industry is the wage leader in the model. Open sector wages respond to deviations of wages from the marginal product of labour, as well as to unemployment. The closed sectors follow the wage developments in the open sector.

Two special characteristics of the Finnish economy have led to some possibly novel specifications. The Finnish financial markets are bank-centred and interest rates applied by banks are mostly institutionally regulated. Therefore, an excess demand for bank loans is probably an important phenomenon and the bank lending rate alone does not sufficiently reflect the relevant cost of finance for firms and households. The problem is made worse by the fact that data for market determined interest rates exists for only a short, recent period. In the model, the problem of the relevant rate of interest is dealt with by means of a disequilibrium model of bank loans. Excess demand for bank credit (credit rationing) is used as an argument in the investment functions along with the administrative interest rates. The structure of the monetary relationships is discussed below in more detail.

Another original feature is the modelling of Finnish-Soviet trade, which is conducted on a bilateral basis. This trade is assumed to be constrained by Finland's demand for Soviet exports (mostly energy). Finland's bilateral exports thus follow her bilateral imports with a lag, reflecting the constraint that the trade must balance over a longer run.

From the point of view of this paper it is useful to note the long-run purchasing power parity constraint and the bilateral trade effects, since these are visible in the simulation results to be presented below.

2.   The structure of the monetary block in BOF3

In spite of some apparently unconventional specifications, the basic thinking behind the monetary-financial block of the BOF3 model is very much in the textbook IS-LM tradition.[2] This means that the influence of the financial markets on the rest of the economy may be analyzed in terms of the supply of and demand for money. The novel features of the model result from an attempt to incorporate into the IS-LM tradition the Finnish money supply institutions as well as to cope with the problem of the missing data on market rates of interest.

The supply of money is not analyzed within the monetary base/money multiplier framework, but instead by credit components of the broad supply of money. To illustrate the model, let us start from the following simplified identities:

Balance sheet of the banks:

$$D = L + H + OB. \tag{1}$$

Here D is bank deposits, L is bank loans to the public, H is net position of the banks vis-a-vis the central bank and OB is other net assets of the banks (inclusive government bonds).

Balance sheet of the central bank:

$$N = R - H + OC. \tag{2}$$

Here N is notes in circulation, R is foreign reserves of the central bank and OC is other assets of the central bank (inclusive government bonds and credit to the public).

---

[2] The monetary equations and their derivation is presented in Tarkka [1983]. The IS-LM analysis of the model is given in Willman [1984].

Balance of payments identity:

$$R = F + FG + X. \tag{3}$$

Here F is private foreign debt, FG is foreign debt of the government and X is the cumulative current account surplus (or deficit).
Money is defined as the sum of notes N and bank deposits D:

$$M = N + D. \tag{4}$$

Substitution the balance sheet identities for N and D, the money supply identity is obtained:

$$M = L + F + FG + OB + OC + X. \tag{5}$$

This identity defines the stock of broad money as the sum of the accumulated current surplus, net domestic and foreign credit raised by the private non-bank sector and net government debt abroad and to the aggregate banking sector.

In this decomposition of the broad money supply, two components are endogenized in the BOF3 model. These are private foreign borrowing and bank loans to the public. Let us consider foreign borrowing first. The analysis of private capital movements is carried out by means of the Kouri-Porter [1974] framework. The virtue of the Kouri-Porter model in this task is that it permits the portfolio analysis of capital movements without requiring data on domestic market rates of interest. The elimination of interest rates from capital movement equations proceeds as follows:

When domestic and foreign assets are imperfect substitutes, the desired net foreign debt of the private sector is a function of the interest rate differential between domestic and foreign interest rates. Disregarding the effects of exchange rate expectations and wealth accumulation, a simplified portfolio equation may take the following form:

$$F = F(r - r_f), \tag{6}$$

where r is the domestic and r_f the foreign rate of interest. Solving for the interest rate differential yields

$$r = r_f + J(F), \qquad J' > 0. \tag{7}$$

This is the risk premium equation for the domestic rate of interest, which is one of the cornerstones of the analysis. The other is the conventional demand for money equation

$$M = M(Y, r - r_D),\tag{8}$$

where Y is nominal income and r_D is the bank deposit rate (i.e., own rate on money). Let us now solve the money supply identity (5) for the private foreign debt F and substitute (8) in for the stock of money:

$$F = M(Y, r - r_D) - L - FG - OB - OCX\tag{9}$$

Substituting the risk premium equation (7) for the domestic interest rate in (9), taking first differences and solving for ΔF, the private capital inflow, gives the Kouri-Porter capital movement equation:

$$\Delta F = -\alpha\big(\Delta L + \Delta FG + \Delta OB + \Delta OC + \Delta X + M_y \Delta Y + M_r(\Delta r_f - \Delta r_D)\big).\tag{10}$$

It is seen that a fraction of other components of the money supply is automatically offset by the capital flow; also the same fraction of changes in the demand for money, evaluated at the foreign interest rate, is automatically satisfied by capital flows. (Note that in (10), ΔX denotes the current account surplus, not its change, since X is the accumulated surplus).

It is worth noting that if the Kouri-Porter model is used along with the money supply identity (5) there is no further need of a demand for money equation in the model, this having been incorporated in the capital flow framework. However, in a model where the domestic rate of interest is included as an explicit variable, this might be solved from a demand for money equation, given the supply of money implied by (10) and (5).

Let us now turn to the other endogenous component of the supply of money, namely, bank loans. As the bank lending rates are usually regulated in Finland, the existence of an excess demand for loans — at least from time to time — is conventional wisdom in Finland. The basis of modelling on the bank loan market in BOF3 is the min condition applicable in this kind of disequilibrium situation:

$$L = \min(L^s, L^d).\tag{11}$$

Here L^s denotes the supply of loans by banks and L^d the demand for loans by the public. The supply of loans function is derived in a dynamic, investment-theoretical framework analogous to the "Tobin's q" theory of fixed investment. This means that the *flow* supply of loans is a function of the differential between the regulated lending rate and the marginal cost of funds to the banks, the call money rate of the Bank of Finland:

$$L^s = L^s(L_L - r_{call}) + L_{-1},\qquad(12)$$

where r_L and r_{call} are the loan and call money rates, respectively, and L_{-1} is the stock of loans inherited from the previous period.

The demand for bank loans is approached from a "monetary" angle which may be simply motivated as follows: the demand for loans is the amount of borrowing from the banks which would be realized in the absence of credit rationing. In no-credit-rationing circumstances the marginal cost of finance for firms and households would clearly be equal to the bank loan rate. Therefore, they would borrow in order to adjust their money holdings until $r = r_L$ or

$$M = M(Y, r_L - r_D).\qquad(13)$$

Note that in (13) the bank loan rate enters as an argument in the demand for money equation. Actually, in BOF3, (13) is interpreted as a long-run equilibrium situation towards which bank lending would gradually drive the existing stock of money in the absence of credit rationing. The demand for loans function may then be written in the following form:

$$L^d - L_{-1} = a\big(M(Y, r_L - r_D) - M_{-1}\big) - b(\Delta F - \Delta FG - \Delta OB - \Delta OC - \Delta X).\qquad(14)$$

Formulation (14) implies that in the absence of credit rationing, and with an exogenously determined lending rate, bank loans will in the long run completely accommodate all changes in the demand for money supply. In the short run this absorption of bank credit is, however, only partial: coefficients in (14) are a and b for sterilization of demand and supply, respectively.

The supply of money identity, the Kouri-Porter Kouri-Porter model and the above-sketched disequilibrium model of bank lending form the monetary sector in BOF3. To get an idea of the monetary-real interaction, the links between the monetary sector and the real side of the model must be examined. It was shown above how the data problem concerning the cost of finance — the market rate of interest — was circumvented by the Kouri-Porter reduction and by embedding the demand for money function in the capital flow and demand for bank loans equations. In the monetary-real interaction the problem of the missing market rate of interest raises its head again, since in the standard IS-LM framework the market rate of interest should transmit the financial impulses to the aggregate demand equations. This problem is dealt with by noting that the implicit market rate of interest is a function of the regulated bank lending rate and the excess demand for bank loans:

$$r = r_L + g(L^d - L).$$ (15)

If excess demand for bank loans is zero, r is equal to r_L. If excess demand for bank loans is positive, the implicit market rate is equal to the regulated rate plus an availability premium. It follows that the regulated lending rate and a measure of excess demand for bank loans can be used together in the aggregate demand equations instead of the market rate. This is in fact the method used in BOF3.

The link from monetary to real phenomena goes through the excess demand for credit variable computed from the bank loan disequilibrium model and through the administrative lending rate. There are also links from real to monetary sectors. These may be analyzed in terms of supply of and demand for money. On the supply side of money they are analyzed via the current account. Similarly the financing of government budget deficits has monetary implications in the model if they are financed through capital imports or from the banks. On the demand side of money, the effects come mainly through nominal income, as is apparent from the discussion above.

The operation of monetary policy in BOF3 is dependent on the state of the bank loan market. If there is excess supply, demand alone determines the actual behaviour of bank lending and the stock of money. In these circumstances discount policy — implemented through the call money rate — appears totally powerless. The proper instrument of monetary policy is then the regulated lending rate which has a direct impact on the aggregate demand. Monetary policy is then "pefectly accomodative", since banks are willing to finance any increases in the demand for money at the prevailing bank lending rate.

By contrast, if there is credit rationing, the domestic component of the money supply is totally exogenous from the point of view of the public. The only accommodation then comes through private capital flows, whch according to the Kouri-Porter equation offset a part of the changes in the demand for and in the supply of money. In these circumstances discount policy, which influences the banks' loan supply, is effective in influencing the supply of money and the prevailing excess demand for loans.

3.   Observations on the actual monetary equations

The precise structure of the monetary block is reported in the model documentation (see footnote 1), but a few comments are perhaps useful before going on to the simulation properties. The monetary and balance of payments block consists of three truly behavioural equations: the short-term private capital flow equation, which is specified in the Kouri-Porter fashion, an equation for bank-notes in circulation, and the disequilibrium equation for bank loans. The demand for bank notes is a simple transactions demand equation with private disposable income as a scale variable. The bank loan equation is obtained by substituting the specified demand and supply functions into the min rule (11) and estimating the resulting nonlinear equation with Nonlinear Least Squares (see Sneessens [1981], for methods).

In addition to the behavioural equations there are the balance-of-payments, central bank balance sheet and the banking sector balance sheet identities. Finally, there are "technical" equations for the own capital of the Bank of Finland, the call money rate, and the excess demand for loans. The call money rate equation is used to deal with situations where the central bank fixes the amount of central bank finance of the banks rather than its price. The excess demand for bank loans is computed from the disequilibrium model of bank lending.

4.   Simulation experiments

In the rest of the paper, results from four simulation experiments are presented. The first is a change in the regulated bank lending and deposit rates, which also serves to evaluate the effects of monetary policy aimed at pegging the market rate of interest; the second is a policy-induced change in the supply of money in the presence of credit rationing by the banks. The third and fourth experiments aim at measuring the degree of crowding-out of fiscal policy appearing from non-accommodative monetary policy.

4.1   A change in the ratio of interest

In the first experiment the regulated lending rate of the banks and the regulated deposit rates are increased by 1 percentage point. The control solution is one with no credit rationing by the banks, so that the implicit market rate also increases by 1 percentage point. This being the case, this experiment may also decribe the effects of monetary policy operating directly through the market rate of interest.

Table 1: The percentage effects on key macroeconomic variables of a permanent increase in interest rates by 1 percentage point. (GDP, imports, and demand components are measured in real terms.)

Year	GDP	IMP	EXP	CTOT	ITOT	PC	WR
1	−0.14	−0.43	−0.03	−0.17	−0.28	0.11	0.01
2	−0.38	−1.13	−0.13	−0.33	−1.21	0.24	−0.04
3	−0.51	−1.46	−0.21	−0.41	−1.95	0.28	−0.19
4	−0.50	−1.47	−0.23	−0.43	−2.12	0.26	−0.35
5	−0.49	−1.48	−0.20	−0.44	−2.16	0.23	−0.48

The simulation experiments are based on a trendlike model scenario over the period 1983–1995. Exchange rates are assumed to be exogenous in all of the simulations.

The results of the experiment are summarized in table 1, where the figures indicate precentage deviations from the control path in the years after the once-and-for-all interest rate increase. It is seen that the increase in the rate of interest has a powerful contractive impact on investment, income, and consumption. The GDP effect seems to stabilize at around 0.5 percent after the third year. Since the marginal propensity to import is high in the model, the increase in interest rates leads to a considerable reduction in imports. The downward reaction in exports may seem perverse at first glance. It is a result of the bilateral trade with the U.S.S.R., and is explained by the reduction of bilateral energy imports leading to a corresponding reduction in bilateral exports.

The Phillips curve effect starts to drive down the wage rate (WR) in the second year after the policy is implemented. Another factor contributing in the same direction is the decrease in productivity caused by the negative GDP effect. The decrease in productivity has also the effect of increasing production cost, which show up as higher prices in private consumption (PC).

From the present result one might conclude that monetary policy is powerless in fighting inflation. This is, however, too hasty a conclusion. One should bear in mind that the simulation is performed under the assumption of fixed exchange rates, and that the tendency to Purchasing Power Parity is rather strong in the model, tying domestic prices in the long run to foreign prices. From the balance-of-payments results (table 2) it is evident that the increase in interest rates strengthens the domestic currency, giving scope to a possible revaluation or diminishing devaluationary

Table 2: The effects on the balance of payments of a permanent increase in interest rates of 1 percentage point. (Effects are in billions of Fim.)

Year	Current account	Capital inflow	Exchange reserve
1	0.329	0.268	0.597
2	0.888	−0.281	1.204
3	1.237	−0.346	2.095
4	1.279	−0.192	3.182
5	1.395	−0.122	4.455

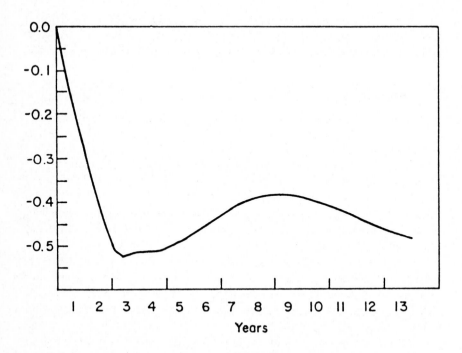

Figure 1: The percentage effect on real GDP of an increase in the market rate of interest of 1 percentage point.

Table 3: The percentage effects on key macroeconomic variables of an increase in the domestic component of money supply of 1 percent of yearly nominal GDP. (GDP, imports, and demand components are measured in real terms.)

Year	GDP	IMP	EXP	CTOT	ITOT	PC	WR
1	0.14	0.46	0.03	0.14	0.58	0.00	0.00
2	0.15	0.40	0.06	0.17	0.45	0.01	0.02
3	0.04	0.11	0.04	0.08	0.07	0.02	0.06
4	0.01	−0.03	−0.00	0.00	−0.07	0.03	0.08
5	0.05	−0.13	−0.04	−0.04	−0.16	0.03	0.07

pressure. This is the channel of anti-inflationary effects in a small, open economy model with fixed exchange rates.

As a point of reference for the balance-of-payments results it is useful to note that nominal GDP in the control solution is 266 billion Fim. in the first year, and 413 billion in the fifth year of the simulated scenario.

In figure 1 the percentage effect of the interest rate increase on real GDP is depicited over a longer (13-year) horizon.

4.2 An increase in the money supply

The next simulation experiment is an increase in the money supply when there is credit rationing by the banks. This experiment might be implemented in various ways with exactly equal results: the basic method of increasing the money supply would be a direct loan by the central bank to the public. Other examples include a suitable manipulation of the call money rate to induce the banks to extend the given amount of new credit, or a capital import by the government which is used to repurchase domestic government bonds.

The performed shock was actually very small, so that in order to make the results more comprehensible, they are scaled up to correspond to a monetary injection of 1 percent of the value of yearly GDP. The injected stock is not reversed, so that money supply remains permanently increased. However, the capital flow equation neutralizes 58% of all shock of money is not as large as the orginal shock.

As in the interest rate experiment, the impact of monetary policy is to a large extent transmitted through fixed investment. The most significant difference from the interest rate experiment is that here the effect is clearly cyclical, whereas in the interest rate simulation the effect on GDP and other key variables seemed more or less permanent.

The cyclical nature of the monetary policy simulation stems from the effects of the current account on money supply. At first the effect of the increase in the supply of money is positive, boosting economic activity and creating a current account deficit. Money flows out of the country through the current account and the orginal expansive effect is over time nullified by this mechanism. The adjustment to the orginal level of activity and to the orginal state of the current account is, however, cyclical and this is why the impact of monetary policy is negative in the medium run (4–11 years). The balance-of-payments effects of monetary policy are presented in table 4. Here the results are again scaled up to correspond a shock of 1 billion Fim, to facilitate interpretation.

The long-run neutrality of monetary policy in this experiment is shown in figure 2, where the long-run time path of the effect on real GDP is depicted. After about 10 years, the GDP effect has converged to practically zero. As is apparent from the effect on prices (see table 3), the neutrality of money does not result from price level adjustment, but rather from the leak through the current account. This is, of course, a result implied by the assumption of fixed exchange rates. A possible anomaly in the results is the parallel reaction of consumer prices in the two simulations: consumer prices rise in both, although the first experiment was contractive, the second was expansive. The reason is a different labour productivity reaction, reflecting the lack of a credit rationing variable in the labour demand equations in the closed sectors.

4.3 Crowding out and monetary policy

In the last two experiments the interaction of monetary and fiscal policy is investigated. The question posed is the following: What proportion of the fiscal policy multipliers are in fact results of the indirect monetization of the budget deficit? It has to be borne in mind that in the IS-LM framework, and with accommodating monetary policy, it is irrelevant whether the government borrows directly from the banks or the households do the borrowing in order to buy the bonds used to finance a budget deficit. This indirect monetization problem is often presented as 'Hicksian" or "transactions" crowding out. In a crowding-out context the question is, what proportion of the fiscal policy multipliers is lost if the central bank acts in a non-accommodative way, fixing the money supply instead of the interest rate.

Table 4: The effects on the balance of payments of an increase in the domestic component of the money supply of 1 billion Fim. (In billions of Fim.)

Year	Current account	Capital inflow	Exchange reserve
1	−0.134	−0.448	−0.582
2	−0.142	0.132	−0.592
3	−0.076	0.054	−0.613
4	−0.056	0.052	−0.617
5	−0.048	0.049	−0.617

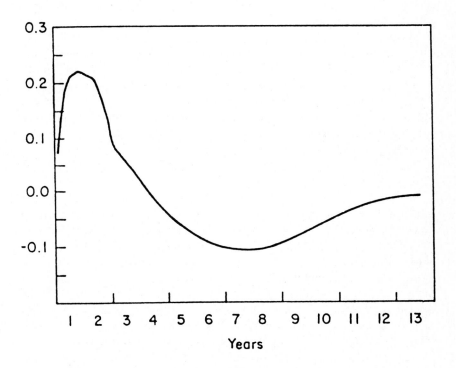

Figure 2: The percentage effect on real GDP of an increase in the domestic component of the money supply of 1 percent of yearly nominal GDP.

In a small, open economy the definition of "non-accommodation" is not as clear as in a closed economy. With a fixed exchange rate and with some capital mobility, there are at least three alternative definitions of "non-accommodative" central bank policy:

(a) the money supply is fixed. In this case the central bank sterilizes the monetary effects of capital movements and the current account.

(b) the domestic component of the money supply is fixed. In this case the central bank keeps bank credit unchanged.

(c) Foreign exchange reserves are fixed. This definition of non-accommodation follows from the likely constraint that fiscal policy cannot lead to a cumulative loss (or accumulation) of reserves. If the exchange rate is to be kept fixed, the central bank must then react to reserve flows induced by fiscal policy.

In the following experiments the definition (c) is accepted. The effects of a bond-financed increase in central government consumption are studied with two alternative assumptions on the monetary policy regime. In the first simulation there is no credit rationing and the market rate of interest is therefore fixed at the level of the regulated bank lending rate. In the second simulation the central bank is assumed to have set a steep call money rate schedule so that a change in the central bank position of the banks leads to a large change in the call money rate. The steepness of the schedule used is approximately equal to the system which prevailed in Finland in the late seventies.

The fiscal policy multipliers are reported in tables 5 and 6. The figures in the tables measure both the effects and the permanent increase in government consumption in millions of Fim (fixed prices). The results are, therefore, expressed as dimensionless multipliers. The size of the fiscal policy shock was .3 percent of GDP in the first year of implementation.

The effects of fiscal policy appear rather strong in the model. The positive impact on real exports is again due to the bilateral trade mechanism, which more than offsets the losses in multilateral exports *in the short run*. In the long run, the effect on total exports turns negative. In interpreting the multiplier on consumption (CTOT) it must be noted that CTOT includes government consumption and therefore the private consumption multiplier is one unit smaller than the effect on total consumption.

In the first two or three years, non-accommodating monetary policy does not seem to matter much. Actually, in the non-accommodative case, the short-run multipliers are slightly larger than in the exogenous interest

Table 5: The multipliers of a permanent increase in central government consumption. Domestic bond finance, *accommodative monetary policy.* (Unit: million/million in fixed prices.)

Year	GDP	IMP	EXP	CTOT	ITOT
1	1.19	0.44	0.05	1.34	0.21
2	1.77	0.88	0.14	1.85	0.63
3	2.13	1.19	0.19	2.16	0.91
4	2.24	1.35	0.17	2.34	1.02
5	2.18	1.42	0.09	2.44	1.04

Table 6: The multipliers of a permanent increase in central government consumption. Domestic bond finance, *non-accommodating monetary policy.* (Unit: million/million in fixed prices.)

Year	GDP	IMP	EXP	CTOT	ITOT
1	1.20	0.45	0.05	1.34	0.23
2	1.80	0.88	0.14	1.87	0.63
3	1.96	1.02	0.17	2.06	0.68
4	1.73	0.94	0.11	2.10	0.52
5	1.40	0.81	−0.01	1.88	0.35

rate case. This is due to the induced capital imports, which in the first case is the domestic capital market. In the medium run, the crowding-out effect begins to be felt, and the fifth-year GDP multiplier is only 64 percent of the accommodating monetary policy case.

The crowding-out effect reduces particularly the multiplier-accelerator effect on investment, which, however, remains positive in the fifth year even in the non-accommodating case, since the central bank must restrict private demand enough to compensate the current account effects of the increase in government spending. The balance-of-payments results are presented in tables 7 and 8.

In the balance-of-payments tables the effects are measured in current prices relative to the increase in government consumption in current prices. The most striking difference between the two alternatives is that in the non-accommodating case, the cumulative loss of reserves is avoided. This is partly due to the depressing effect on domestic demand of the monetary

Table 7: The effects on the balance of payments of an increase in central government consumption. Domestic bond finance, *accommodative monetary policy.* (Unit: million/million, current prices.)

Year	Current account	Capital inflow	Exchange reserve
1	−0.45	0.55	0.10
2	−0.78	0.45	−0.23
3	−0.97	0.32	−0.88
4	−1.04	0.19	−1.73
5	−1.05	0.09	−2.69

Table 8: The effects on the balance of payments of an increase in central government consumption. Domestic bond finance, *non-accommodating monetary policy.* (Unit: million/million, current prices.)

Year	Current account	Capital inflow	Exchange reserve
1	−0.46	0.50	0.04
2	−0.78	0.69	−0.05
3	−0.81	0.87	0.01
4	−0.69	0.66	−0.02
5	−0.58	0.61	0.01

policy, which serves to improve the current account relative to the accommodating monetary policy alternative, but a larger effect is that the tighter monetary policy induces a private capital inflow sufficient to finance the deficits in the current account and in the budget. As might be expected, in the long run the non-accommodating monetary policy alternative nullifies all fiscal policy effects on activity, since the current account balance must be unaffected by the fiscal policy in the long run. The remaining effect of the increase in government consumption is then a corresponding decrease in private investment. The long-run GDP effects of fiscal policy are depicted in figure 3, where the solid line (1) denotes the time path of the fiscal policy multiplier in the accommodating monetary policy case, and the broken line (2) denotes the time path of the multiplier in the non-accommodating

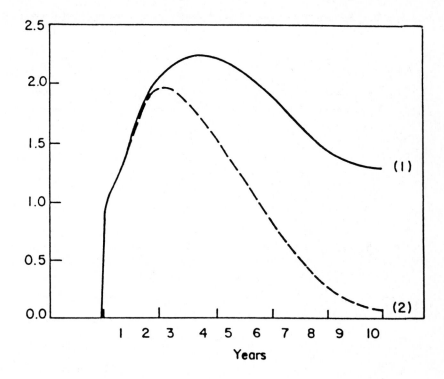

Figure 3: The real GDP multipliers of central government consumption
in the cases of accommodating monetary policy (1) and non-
accommodating monetary policy (2).

monetary policy case.

5.   Conclusion

It has not been the aim of this paper to give a comprehensive account
of the simulation properties of BOF3. The concentration on the most
important aspects of the monetary-financial linkages in the model has made
it necessary to exclude many interesting questions. An interested reader
may refer to some earlier published simulation results (see eg., Chan-Lee
and Kato [1984], and Lybeck et al. [1984]; in Finnish also Tarkka [1984].

In the last year or so, the banks have become very active in the so-
called "grey" market of short-term deposits, where the rate of interest

is unregulated. This development has effectively endogenized the money supply so that the Bank of Finland's call money rate now determines the opportunity cost of short-term funds to the Finnish firms. The monetary mechanism appears to operate very much like the case of no credit rationing dealt with in the present paper, even if the market rate of interest is higher than the regulated rate and there is excess demand for loans granted at the regulated interest rates.

The development of a more institutionalized short-term money market would remove the data problem on the domestic short rate of interest, which has troubled Finnish monetary economists in the past. It would also necessitate the endogenization of the market rate or "grey" deposits at the banks in the BOF3 model, now treated exogenously within the "other items" of the banks' balance sheet.

References

Bank of Finland [1984], "The BOF3 Quarterly Model of the Finnish Economy", Research Department, TU 14/84.

Bank of Finland [1972], "A Quarterly Model of the Finnish Economy", series D:29.

Chan-Lee, James and Hiromi Kato [1984], "A Comparison of Simulation Properties of National Econometric Models", *OECD Economic Studies, Spring.*

Kouri, Pentti and Michael Porter [1974], "International Capital Flows and Portfolio Equilibrium", *Journal of Political Economy, 86.*

Lybeck, Johan et al. [1984], "A Comparison of Simulation Properties of Five Nordic Macroeconometric Models", *Scandinavian Journal of Economics, 86,* 35–51.

Waelbroeck, J. [1976], *The Models of Project LINK.* Amsterdam: North-Holland Co.

Sneessens, Henri [1981], *Theory and Estimation of Macroeconomic Rationing Models.* New York: Springer Verlag.

Tarkka, Juha [1983], "Suomen kansantalouden neljännesvuosimalli BOF3: Rahamarkkinat ja masutase", Bank of Finland Research Department, TU 16/83.

Tarkka, Juha [1984], "Suomen kansantalouden netjännesvuosimalli BOF3: Mallin käyttäytyminen simulointikokeissa", Bank of Finland Research Department, TU 4/84.

Willman Alpo [1984], "Suomen kansantalouden neljännesvuosimalli BOF3: Mallin makroteoreettinen luonne ja tärkeimmät ominaisuudet", Bank of Finland Research Department, TU 13/84.

Macroeconomic Medium-Term Models in the Nordic Countries
O. Bjerkholt and J. Rosted (Editors)
© Elsevier Science Publishers B. V. (North-Holland), 1987

MODAG A:
A Medium-Term Macroeconomic Model of the Norwegian Economy*

by

Ådne Cappelen and Svein Longva

Research Department,
Central Bureau of Statistics,
Oslo, Norway

1. Introduction

Most Norwegian macroeconomic models have been developed for economic policy purposes and reside within government agencies. The Norwegian planning system is an integral part of government decision-making and the models have for many years been an integrated part of the planning environment. The two main policy documents are white papers called, respectively, the "National Budget" (an annual plan and economic report) and the "Long Term Programme" (a quadrennial programme which also includes a long-term perspective). Macroeconomic models play an important part in improving communication, understanding and consistency within the planning process.

The use of a macroeconomic model while analyzing alternative economic policies within the decision-making process of the government is quite different from that of providing the best possible forecasts of the

* The authors would like to thank Inger Holm, Roar Bergan, Øystein Olsen and Nils Martin Stølen who have participated in the construction, updating and use of MODAG A from 1982 to 1985, Olav Bjerkholt for useful comments to an earlier draft of this paper, and Heidi Munkelien for expert word processing.

development of the national economy. Ragnar Frisch expressed this distinction very succinctly many years ago:

> How can it be possible to make a projection without knowing the decisions that will *basically influence* the course of affairs? It is as if the policy maker would say to the economic expert: "Now you expert try to guess what I am going to do, and make your estimate accordingly. On the basis of the *factual* information thus received I will then decide what to do". The shift from the on-looker viewpoint to the decision view-point must be founded on a much more coherent form of logic. It must be based on a decision model, i.e. a model where the *possible* decisions are built in *explicitly* as essential variables. (Frisch [1961], p.4).

The Norwegian use of macroeconomic models adheres to this view with due regard to the partial nature and structural limitations of existing models. Economic policy is formulated, analyzed, and implemented within the framework of economic models with important policy instruments specified in great detail.[1]

A distinctive feature of the Norwegian model-building tradition is the use of detailed multisectoral input-output based models. Short and medium-term planning of the Norwegian economy in the last 20–25 years has been based on such models, where also elements from the Scandinavian model of inflation and Keynesian macro theory play a central role. These models are oriented towards *demand management* and *incomes policy* formulation. While demand management is mainly the responsibility of the central government, the formulation of an income policy involves also the labour market organizations, etc., especially in connection with the income settlements, cf. Cappelen and Longva [1984]. A decision model in the sense of Frisch, called MODIS IV, forms the core of the model system (see Bjerkholt and Longva [1980]).[2] MODIS IV is an "open" model in the sense that much is left unexplained and is instead determined exogenously. The model serves mainly as a tool for securing consistency in the policy-making

---

[1]   Some recent general references to the use of models in economic planning in Norway are Aukrust [1978], Bjerkholt and Longva [1980], and Johansen and Strand [1981]. See also Bjerkholt [1983] and Larsen and Schreiner [1985].

[2]   The first version of MODIS became operational in 1960 (see Sevaldson [1964]). The first coherent presentation of what later came to be known as the Aukrust model or the Scandinavian model of inflation is given in Utredningsutvalget [1966a, 1966b]. Later references are Aukrust [1970, 1977] and Edgreen, Faxen and Odhner [1973]. The short-term version of the inflation model was included in MODIS as early as 1965. MODIS IV has approximately 200 commodities and 150 production sectors.

process, but it also serves as a system for gathering, evaluating and presenting sectoral information. The shortcomings of MODIS IV with regard to its theoretical content and some of its other weaknesses are "compensated" to some degree within the administrative environment of the model. The "openness" of MODIS IV has in fact been regarded as a virtue, given the role the model plays in the administrative planning process.

The demand and incomes policy orientation of the MODIS model is in contrast to the long-term general equilibrium model MSG where the factors influencing growth (growth in labour force, capital accumulation and technical progress) and the corresponding equilibrium prices, i.e., supply-side factors, are the driving forces (see Johansen [1960, 1974]) and Longva, Lorentsen and Olsen [1985]). The separate modelling approaches for short and medium-term and for long-term planning reflect the fact that the explicit policy instruments in Norway are related mostly to demand management and income policy.

In this paper we shall present the main structure of an annual, medium-term macroeconomic model called MODAG A. It is a complete and self-contained model, but for policy application it is designed to be used as a supplementary model to MODIS IV. The incomplete character of the MODIS model and the increased emphasis on market oriented economic policies in recent years have naturally raised the question of extending the model system to also include models with more behavioural relationships. The sheer size of MODIS IV and the fact that the model is meant to be deeply embedded in the administrative planning routines have in practice prevented the extension of MODIS IV to comprise more behavioural relationships.

The first version of MODAG A became operational in 1983 and has been further developed since then. Like MODIS, MODAG A is designed mainly for demand management and income policy analysis. Even though MODAG A contains a more comprehensive set of behavioural relations than MODIS IV, the Norwegian economy is of course not completely modelled. MODAG A is meant to reside within a planning environment and be used together with other models as a tool, and not as a "black box", in preparing planning-documents and carrying out policy analysis. The commodities and sectors in MODAG A are aggregates of those in MODIS. Model blocks of MODIS, i.e., submodels for direct and indirect taxes, may be used to transform in a consistent way the specific and detailed changes in policy instruments as specified in that model into the broader aggregates of MODAG A.

This paper is organized as follows. The main features of MODAG A are presented in section 2 and in Appendix B. A discussion of "missing equations", i.e., important variables and relationships that are exogenous in the model but endogenous in the economy, is also included. Section 3 and Appendix A contain a more detailed description of the main submodels. Those readers who are not interested in the details of the model may skip this section. The empirical characteristics of the complete model are illustrated by impact analysis (multipliers) in section 4. Conclusions are drawn in section 5.

2.   Main features of MODAG A

MODAG A is an input-output based model intended for use in medium-term macroeconomic planning and policy analysis. The structure of MODAG A is obviously influenced by MODIS IV, which as mentioned in the introduction, combines certain elements of the Scandinavian model of inflation, with its distinction between exposed and sheltered commodity markets, Keynesian macro theory and input-output modelling. The Norwegian national accounting system forms the conceptual framework and the empirical basis of the model. Most parameters of the various submodels are estimated econometrically from national accounts time series, whereas the coefficients of the input-output structure are estimated from national accounts for the base year of the model. The model is rebased every year, and the base year will normally only lag one or two years behind the current year.

The description of the commodity flows is one of the main elements of MODAG A. Just as in the national accounts, commodity transactions are represented by means of two commodity × sector-matrices, one for the flow of commodities *to* each sector and one for the flow of commodities *from* each sector. The principal concept for evaluating commodity flows is (approximate) basic values. The commodity flows are flows between (functional) sectors.[3]   MODAG A has 41 commodities, 33 production sectors and 19 categories of private consumption. Real capital and investments are grouped into 8 categories for each of the production sectors.

In modelling the commodity markets the notion of a small price-taking economy producing competing commodities identical to goods produced in other countries is modified by assuming that the same commodity with different countries of origin (domestically produced or imported) or delivered

---

[3] A more comprehensive discussion of these concepts is given in Bjerkholt and Longva [1980].

to different markets (domestic or foreign market) are imperfect substitutes (cf. Armington [1969]). This means that the model has been constructed on the assumption that it is possible to identify separate price equations and demand curves for competing Norwegian products both on foreign and domestic markets.

2.1   The main model blocks

In the description of the model, see figure 1, it is convenient to make a distinction between the price part and the quantity part, even though MODAG A, as opposed to MODIS IV, is formally a simultaneous model in prices and quantities. The *quantity part* is mainly a demand driven model while the *price part* is supply or cost orientated. As may be seen in the lower part of figure 1, the demand components distinguished in MODAG A are private consumption, gross investment in industries, government expenditures on goods and services for consumption and investment purposes, exports and changes in inventories. In addition we have the intermediate demand for material input from the production sectors, which is handled by input-output relations. Government expenditures and most changes in inventories are exogenous variables in the model.[4]

Private consumption, income, and direct taxes

Private consumption is determined endogenously in the consumption and income model by a macro consumption function and a system of demand functions. The macro consumption function determines private consumption as a function of real disposable income accruing to each socioeconomic group (wage earners, self-employed persons, pensioners) as well as of consumer credit supply. Current income consists of wages (determined by exogenous estimates of wage rates and endogenously determined employment in industries, and exogenously given government employment), endogenous "consumption-motivating operating surplus" (dependent on operating surplus margins and production), and exogenously given government transfers and net interest income to households. By deducting endogenously determined direct taxes and deflating by the consumer price index we arrive at real disposable consumption-motivating income. Direct taxes are determined through estimates of average and marginal macro tax rates. These

---

[4] Government consumption, i.e., government purchases of goods and services for consumption purposes, plus depreciation of government consumption capital, less the sales of services to the private sector (fees), are endogenously determined since the latter two items are endogenous in MODAG A.

tax rates are generated in a separate micro based model for direct taxes. Total private consumption is allocated among the consumption categories through a system of demand functions with total consumption expenditures and prices as the explanatory variables.

Exports

Exports of resource-based products (e.g., crude oil and natural gas) are assumed to be supply-determined and given exogenously in the model. Due to difficulties in determining stable export relations the same is true for exports of ocean transport services and some minor services. For most manufactured goods and some services, covering about thirty-five percent of total exports, demand equations determine exports as a function of exogenously given world market growth "indicators" and of the ratio between the Norwegian export price and an exogenously given competitive price.

Domestic production, inventory changes and imports

Exogenously and endogenously determined commodity demand is subdivided into domestic production, changes in inventories and imports in the commodity balance equations. The import of most manufactured goods, covering about fifty percent of total imports, is determined by endogenously calculated changes in the import share of each commodity. Changes in import shares are determined in the import share model. In this submodel the change in each import share is assumed to be a function of the ratio between the domestic and the import price. The import share for each commodity is demand (purchaser) differentiated, so that changes in the demand composition also influence the demand for imports. Changes in inventories of imported goods are exogenously given. This is also true for changes in most inventories of domestically produced goods. For certain important export orientated products (paper and paper products, industrial chemicals and metals) inventory changes are functions of changes in demand, but after some time inventories again return to "normal".[5] For given demand, imports and inventory changes, Norwegian production is determined residually. For the resource-based industries, production is exogenously given and imports of these products are usually determined residually from the commodity balance equations. The same is the case for non-competitive imports.

---

[5] See Persson [1982] for a more detailed discussion of inventory behaviour.

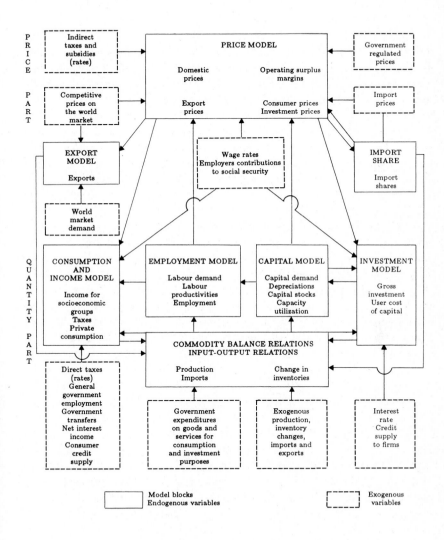

Figure 1: The main structure of MODAG A.

Factor demand (labour, capital, materials and energy)

The demand for both labour and capital (primary factor demand) is derived from the assumption of cost-minimizing behaviour. Production is modelled as a function of labour hours and the capital stock in place, while materials and aggregate energy input are related to output by fixed coefficients in quantity input-output relations.

In the capital model, the desired capital stock by industry is modelled by assuming that producers minimize long-run costs of labour and capital for any given output, making the desired capital stock dependent on the level of production and relative-factor prices. Depreciation in constant prices is calculated as a function of time series for gross investment and depreciation rates according to capital category and industry. The depreciation rates are aggregates of those in the national accounts and is based on a linear survival function for each vintage of capital, cf. Biørn [1983]. Gross investment by (private) industry is modelled in the investment model by assuming the presence of capital adjustment costs and that the speed of adjustment to the optimal level of capital stock depends on internally generated funds (approximated by gross operating surplus) and credit supply. Investments in oil and gas extraction and ocean transport, covering forty percent of private gross investments, are exogenously given. The production capacity in each industry is assumed to be proportional to the real capital stock adjusted by a trend.

In the employment model, labour demand is modelled by assuming that short-run labour costs, inclusive hiring and firing costs, are minimized given current output and the capital stock at the end of the previous year. Employment is thus determined by output and the capital stock through a partial adjustment mechanism. When labour input has been determined, labour productivity can be calculated. Labour productivities are included in the equations for variable unit costs in the price model.

Prices

In the price part of MODAG A (see the upper part of figure 1), commodity prices, price indices for various final demand groups, as well as gross operating surplus margins are determined. Each commodity can in MODAG A, in principle, have three different prices; an import price, a price for the domestically produced commodity sold on the domestic market (a domestic price) and an export price. Import prices are stipulated exogenously, based on assumptions about international price developments, i.e., we assume an infinitely elastic supply of imports. The domestic prices of commodities that are directly determined by negotiations, i.e., agricultural prices, or by government regulations are exogenous in MODAG A. The remaining domestic prices and export prices (apart from prices of crude oil, natural gas and ocean transport services which are exogenous) are determined endogenously in the price model by a set of price equations that determines prices as functions of variable unit costs, prices on competing foreign products and capacity utilization indices. Variable unit costs are defined as the sum of labour, energy and material input costs, calculated per unit produced. The labour-input cost per unit produced is determined by the wage rate per man-year, the tax rate for employers' contributions to social security and labour productivity. The material and energy-input cost is determined through the input-output relations, the changes in import shares, and the indirect tax and subsidy rates. The estimated importance of variable unit cost versus the competitive price index varies between goods and is normally related to the size of the market share and to the homogeneity of the products. Changes in the competitive prices are important in the determination of export prices and of domestic prices of commodities produced and marketed domestically under strong foreign competition (exposed domestic prices). Changes in variable unit costs determine the domestic prices of commodities sheltered from foreign competition (sheltered domestic prices). The market situation indicated by capacity utilization indices influences price-setting on certain export markets and mainly for manufactured goods, whereas services are virtually unaffected. Price equations are made dynamic by assuming that prices have lagged responses to changes in unit costs and competitive prices.

2.2   The interrelation between prices and quantities and the working of the model

In the presentation above we have looked at the most important submodels of MODAG A. As mentioned, these submodels constitute a simultaneous system. However, the main effects in MODAG A run from the price part to the quantity part. As we can see from figure 1 the quantity part of the model can only affect the price part through changes in labour productivities and capacity utilization. The estimated effects of changes in capacity utilization are, in fact, fairly modest, so that the primary influence is through labour productivity, which may change considerably in the short run if labour adjusts slowly to changes in production. However, the significance of this for price setting, even in industries where cost-plus pricing is dominant, is dampened by the sluggishness of the price adjustments. On the other hand, for the operating surplus margin the effect of changes in labour productivity may be considerable. Labour productivity in the long run will be affected both by changes in production (because of increasing returns to scale) and the capital stock. Quantity changes thus have some endogenous effects on prices also in the long run.

By contrast the effects running from the price part to the quantity part are strong even in the short run. The effects work partly through factor prices such as wage rates and operating surplus margins, and partly through commodity prices (consumer, export and import prices).

From what has been said above concerning producer behaviour it follows that prices adjust to changes in costs and competitive prices, whereas they are only to a limited degree influenced by changes in demand. Changes in demand, however, will rather quickly influence production and inventories.[6] Output may therefore be said to be determined from the demand side whereas prices are almost independent of demand.

This description of producer behaviour applies mainly to the manufacturing and service industries. For the resource-based industries (agriculture, forestry, fishing, hydroelectricy production and crude oil and natural gas extraction) in addition to ocean transport, which are very important in Norway, output may be said to be supply determined (capacity constrained). In the present version of MODAG A production, employment, investment, exports and prices are usually exogenously given for these industries with either changes in inventories or imports determined endogenously. Due to the importance of these industries for the Norwegian economy, MODAG A can therefore not be characterized as a completely demand and cost driven model. The relative importance of these industries for the Norwegian economy is brought out in table 1.

If, in order to simplify, we ignore the effects going from the quantity part of the model to the price part, the model appears as a recursive structure, since the price and the import share models may be viewed as independent of the quantity part. The workings of the model can then be explained as follows. From exogenous estimates of wage rates, indirect tax and subsidy rates and foreign market prices, the price model and the import share model, as a simultaneous system, determine domestic prices, export prices, operating surplus margins and import shares. Prices and operating surplus margins enter the private consumption and income model and the investment model of the quantity part. Together with exogenous estimates of wage rates, certain income components (government trans-

---

[6] See, for example, Bruno [1979] for a model which has certain similarities to our formulation of producer behaviour.

Table 1: Relative importance of supply determined industries in the Norwegian economy (in percentages).

	Value-added	Exports	Investment	Employment
Resource-based industries	26.5	39.0	40.5	9.0
Ocean transport	2.5	15.5	3.0	1.5
General government	13.5	0.5	11.5	23.5
Other sectors	57.5	45.0	45.0	66.0
Total	100.0	100.0	100.0	100.0

The percentages are based on figures from the 1984 national accounts.

fers and interest flows) and direct tax rates, private consumption demand is determined as a function of the level of production. For exogenously given wage rates, the nominal rate of interest and credit supply investment demand are also determined as a function of production. Export prices and exogenous estimates of competitive prices and world market demand determine exports. Together with estimates of exogenous demand and endogenous import shares, production is then determined through a traditional multiplier mechanism.

2.3   The partial nature of the model

In MODAG A there are a number of important economic variables which are exogenous in the model, but may be regarded as endogenous in the economic system of which the model is only a partial representation (model-exogenous but economy-endogenous variables). This applies *inter alia* to:

- wage formation and labour supply
- financial variables.

Wage formation and labour supply are exogenous in the model as it is presented in this paper.[7] This means that the most important "supply-side" effect and resource constraint in an economy like the Norwegian one, with its near full employment, is left out of the model. When MODAG A is used

---

[7] Wage formation and labour supply equations are included, however, in the latest version of MODAG. This version of the model, which is called MODAG W, is still in the experimental stage.

for policy purposes its administrative environment comprises a submodel developed by the Ministry of Finance in which wages and salaries are endogenized by wage formation equations (see Eriksen and Qvigstad [1983]). When MODAG A is used in studies related to income policy, which may be viewed as an attempt to reach a "feasible" wage development without relying on the labour market as a regulator, the absence of a wage formation block is in accordance with the use of the model.

Financial variables do play an important role in the present version of MODAG A. In particular, increased credit supply by state and private banks influences significantly both consumer spending and private investment. The nominal interest rate enters the investment equation in many industries and net interest income for households is important in determining total consumption. All these variables however are exogenous in the model. There is no feedback from the real side of the economy to the financial as the model is now formulated. With reference to the IS-LM diagram in macroeconomic textbooks, we may say that MODAG A is a disaggregated model of the IS-curve only. This is obviously a serious shortcoming, but it must be viewed in light of some institutional characteristics of the Norwegian economy. During most of the post-war period the financial sector has been subject to elaborate regulation by the government. A very detailed financial model is used by the government in order to work out the implications for the financial sector of developments on the real side of the economy. Certain deregulations in the financial markets in recent years has however increased the need for developing integrated models. The switches of "regimes" may make the estimation of such models difficult.

2.4   Other main shortcomings

In addition to the "missing" model blocks discussed above there are, of course, many parts of the model as it is now formulated and estimated which are not satisfactory. This applies to the modelling of supply behaviour for exposed industries, which in the medium term probably face given prices both on the domestic and the world market. Marginal costs and not demand should then determine the level of production, i.e., the export demand equations are replaced by export supply equations.

Another part of the present version of MODAG A which is not modelled in a satisfactory way is factor demand. Two aspects are important in this area: the substitution between production factors, and whether to impose constant returns to scale or allow increasing returns to scale. In the present model version there is substitution between labour and capital in more than half of the industries (mainly in manufacturing) and between fuels and electricity in most sectors, but no substitution between primary inputs and material inputs. The model specification also allows for increasing returns to scale. Obviously, how we model the production structure is of importance for the long-run solution of the model.

A third aspect of the model which will be important to study more closely is the specification of expectations. This theme has been the subject of heated debates in macroeconomics for some years but no clear conclusion has emerged so far. Our specification varies between traditional adaptive or backward-looking expectations and myopic but perfect foresight. Our present choices are more dictated by goodness of fit and restrictions on the sign of parameters than by the goal of modelling expectations more explicitly.

3.   A closer look at some of the submodels

In this section, we want to examine more closely some of the submodels of MODAG A. The submodels for private consumption and direct and indirect taxation are almost the same in MODAG A as in MODIS IV. The description of these submodels in the following is therefore rather brief. A survey of the most important price and quantity elasticities in the submodels of MODAG A is presented in tables A.1 to A.8 in Appendix A.

3.1   Exports

In MODAG A export demand equations have been introduced for about half of the commodities, covering thirty-five percent of total exports. Exports of resource-based products such as crude oil and natural gas, fish and agricultural products, etc., covering about forty percent of total exports, are assumed to be capacity-constrained and thereby supply-determined. Capacity changes in production of these commodities are strongly influenced by economic policy and exports are therefore exogenously fixed, given the medium-term character of the model. For export of ocean transport services, exports of some minor services and second-hand real capital, etc., we have been unable to establish stable export equations (cf. also table A.1 in Appendix A).

The implemented export equations cover most of the exports from manufacturing industries. A basic feature of the specification of these equations is that the volume of exports is assumed to depend on world market demand. Thus we assume that Norwegian producers face specific demand curves on the world market which may be represented by

$$A_t = f\left(\frac{P_t^A}{P_t^K}, V_t\right).\tag{3.1}$$

(3.1) expresses the assumption that the volume of Norwegian exports A, is a function of the ratio between the Norwegian export price P^A, and a price index for competing commodities P^K, and a variable V which denotes the size of the world market. The usual argument for adopting a specification like (3.1) is that Norwegian-produced commodities are imperfect substitutes for commodities originating in other countries. For given prices exports are then determined on the demand side. This is an argument which may be reasonable for relatively detailed groups of manufactured goods. For more homogeneous commodities, the assumption that there exist separate demand curves for Norwegian commodities is reasonable only if they constitute a considerable share of the total amount of the commodity available on the world market. However, for small countries this will only be the case for a few commodities and it is customary to assume that exports may be better modelled by constructing a so-called *small-open-economy-model*. This implies that exports are assumed to consist of homogeneous commodities that are sold at given prices on the world market. Exports are thereby determined by supply conditions. For three staple commodities (paper and paper products, industrial chemicals and metals) we have attempted to estimate a more supply-oriented model for exports, with exports dependent upon export prices (the producers are assumed to be price-takers)[8], capacity and factor prices. This formulation was unfortunately not successful. The capacity variables were the only variables which seemed to have any significance, whereas the relative-factor prices and therefore export prices were insignificant. Therefore, also for these commodities exports are determined by demand functions in the present version of MODAG A. Work will continue, however, on the construction of alternative models for these commodities.

In the model we have generally chosen the following log-linear form:

$$\log A_t = C_A + a_1 \log\left(\frac{P^A}{P^k}\right)_t + a_2 \log V_t,\tag{3.2}$$

where C_A, a_1 and a_2 are coefficients. a_1 and a_2 may be interpreted as

---

[8] See also the modelling of export prices in section 3.3.

price and income elasticities, respectively. Estimates have been made for two different dynamic formulations of this relation. In the first formulation a two-year price lag is stipulated, i.e.,

$$\log A_t = C_A + a_1^0 \log\left(\frac{P^A}{P^K}\right)_t + a_1^1 \log\left(\frac{P^A}{P^K}\right)_{t-1}$$
$$+ a_1^2 \log\left(\frac{P^A}{P^K}\right)_{t-2} + a_2 \log V_t \, . \tag{3.3}$$

The coefficient a_1^0 expresses the *immediate* effect of a relative price change on export demand, whereas a_1^1 and a_1^2 express the lagged effects of price changes. In the second formulation we have assumed that equation (3.2) expresses the expected demand, and that there is sluggishness in the export adjustment (*partial adjustment*). Changes in actual exports are considered to be dependent upon the difference between expected demand and actual export the year before

$$\log A_t - \log A_{t-1} = \lambda(\log A_t^D - \log A_{t-1}) \, , \tag{3.4}$$

where $\log A_t^D$ is given by (3.2). (3.4) inserted into (3.2) gives

$$\log A_t = \lambda C_A + \lambda a_1 \log\left(\frac{P^A}{P^K}\right)_t + \lambda a_2 \log V_t + (1 - \lambda) \log A_{t-1} \, . \tag{3.5}$$

Equations (3.3) and (3.5) are estimated using annual data covering the period 1962 to 1981. For the volume of Norwegian exports and for export prices, data from the national accounts have been used, whereas the figures for world market demand are based on consumption and investment data for Norway's major trading partners (various OECD countries), see Tveitereid and Lædre [1981]. As indicator of the competitive price for Norwegian exports of various commodities we have in some cases used the corresponding price index for the world market indicator and in other cases the import prices of the corresponding MODAG commodity.

For most commodities the ordinary least squares (OLS) have been used in the estimation. For some commodities, however, the instrument variables method gave more accurate and reasonable estimates. The results may be summarized in the following way (cf. also table A.1 in Appendix A):

(i) The estimated parameters indicate a considerable sluggishness in export adjustment. Equation (3.5) is preferred for all commodities. The long-run elasticities of changes in both relative prices and market volume for many commodities are larger (in numerical values) than the corresponding immediate effects.

(ii) In general, the results imply reasonable price elasticities. However, for four of the commodities and for all services the estimates of (long-run) price elasticities are less than 1 in absolute value. If we weigh the elasticities together by using the export values for 1984 as weights we get an average price elasticity (for the commodities for which export equations have have been specified) of approximately −1.3.

(iii) All estimated (long-run) world market growth elasticities are, with one exception, greater than 1. The average export weighted market demand (income) elasticity is close to 1.7.

The specification and the estimation of the export model are discussed in detail in Bergan and Olsen [1985].

3.2   Imports

The commodity imports in MODAG A are, with two exceptions (ships and oil platforms, and electricity), determined endogenously. The determination of imports, however, is different for different groups of commodities. For so-called non-competitive imports (commodities of which, by definition, there is no comparable Norwegian production), imports are demand-determined directly from the commodity balance equations. This is also the case for imports of resource based commodities (primary industry products, crude oil, and natural gas). In MODAG A the production of these commodities is stipulated exogenously and imports are thereby determined residually. For the remaining commodities, imports are determined with the help of import shares (imports of the commodity relative to domestic use). For manufacturing goods covering about fifty percent of total imports, these import shares are specified and estimated as functions of the ratio between the domestic and the corresponding import price (cf. also table A.2 in Appendix A). For the imports of services (except tourism), the import shares are changed exogenously.

As is the case for the export model, the specification of the import share equations in MODAG A is based on the assumption of separate demand curves facing Norwegian producers. For given prices, it is also assumed that quantities on the domestic market are determined by demand. The same objections may be raised to this model formulation as the objections in the previous section regarding the determination of exports.

Especially for relatively homogeneous products there is reason to believe that supply-side variables are important factors in the allocation of demand between Norwegian production and imports.

The specified import share relations in MODAG A are, however, as mentioned above, derived as demand functions. Consumers and producers are assumed to minimize their total expenditures for purchase of a commodity, whether imported or produced domestically. Total demand for the commodity concerned is defined as a CES-aggregate homogeneous of degree 1 in the input of domestically produced commodity and imported commodity. The elasticity with respect to domestic market growth (the demand or income elasticity) is thus assumed to be 1. The specification is based on the assumption of weak separability in demand between the input of this commodity and other commodities. The *ratio* between imports and Norwegian production of corresponding commodities may thereby be expressed as a function of the price ratio between these two commodities alone.[9] More precisely, in MODAG A the following set of import share equations are specified:

$$DIS_t = \left[IS_0 + (1 - IS_0) \left(\sum_{T=t-2}^{t} (P^N/P^I)_T^{\theta_T} \right)^{1-\sigma} \right]^{\sigma/(1-\sigma)} \qquad (3.6)$$

This relationship determines the import share index of a commodity, DIS (the import share relative to the import share in the base year (IS_0)), as a function of the ratio between domestic price (P^N) and import price (P^I). The parameter σ is the elasticity of substitution between imported and Norwegian goods. The θ's are lag parameters, and express the fact that it may take time before changes in relative prices have completed their effects on the allocation of demand between Norwegian and imported goods.

Equation (3.6) is estimated for the manufactured goods in the model on the basis of national accounts data for 1962 to 1980. Ordinary least squares (OLS) was used in the estimation. For some of the commodities in MODAG A, equation (3.6) has also been estimated with the inclusion of a trend term in order to investigate the possibility that some variables may have been left out. The results can be summarized in the following way (cf. also table A.2 in Appendix A):

(i) As a result of the relatively limited number of observations, *a priori* restrictions on the lag structure in the model were imposed. The specification which fitted the data best was chosen. For most commodities

---

[9] The assumption of a homothetical aggregate would have sufficed for this result.

this resulted in a specification where about 50 per cent of the effect of a relative price change on the import share was realized the first year. For three commodities — textiles and wearing apparels, wood and wood products and paper and paper products — a specification without lag effects gave the best results, while the *immediate* effect was estimated to be zero for mining products.

(ii) The estimates of the elasticity of subsitution vary for most products from 1.0 to 1.5. Exceptions are paper and paper products and printing and publishing, with substitution elasticities less than 1, and industrial chemicals and chemical and mineral products where this essential parameter was estimated to be approximately 2. The corresponding direct price elasticities — which are defined as the substitution elasticities multiplied by the cost shares — vary from about 0.5 to a little over 1 in absolute value. Using the import values for 1984 as weights we get an average long-run price elasticity of approximately −0.75.

(iii) For some groups of commodities, mainly consumer goods (textile and wearing apparels, paper and paper products, printing and publishing, beverages and tobacco) equation (3.6) also includes a trend. There are tendencies toward auto-correlation in the error term and the effects of relative prices are insignificant. By introducing a trend, the estimation results for these commodities become much more satisfactory. For these commodities the (significant) trend indicates an autonomous increase in the import shares by about 8 percent per annum. These results should be viewed in the context of the specified model and its possible inherent weaknesses, which were pointed out above. Of obvious importance is the assumption of identical income elasticities for Norwegian goods and imports, and the fact that Norwegian production of many commodities may be determined by supply-side factors so that imports are determined residually and not according to import share relations.

The import model is documented in more detail in Stølen [1983].

3.3 Prices

As MODAG A is a simultaneous model in prices and quantities, we speak of the *price-model* here as that part of the model where the price and cost equations are specified. In MODAG A each commodity has three associated prices, dependent on its origin and destination. We distinguish between the *import price*, the *domestic price* and the *export price*. The differentiation between the import price and the price of the domestically produced commodity sold on the domestic market (domestic price) can be justified by pointing out that imports and domestic production of the same commodity will not be perfect substitutes. The differentiation between domestic price and export price can be justified in the same way, but in this case the possibility of price discrimination should be added. The differentiation between export and domestic price implies that the simple *law of one price* in the Scandinavian model of inflation needs to be somewhat modified. Firms may be especially exposed to competition on the export market while on the domestic market they may occupy a sheltered position if they actually (or potentially) have very little competition from imports.

The prices of energy (crude oil, natural gas and electricity) and some prices of primary industry products are exogenous, as is the production of these goods. The resource-based (*extractive*) production is determined by supply at given prices which are either genuinely exogenous to the Norwegian economy, such as crude oil and natural gas prices, or are determined administratively such as agricultural prices or electricity prices. The model however is not explicit on this point.

If we ignore the dynamic specification, the equations for the endogenously determined prices in MODAG A can generally be written in the following way:

$$\log P_t^N = C_P + a \log UC_t + b \, CAP_t + c \, CAP_t^2 + (1-a) \log P_t^I, \quad (3.7)$$

where P^N is either the export or the domestic price, UC is the unit-variable cost (wages and material input costs), CAP is a capacity utilization index and P^I is the import price. C_p, a, b and c are coefficients. Homogeneity of degree 1 in absolute prices is assumed.

The price equations are made dynamic by assuming partial adjustment. This lag distribution is obviously very simple and restrictive, but it requires few extra parameters and can be justified by the slowness of adjustment to changes in unit costs and competitive prices. We have experimented with other lag formulations as well, such as lagged changes in unit costs or import prices which are significant for some products.

Price equations are estimated on the basis of annual data from the national accounts for the period 1962 to 1984. A variable representing the effect of price controls was included and found significant in most domestic price equations for services.[10] The results of the estimation may be briefly

---

[10] We have also tested whether the increase in the degree of foreign competition as measured by the import share has had any influence on the domestic price. With

summarized as follows:

(i) *Domestic prices.* The service industries, including building and construction, seem to follow a mark-up pricing rule. The same is true for some of the manufacturing industries (production of food and of beverages and tobacco). These industries may, as in MODIS IV, be classified as sheltered industries. The other industries are to varying degrees exposed to import competition as indicated by the estimate of a in (3.7), and may be classified as exposed industries (cf. also table A.3 in Appendix A).

(ii) *Export prices.* For traditional Norwegian exports (paper and paper products, industrial chemicals and metals) export prices are heavily influenced by world market prices but (domestic) unit costs also seem to play a significant role. One possible explanation of this result may be that Norwegian producers have market shares that allow them some freedom to set prices even on markets for staple goods. For those exposed industries which are primarily oriented towards the domestic market and for which the export markets are secondary, we found that export prices and domestic prices have developed fairly similarly. For sheltered industries the mark-up pricing rule gives a reasonable description of export price determination (cf. also table A.4 in Appendix A).

(iii) The estimation results show that on the average more than half of the total effects on prices of changes in costs and competitive prices appear during the first year.

(iv) In general, changes in capacity utilization do not seem to have very much impact on prices. However, for industries exposed to foreign competition capacity utilization does affect price behaviour and in some industries the effect is U-shaped, i.e., at very low capacity utilization there is short-run increasing returns. This is in accordance with the employment model.[11]

We have thus obtained results which correspond reasonably well to the more or less *a priori* assumptions about price behaviour which have for a long time characterized Norwegian macro models. On the other hand our results

---

one exception we were not able to find any significant effects.

[11] Due to the way in which unit costs are defined, including current and not normalized labour productivity among other things, increased production would result in lower prices in the short run because of increased productivity even without the U-shaped capacity term in the price equation.

give a somewhat different picture of price formation from empirical studies based on statistical data from the 1960's, where the degree of costs passed on to prices in exposed industries was clearly higher (Ringstad [1974]). One explanation of this difference may be that the Norwegian economy was more sheltered in the 1960's than it was in the 1970's and that this change has modified pricing behaviour.

3.4 Factor demand

In MODAG A the factors of production are separated into four main groups: real capital, labour, materials, and energy. In general the model assumes substitution between labour and capital whereas the inputs of materials and total energy are used in fixed proportions to gross output. However, there is substitution between the two energy commodities fuels and electricity based on the assumption that producers minimize total energy costs, where total energy is a CES-aggregate of the two energy commodities.

The demand for capital is derived from the assumption that producers minimize long-run costs of labour and capital for any given output. Labour demand is modelled by assuming that short- run labour costs are minimized given current output and the capital stock by the end of the previous year. The submodels are presented in more detail below.

Employment

MODAG A distinguishes between wage earners and self-employed persons. The number of persons in the latter group is exogenously given. The employment of wage earners, however, is determined endogenously with the exception of local and central government, ocean transport and resource based industries, covering about thirty percent of the total employment (cf. also table A.5 in Appendix A).

Short-term demand for labour (wage earners) by industry is modelled assuming that, for given production X and the capital stock K, industries minimize their short-run labour costs. The number of employees, N, is a quasi-fixed factor with adjustment to the desired level occurring gradually because of the costs (*hiring and firing costs*) associated with rapid adjustment. The number of hours worked per worker, H, is the only completely flexible factor in the short run. Using a simplified version of the relation between hourly wages and actual hours worked it can be shown that the optimum number of hours per worker equals normal working hours H^N (see Bergland and Cappelen [1981]).

The production functions for the manufacturing industries do not have constant marginal elasiticities with regard to labour as is the case with, e.g, the Cobb-Douglas function. Instead, we have chosen a production function where the elasticity of labour decreases in proportion to increases in the capacity utilization rate CAP. For the other industries Cobb-Douglas production functions have been chosen.

The short-run production function for each of the manufacturing industries is specified as

$$X_t e^{\theta CAP_t} = AN_t^\alpha H_t^\beta e^{\varrho t}, \qquad (3.8)$$

where θ, α, β, A and ϱ are positive constants. The elasticity of labour with regard to X is $\alpha/(1 + \theta CAP)$ which decreases as CAP increases.

The capacity utilization rate is estimated as a modified Wharton index:

$$CAP_t = \gamma_t \frac{X_t}{K_t} \qquad \gamma_t > 0, \qquad (3.9)$$

where γ_t is the trend-through-peak capital-output ratio. The elasticity of substitution between labour and capital implied by (3.8) and (3.9) varies between 0.5 and 1.0.

From the assumptions outlined above, we can express the desired number of employees in each industry as a function of X, CAP (or $\log K$ for industries outside manufacturing) and H^N. By imposing a partial adjustment mechanism with λ representing the adjustment parameter we obtain:

$$\log N_t = C_N + \frac{\lambda}{\alpha} \log X_t - \frac{\lambda\beta}{\alpha} \log H^N$$
$$+ \frac{\lambda}{\alpha}(CAP_t - \varrho t) + (1 - \lambda) \log N_{t-1}. \qquad (3.10)$$

The estimation is based on data from the national accounts from 1962 to 1979. The OLS method of estimation was used. In the estimation we did not get accurate estimates of the effects of H^N, and this variable was therefore left out of the model.[12] The most important results may be summarized as follows (cf. also table A.5 in Appendix A):

(i) Generally, the estimation results indicate increasing returns to scale. For most manufacturing industries the elasticity of labour demand with regard to production (current output) is close to 1 at full capacity

---

[12] With annual data, H^N has a trend development which makes it difficult to distinguish the effect of H^N from the trend term.

utilization. The trend term, which expresses technological change (the parameter ϱ), is zero for many of the manufacturing industries and has a low value for the others. This is probably due to the estimated increasing returns to scale.

(ii) For other industries (service industries as well as the building and construction industry) the estimates show an elasticity of labour with regard to production of less than 1 and insignificant technological trend terms, but the returns to scale here are lower than in the manufacturing industries. This is partly because significant estimates of the parameter for real capital stock were found only for the building and construction industry and for the wholesale and retail trade.

(iii) For manufacturing industries using unskilled labour we obtained relatively high figures (0.7–0.8) and clearly significant estimates of the adjustment parameter λ. This indicates a rapid adjustment of labour. For other manufacturing industries λ was estimated to be between 0.4 and 0.6, i.e., a much slower adjustment. For other industries than manufacturing the estimates of the adjustment parameter vary greatly from industry to industry. The results for the building and construction industry are close to those we obtained in the manufacturing industries which use a great deal of skilled labour.

Capital and investment

Assuming firms minimize long-run factor costs to any given output level, the desired capital stock K_t^D may be written as a function of relative factor prices and output:

$$K_t^D = f\left(\frac{p_t^J}{w_t}, X_t, t\right) \tag{3.11}$$

where X is the level of output, p_t^J is the user cost of capital and w_t the wage rate per man-year. p_t^J is defined in accordance with the framework of Biørn [1984] (see also Bergan et al. [1985]), and depends on investment prices, tax rates, the interest rate and depreciation rates.

In the presence of adjustment costs it is optimal for firms to adjust their capital stock only partially towards the desired or optimal level:

$$K_t - K_{t-1} = \lambda(K_t^D - K_{t-1}). \tag{3.12}$$

Due to imperfect capital markets and the existence of credit rationing during the estimation period the speed of adjustment λ is assumed to depend on internally generated funds approximated by gross operating surplus RYR and credit supply to firms $KREDB$, both in real terms, in the following way:

$$\lambda = \lambda_0 + \lambda_1 \frac{KREDB_t + \sum_{\ell=1}^{4} \beta_{t-\ell} RYR_{t-\ell}}{K_t^D - K_{t-\ell}}. \qquad (3.13)$$

This way of specifying λ assumes that K_t^D is always different from K_{t-1} which may be a reasonable approximation for the industries in the period we are studying. We admit, however, that our specification is rather *ad hoc*.

Substituting (3.13) and (3.11) into (3.12) we obtain

$$K_t - K_{t-1} = \lambda_0 f\left(\frac{p_t^J}{w_t}, X_t, t\right) - \lambda_0 K_{t-1}$$
$$+ \lambda_1 \left(KREDB_t + \sum_{\ell=1}^{4} \beta_{t-\ell} RYR_{t-\ell}\right). \qquad (3.14)$$

By definition $K_t - K_{t-1} = J_t - D_t$, where J is gross investment and D is depreciation. If we as a simplification assume $D_t = \delta K_{t-1}$, we have the following equation for gross investment by industry:

$$J_t = \lambda_0 f\left(\frac{p_t^J}{w_t}, X_t, t\right) + (\delta - \lambda_0) K_{t-1}$$
$$+ \lambda_1 \left(KREDB_t + \sum_{\ell=1}^{4} \beta_{t-\ell} RYR_{t-\ell}\right). \qquad (3.15)$$

To simplify further, the f-function is assumed to be linear. Almon-lag distributions (normally of length 1 to 4 years) are specified for production, relative factor prices and gross operating surplus.

Investment equations like (3.15) have been implemented for 20 of the 28 private industries in the model, once again leaving out most of the resource-based industries and ocean transport (cf. table A.6 in Appendix A). The estimation is based on data for the period 1962–82. The results vary a lot between industries but some systematic differences occur:

(i) Output is the main explanatory factor in manufacturing. However, only gross operating surplus seems to have any influence on investment in the export oriented industries (paper and paper products, industrial chemicals and metals). Strictly speaking this implies that the model (3.15) is rejected for these industries.

(ii) Relative factor prices seem to have some impact on investments in labour-intensive industries. Credit supply does not seem to be an important factor in determining investment in a disaggregate study like ours.

A problem is that the estimated values of $(\delta - \lambda_0)$ are often positive or very close to zero. In some cases (3 out of 20) we have had to implement equations with $(\delta - \lambda_0 = 0)$. This implies that when production or relative factor prices change the investment process will persist for a very long time until the new desired capital stock is reached. The model may therefore produce some implausible short-run and medium-term results. A detailed presentation of the empirical results is given in table A.6 in Appendix A.

Gross investment in housing, JH is determined by an equation quite different from (3.15) due to the fact that the decisions to invest in housing are made by households, not firms. The chosen equation is:

$$JH_t = C_{JH} + 0.0668(RWE_{t-1} + RSE_{t-1}) - 0.048KH_{t-1}$$
$$18600r_t - 13600 \left(\frac{P^{JH}}{P^C} \right)_t + \text{demographic variables}. \tag{3.16}$$

Only lagged real disposable incomes for wage earners, RWE, and for the self-employed, RSE (see section 3.6), are included because we do not believe that pensioners are important investors in housing. The demographic variables, which consist of a breakdown of the total population between 20 and 60 years, also seem to indicate that people belonging to the oldest age group 40–60 years do not contribute much to investment in housing compared to younger age groups with equal income. KH is the real capital stock in the housing sector. We tried, without success, to include a variable showing the increase in (real) credit supply from the state bank for investment in housing. The variable r is the nominal rate of interest in commercial banks. The variable P^{JH}/P^C is the relative price between new houses and consumer goods.[13]

---

[13] The investment analysis is further documented and discussed in Bergan et al. [1985].

Electricity and fuels

We assume that the energy aggregate by industry is a linear homogeneous function of electricity E and fuels F and is related to gross output by fixed coefficients. Assuming the CES-function we have:

$$1 = \left[\delta_E \left(\frac{a_E}{\delta_E} \right)^{-\varrho} + \delta_F \left(\frac{a_F}{\delta_F} \right)^{-\varrho} \right]^{-1/\varrho} \qquad \delta_F = 1 - \delta_E \qquad (3.17)$$

where a_E and a_F are input coefficients and δ_E, δ_F and ϱ are parameters. We assume that producers minimize the cost of using electricity and fuels. It then follows that:

$$\frac{a_E}{a_F} = \frac{\delta_E}{\delta_F} \left(\frac{P_E^C}{P_F^C} \right)^{-\sigma} \qquad (3.18)$$

where $\sigma = 1/(1 + s)$ is the elasticity of substitution between electricity and fuels and P_E^C/P_F^C the relative price. (3.18) is estimated adding the lagged input-coefficient ratio, so that this ratio is partially adjusted to its optimal level given by (3.18) when the relative energy price changes. The short and long-run effects of an increase in the price of electricity on the relative use of electricity compared to fuels are given in table A.7 in Appendix A. The general result is that the estimated elasticity of substitution centers around 1, with one or two important exceptions — manufacturing of paper and paper products where it is 0.5 and manufacturing of metals where σ is almost 0. The latter result is important since this sector uses a quarter of total electricity production in Norway.[14]

3.5   Direct and indirect taxes

Direct taxes are treated in the same way in MODAG A as in MODIS IV. In the models, direct taxes are paid according to different socioeconomic groups (wage earners, self-employed persons, pensioners). The taxes are determined by a two-step procedure. In a separate micro-based model, average and marginal macro tax rates are calculated for each socioeconomic group. For given tax rates direct taxes are determined by relationships of the type:

$$T_t = \left[t_g \frac{Y_0}{N_0} + t_m \left(\frac{Y_t}{N_t} - \frac{Y_0}{N_0} \right) \right] N_t + TX_t \qquad (3.19)$$

---

[14] Energy demand in MODAG A is presented more fully in Bye and Frenger [1984].

where T is total direct taxes (for each socio-economic group), TX is exogenous (income independent) direct taxes, t_g and t_m are the average and marginal macro tax rates, respectively. Y/N is income (liable to taxes) per taxpayer. The number of taxpayers N is exogenous for self-employed persons and pensioners. The number of taxpaying wage earners is assumed to be proportional to the number of man-years worked by wage-earners.[15]

The tax rates t_g and t_m are calculated in a separate model as mentioned above. The actual rules of the tax system are included in this model, in addition to information on income distribution and on the number of taxpayers in the various income groups. Assumptions on income growth in the forecasting years are also included. In order for marginal tax rates to be correctly estimated, the (exogenous) assumptions of income growth (the variable Y/N) in the separate model ought to correspond fairly well with the endogenously determined income development in the macro model. Iterative calculations may therefore be necessary if deviations are too large.

The treatment of *indirect taxes* and subsidies is extremely simplified in the MODAG model compared to MODIS IV. This is partly because it is almost impossible, at MODAG's level of aggregation, to link each indirect tax and subsidy directly to commodities in the same way as it is done in MODIS IV. More important, however, is the fact that without the simplifications the MODAG model would have had a great number of additional variables and a far more complicated model structure. In practice, the model uses only rates for nonrefundable value-added taxes and other value taxes (net), since quantity taxes and subsidies are interpreted as value taxes (net). The indirect tax rates used in MODAG A are generated by MODIS simulations, since routines have been developed to convert MODIS results to estimates of exogenous variables in MODAG A.[16]

3.6 Private consumption

The private consumption model in MODAG A consists of three parts:

(i) equations which determine consumption-motivating income according to socioeconomic groups (wage earners, self-employed persons, pensioners)

(ii) a macro consumption function which determines total consumption as a function of real disposable consumption-motivating income according

---

[15] See Bjerkholt and Longva [1980] pp. 137–144 for a further discussion.

[16] For a discussion of the treatment of indirect taxes in MODIS, see Bjerkholt and Longva [1980] pp. 144–160.

to socioeconomic groups.

(iii) a linear expenditure system which, based on the macro consumption
function's estimate of total consumption and relative prices, determines the consumption of each consumption category.

Consumption-motivating income by socioeconomic group (wage earners
WE, self-employed *SE* and pensioners *TE*, which is, in general terms, defined as:

$$WE = g_{WW}\, YW_t + g_{EW}\, YE_t + g_{UW}\, YU_t + g_{TW}\, YT_t - TW_t$$
$$SE = g_{WS}\, YW_t + g_{ES}\, YE_t + g_{US}\, YU_t + g_{TS}\, YT_t - TS_t \qquad (3.20)$$
$$TE = g_{WT}\, YW_t + g_{ET}\, YE_t + g_{UT}\, YU_t + g_{TT}\, YT_t - TT_t\,.$$

YW is wages and salaries.[17]

Total wages and salaries are determined by multiplying the model estimate of the number of wage earners by industry, with exogenously given
wage rates. Income from self-employment *YE* is determined as shares of the
operating surplus (which is endogenous) in each industry. Transfers *YU*
are exogenous, as is net interest income *YT*. Each kind of income is allocated among the three socioeconomic groups by means of a set of shares,
represented by the *g*-parameters, derived from income statistics. Direct
taxes (*TW, TS, TT*) are determined by the tax equations (see (3.19)).

Total private consumption excluding health care consumption, which is
exogenous, is determined by the following aggregate consumption function,
estimated on the basis of national accounts data from 1962–82:

$$C_t = C_C + 0.652R_t + 0.217R_{t-1} + 0.714KREDH_t$$
$$R_t = RWE_t + 0.623RSE_t + 0.905RTE_t\,, \qquad (3.21)$$

where *RWE* is the wage-earners' real disposable consumption-motivating
income, *RTE* is the same for the pensioners and *RSE* for the self-employed,
while *KREDH* is the real value of the increase in credit supply to households. The ratios between the marginal propensities to consume of the
various socioeconomic groups are estimated using cross-sectional data (see
Cappelen [1980]). The estimated propensity to consume proved to be very
stable when the estimation period was changed. The long-run marginal

---

[17] In this presentation we ignore some minor differences between tax liable income
and consumption-motivating income before taxes. For a short discussion of this
see Cappelen, Garaas and Longva [1981], section 4.2.6.

propensities to consume are 0.87 for wage-earners, 0.54 for the self-employed and 0.79 for pensioners.

The total consumption arrived at by (3.21) is allocated according to consumption categories by a set of linear expenditure relations (LES):

$$C_{jt} = \alpha_j + \beta_j \frac{P_t^C C_t - \sum_k \alpha_k P_{kt}^C}{P_{jt}^C} + \gamma_j CU_t, \qquad (3.22)$$

where C_j is the consumption of category j and P_j^C is a price index for this consumption category, calculated as a weighted sum of domestic and import prices. P^C is the price index for total consumption C which is also used to deflate the variables included in the macro consumption function. CU represents foreigners' consumption in Norway and is endogenously determined in the export model. The parameters of (3.22) are estimated indirectly by using estimates of income elasticities from various sources (mainly cross-section studies) and budget shares and a formula for translating these estimates to the parameters of (3.22) (cf. Bojer [1966]).

For the two energy categories, electricity and fuel, the model is somewhat more complex. As energy is a CES-aggregate of the two inputs, electricity and fuel, we may write the dual price index PU^C as:

$$PU_t^C = \left(\delta_E P_{Et}^{C1-\sigma} + \delta_F P_{Ft}^{C1-\sigma}\right)^{1/(1-\sigma)}, \qquad \delta_F = 1 - \delta_E \qquad (3.23)$$

where δ_E and σ are estimated coefficients. Assuming that consumers minimize the cost of buying electricity (C_E) and fuel (C_F) we arrive at the following equation from which δ_E and σ have been estimated:

$$\frac{C_{Et}}{C_{Ft}} = \frac{\delta_E}{1 - \delta_E} \left(\frac{P_{Et}^C}{P_{Ft}^C}\right)^{-\sigma} \qquad (3.24)$$

We have estimated (3.24) using OLS and experimented with different lag-specifications using national accounts data for 1962–1984. The result for σ centered around 2 with substantial lag-effects in relative prices. We have chosen, however, to implement the model without lags mainly to make the model simple. But there are also reasons to believe that consumers will adapt more quickly to changes in relative energy prices in the future than what we have observed as responses to changes due to OPEC I and II.

The demand equations for electricity and fuel may now be written as (see Frenger [1985]):

$$C_{it} = \alpha_i + \beta_u \delta_i (PU_t^C / P_{it}^C) \left(P_t^C C_t - \sum_k \alpha_k P_{kt}^C \right) / P_{it}^C, \quad i = E, F. \quad (3.25)$$

Note that in (3.22), which determine consumer demand for non-energy goods, one of the P_{kt}^C is PU_t^C as given by (3.23). With this model specification electricity and fuel are alternative in demand, whereas energy in total is complementary to other goods as is generally the case in the LES.

4. Multipliers estimated by MODAG A

We have carried out some simple model calculations to illustrate the main features of the model. Hopefully the results can also be used to shed some light on the workings of the Norwegian economy. However, as clearly indicated in the discussion above, MODAG A is not a complete model of the Norwegian economy. Several important groups of variables which are obviously endogenously determined in the economy are treated as exogenous in the model. This applies both to variables that should interact simultaneously with other specified variables of the model, e.g., wage rates and financial variables, and to variables that are determined by economic and other processes not included in the present model, e.g., production, investment and exports of industries based on natural resources. This means that the model will, at least for some types of sensitivity analysis yield unrealistic, counter-intuitive or even adverse results.

The usefulness of MODAG A can only be reviewed when the model is regarded in its proper setting, i.e., as a tool in a planning or a policy-analysing process. The empirical characteristics of MODAG A presented below will therefore first and foremost illustrate the functioning of the model as such and only with certain qualifications the working of the Norwegian economy. It is not the purpose of this paper to give a comprehensive presentation of the working of the Norwegian economy.

For the calculations below our point of departure has been a reference scenario for the Norwegian economy calculated with the use of MODAG A. Along this reference scenario we have calculated multipliers which represent the impact of sustained changes in exogenous variables on important model determined (endogenous) variables. Both the effect on the endogenous variables and the change in the exogenous variables are measured as deviations from the reference scenario. Because of lagged adjustments to changes in exogenous variables, deviations (in relation to the reference scenario) are calculated for up to ten years after the change has taken place. After five years most effects however are minor, the major ones already visible.

Below are presented some of the main effects of sustained increases in a selection of important exogenous variables.

Wage rates

Figures 2 and 3 show some of the main effects of a 1 percent sustained increase in wage rates from 1984. This implies a change in the distribution of income between households, general government and private enterprises. Higher wages increase the nominal income of households while operating surplus (profits) in private enterprises is reduced. The increase in consumer demand is the most important quantitative short-run effect of increased wages. The increase in tax revenues is larger than the increase in government wage costs. A wage increase thus increases the government budget surplus. This is due to the fact that, except for taxes related to crude oil and natural gas production, most taxes in Norway are related to wages, either directly, as taxes on income or on wage costs in the business sector, or indirectly, as taxes on consumption.

Another effect of higher wage rates comes via changes in the relative prices of commodities, i.e., changes in price-competitiveness, as domestic and export prices increase in relation to world market prices. Thus the volume of endogenous exports decreases, but the effect is small in the short run. The reason why endogenous exports are not reduced more is the relatively small effect of wage increases on costs in many export-orientated industries and a price elasticity only somewhat above 1 in the long run, as mentioned in section 3.1. In addition, exports from resource-based industries and ocean transport are exogenously given in the model. The increase in imports in the short run is due both to higher import shares and higher domestic demand. In the long run the loss in price-competitiveness becomes more important and imports increase even though total demand is reduced.

Higher wage rates also change the relative (primary) factor price of labour and capital and demand for capital increases as capital is substituted for labour. However, from figure 3 we can see that, in spite of increased capital intensity, the effect on employment is smaller than on production in the longer run. This is partly explained by the shift from exposed (and labour-extensive) industries to sheltered (and labour intensive) industries, in addition to the effects of increasing returns to scale. The total effect of

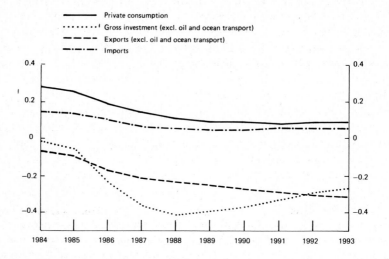

Figure 2: Effects on main components of GDP (in percent) of a 1 percent increase in wage rates.

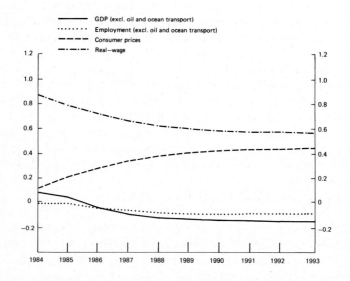

Figure 3: Effects on GDP, employment and consumer prices (in percent)
of a 1 percent increase in wage rates.

higher wage rates on investment demand is negative due to the reduction in total demand (in the long run) and in operating surplus (profits).

The effect of 1 percent higher wage rates on consumer prices is low in the short run, approximately 0.1 percent, but increases over a long period to somewhat above 0.4. The estimated inertia in price behaviour is mainly due to the partly government regulated industries like transport and housing, where the lags between cost and price increases, are rather long. This delayed effect on consumer prices is the main reason why production increases in the short run and decreases in the long run. Export prices (exclusive oil and gas prices) increase in the long run by about 0.3 which is lower than the effect on consumer prices.

In the long run the employment real wage elasticity (exclusive oil, ocean transport and government) is slightly below −0.2.

World market prices

Figures 4 and 5 show the effects of a 1 percent sustained increase in the level of world market prices from 1984 compared to the reference path. By world market prices we mean all prices on imports and on competitive goods on the world market in addition to some domestic and export prices which are believed to follow world market prices rather closely (oil and gas prices, prices on ocean transport services, forestry products and fish). The importance of world market prices for the Norwegian economy is clearly revealed in figure 5. Consumer prices increase by 0.3 percent the first year and almost 0.5 in the long run. Prices on investments and exports (exclusive oil and gas prices) increase in the long run by as much as 0.6 and 0.8 percent, respectively.

World market prices are very important for variable unit costs in manufacturing. Actually, the effect on variable unit costs in manufacturing of an increase in world market prices is slightly higher than the effect of increased wage rates (both between 0.40 and 0.45). This illustrates the specific type of openness that is characteristic for the Norwegian economy and explains to a large extent why changes in wage rates have a perhaps surprisingly small effect on exports and import shares as long as important quantitative elements of supply-side behaviour are disregarded as is the case in MODAG A.

The increase in consumer and investment prices leads to lower consumer demand, production and investment. However, after the initial reduction in investment the deviation from the reference scenario is reduced as investment picks up in the most export-oriented manufacturing industries where production and operating surplus increase considerably. The

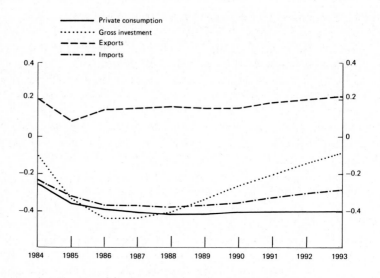

Figure 4: Effects on main components of GDP (in percent) of a 1 percent increase in world market prices.

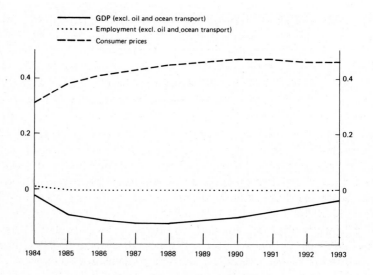

Figure 5: Effects on GDP and consumer prices (in percent) of a 1 percent increase in world market prices.

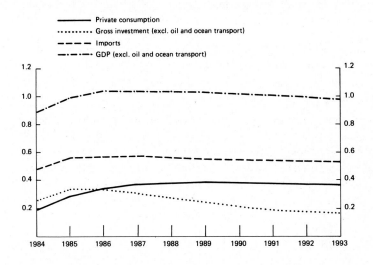

Figure 6: Effects on main components of GDP of an 1 billion NOK increase in government purchases of goods in fixed-1984 prices. (Changes in billion NOK).

rather small change in relative prices between domestic and foreign products implies that exports and import shares do not change very much.

The reason why the impact on the volume of exports declines from 1984 to 1985 is that the increase in the export volume in 1984 increases capacity utilization in many important export-oriented industries, which raises their export prices the next year. When investments in these industries pick up, capacity is increased, export prices are lowered and exports are increased again.

Government expenditures on goods for consumption purposes

Figure 6 shows the effects on main components of GDP of a one billion NOK sustained increase in government expenditures on goods for consumption purposes. (In 1984 total GDP was approximately 450 billion NOK.) Thus the first-year multiplier is 0.9 and the second-year multiplier is 1.0, which is also very close to the multipliers of the following years. Price effects are negligible in all years, but due to pro-cyclical behaviour of productivity and increasing returns to scale, prices fall slightly.

The lagged response of increased government expenditure is partly due to lags in the macro consumption function and in the investment equations. The lags in the employment equations are also important. Gross investments reach a peak after three years while private consumption continues to increase for much longer. Thus the GDP multiplier is almost constant and falls only after six to seven years. The movements in imports mirror changes in gross investment goods rather closely as import shares for investment goods are relatively high.

In the version of the model presented in this paper there are, almost by definition, no long-run *crowding-out* effects in the private sector either through changes in wage rates, exchange rates or financial variables since these variables are exogenous. Initially there is a small crowding-out effect on exports due to increased capacity utilization and a loss of price competitiveness on export markets. In the long run, as investment increases capacity, this effect on export prices vanishes.

World market demand

In MODAG A world market demand is proxied by a weighted sum of consumption and investment in the eight most important trading countries for Norway. In the simulations presented here these market indicators are increased by 1 percent every year from 1984 and onwards. As only 35 percent of total exports are endogenous in MODAG A, the change in demand has only moderate effects on production in Norway. The effects on some macroeconomic variables are shown in figures 7 and 8.

The short-run effect on exports (traditional goods) is 0.7 percent due to lags in the export equations. Export prices (exclusive oil and gas prices) increase quite substantially during the first years because of increased capacity utilization in export-oriented industries. As profits and production increase and investment follows suit, capacity is increased and export prices return to the reference path. This improves price-competitiveness and exports continue to increase.

Prices on investment goods decline when investment increases, as there are almost no capacity effects on these prices and the pro-cyclical effects on productivity and increasing returns to scale reduce unit costs. This also explains some of the increase in investments which continues, although at a moderate pace, even after ten years. A long-run stable solution is not visible after ten years, but judging from figures 7 and 8, a stable solution will be reached later.

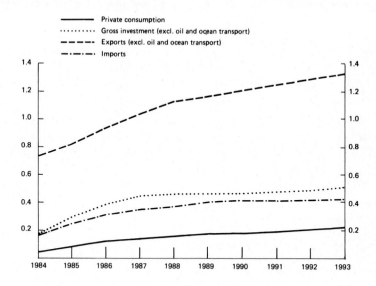

Figure 7: Effects on main components of GPD (in percent) of a 1 percent increase in world market demand.

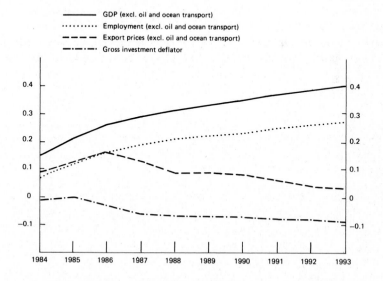

Figure 8: Effects on GDP, employment and prices (in percent) of a
1 percent increase in world market demand.

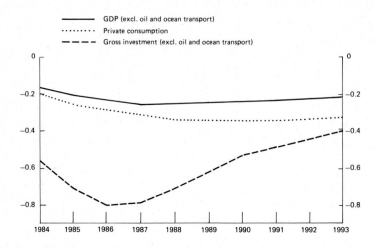

Figure 9: Effects on GDP, private consumption and investment of a 1
percentage point increase in interest rates.

Interest rate

Interest rates are exogenous in MODAG A. The main interest rate indicator
in the model is the average rate on loans from commercial banks. This
rate enters the user-cost term in the investment equations. Net financial
income for households is also exogenous and in the simulations this income
is changed by the same factor as the interest rate, implying a constant
interest rate margin in the financial sector. Figure 9 shows the effects
on GDP, private consumption and investment of a 10 percent increase of
these interest variables, equivalent to an increase in the rate of interest of
approximately 1 percentage point, from 1984 and onwards. As is seen from
figure 9 there is a rather substantial negative effect on gross investment
(exclusive oil, ocean transport and government). The largest effect is on
gross investment in housing which in the long run is reduced by 1 percent.

The effect on consumption is mainly due to higher interest payments,
but in the longer run lower investments reduce the capital stock and increase unit costs compared to the reference scenario. Thus prices will
increase somewhat. In addition, the rate of interest affects consumer prices
directly via the price on housing services. The long run effect on consumer
prices is 0.25 and this price increase further reduces consumer demand. Em-

ployment is not much affected by higher interest rates. This is of course a result of the lower capital stock due to the higher user cost of capital when interest rates are increased.

5. Some main conclusions

In reviewing the empirical characteristics of the working of the Norwegian economy, especially the *openess of the economy*, the importance of *resource-based industries* and the existence of many partly or totally *government regulated industries* must be taken into account. In using MODAG A as a tool in such an analysis the absence of a model of the financial markets, wage formation and supply behaviour for the resource-based industries makes the model analysis only partial. Having these very important qualifications in mind when interpreting the results, some of the main empirical characteristics of MODAG A are the following:

(i) *Domestic cost increases* (mainly increases in wage rates) have a strong impact on the development of consumer and investment prices and a much smaller impact on export prices. The net effect on the activity level (GDP and employment) is negative but rather small. The net effect on exports and imports is significantly negative (exports decrease and imports increase).

(ii) Increases in *world market prices* world market price effects are decisive for the development of export and investment prices but consumer prices are also strongly influenced. The net effect on the activity level (GDP and employment) is negative but rather small. The net effect on exports and imports is significant (imports decrease and exports increase).

(iii) Increases in *government expenditures* (on goods) have an expansionary effect on the economy, whereas the effects on prices are negligible.

(iv) Increases in *world market demand* have a strong impact on the domestic activity level (GDP and employment) whereas the effects on prices are small.

Appendix A   Survey of important price and quantity elasticities in the submodels of MODAG A

Table A.1: Determinants of exports.

Commodity	Shares of exports in 1984*	Elasticities w.r.t.			
		Relative prices		Market growth	
		1 year	Long-run	1 year	Long-run
Agricultural products	0.3	X	X	X	X
Forestry products	0.1	X	X	X	X
Fish	0.5	X	X	X	X
Mining products	0.7	X	X	X	X
Food products	3.9	−0.26	−0.39	0.59	0.89
Beverages and tobacco	0.1	−0.67	−0.92	1.68	2.29
Textiles and wearing apparels	0.5	−0.50	−1.50	0.35	1.08
Wood and wood products	0.6	−0.50	−1.02	1.07	2.16
Paper and paper products	2.9	−1.37	−1.86	1.04	1.41
Industrial chemicals	3.0	−0.68	−1.00	1.31	1.93
Refined petroleum products	2.4	X	X	X	X
Other chemicals and mineral prod.	2.4	−0.47	−0.93	1.48	2.92
Iron, steel and metal	9.2	−1.77	−1.77	1.42	1.42
Machinery and metal products	5.3	−0.15	−1.90	0.48	2.06
New ships and oil platforms	0.9	X	X	X	X
Printing and publishing	0.1	−1.10	−1.51	1.67	2.15
Electricity	0.3	R	R	R	R
Wholesale and retail trade	3.0	−0.38	−0.67	1.03	1.81
Crude oil and natural gas	36.4	X	X	X	X
Oil drilling	1.1	X	X	X	X
Pipeline services	1.3	X	X	X	X
Ocean transport	16.1	X	X	X	X
Domestic transport	2.2	−0.22	−0.37	1.34	2.23
Government services	0.2	X	X	X	X
Re-export of non-compet. imports	0.4	X	X	X	X
Second-hand ships and platforms	2.5	X	X	X	X
Tourism	2.5	−0.31	−0.31	1.77	1.77
Other services	0.9	X	X	X	X
Correction for oil fields	0.9	X	X	X	X

X means that the export of this commodity is exogenously determined.

R means that the export is endogenously determined by the commodity balance equation.

* in percent

Table A.2: Determinants of imports and import shares.[1]

Commodity	Shares of imports in 1984*	Relative price elasticities	
		1 year	Long-run
Agricultural products	0.8	R	R
Forestry products	0.2	R	R
Fish	0.0	MX	MX
Mining products	0.7	−0.00	−0.76
Food products	1.8	−0.60	−1.19
Beverages and tobacco	0.3	MX	MX
Textiles and wearing apparels	5.5	−0.33	−0.33
Wood and wood products	2.2	−0.68	−0.68
Paper and paper products	1.6	−0.76	−0.76
Industrial chemicals	3.2	−0.49	−0.99
Refined petroleum products	2.7	R	R
Other chemicals and mineral prod.	10.2	−0.45	−0.90
Iron, steel and metal	5.0	−0.19	−0.37
Machinery and metal products	21.7	−0.39	−0.77
New ships and oil platforms	6.7	X	X
Printing and publishing	0.7	−0.28	−0.57
Electricity	0.0	X	X
Wholesale and retail trade	0.6	MX	MX
Crude oil and natural gas	2.0	R	R
Oil drilling	0.4	MX	MX
Other services	1.6	MX	MX
Non-competing imports	24.5		
− Food	1.8	R	R
− Manufacturing products	4.0	R	R
− Gross expenditure for shipping	13.0	R	R
− Gross expenditure in oil drilling, etc.	2.3	R	R
− Other	2.9	R	R
Tourism	7.0	R	R

X means that the import of this commodity is exogenously determined.

MX means that the import share is exogenously determined.

R means that the import is determined from the commodity balance equation.

* in percent

[1] All market growth (income) elastiticities are unity as long as the composition of demand is unchanged.

Table A.2: Determinants of domestic prices.

Commodity	Elasticities with respect to						
	Unit costs		World market price		Capacity utilization[1]		Price controls[2]
	1 year	Long-run	1 year	Long-run	1 year	Long-run	1 year
Agricultural products	X	X	X	X	X	X	X
Forestry products	0.281	0.310	0.627	0.690	0.400	0.500	0.000
Fish products	0.283	0.433	0.370	0.567	0.000	0.000	0.000
Mining products	0.248	1.000	0.000	0.000	0.000	0.000	0.000
Food products	0.530	1.000	0.000	0.000	0.000	0.000	-0.015
Beverages and tobacco	0.703	1.000	0.000	0.000	0.000	0.000	0.000
Textiles and wearing apparels	0.395	0.764	0.122	0.236	0.300	0.600	-0.023
Wood and wood products	0.287	0.664	0.135	0.336	-0.100	-0.300[3]	0.000
Paper and paper products	0.313	1.000	0.000	0.000	1.500	4.700	0.000
Industrial chemicals	0.329	1.000	0.000	0.000	0.000	0.000	0.000
Petrol	0.258	0.386	0.410	0.612	0.000	0.000	0.000
Other fuels	0.209	0.225	0.721	0.775	0.000	0.000	0.000
Other chemicals and mineral products	0.739	0.922	0.063	0.078	0.500	0.700	0.000
Iron, steel and other metals	0.106	0.228	0.357	0.772	0.000	0.000	0.000

X means that the domestic price of this commodity is exogenous.

[1] Due to the U-shape of the cost-curves in some industries this effect is calculated when capacity utilization increases from 0.95 to 0.96.

[2] In the long run the direct effect of price control is assumed to be 0, i.e., it is assumed that the control is lifted as has been the case with all controls historically.

[3] Variable costs reach a minimum when capacity utilization is 96 percent.

Table A.9: Determinants of domestic prices (continued).

Commodity	Elasticities with respect to						
	Unit costs		World market price		Capacity utilization[1]		Price controls[2]
	1 year	Long-run	1 year	Long-run	1 year	Long-run	1 year
Machinery and metal products	0.941	1.000	0.000	0.000	0.000	0.000	-0.076
Ships and oil platforms	0.703	1.000	0.000	0.000	0.000	0.000	0.000
Printing and publishing	0.431	0.901	0.047	0.099	0.000	0.000	-0.029
Electricity	X	X	X	X	X	X	X
Construction	0.722	1.000	0.000	0.000	0.000	0.000	0.000
Wholesale and retail trade	0.449	1.000	0.000	0.000	0.000	0.000	-0.065
Crude and natural gas	X	X	X	X	X	X	X
Oil drilling	X	X	X	X	X	X	X
Ocean transport	X	X	X	X	X	X	X
Domestic transport	0.311	1.000	0.000	0.000	0.000	0.000	-0.047
Banking and insurance	0.971	1.000	0.000	0.000	0.000	0.000	0.000
Housing services	0.305	1.000	0.000	0.000	0.000	0.000	-0.024
Other services	0.262	1.000	0.000	0.000	0.000	0.000	-0.030
Government fees	0.700	1.000	0.000	0.000	0.000	0.000	0.000
Non-competing imports	X	X	X	X	X	X	X

X means that the domestic price of this commodity is exogenous.

[1] Due to the U-shape of the cost-curves in some industries this effect is calculated when capacity utilization increases from 0.95 to 0.96.

[2] In the long run the direct effect of price control is assumed to be 0, i.e., it is assumed that the control is lifted as has been the case with all controls historically.

Table A.4: Determinants of export prices.

Commodity	Elasticities with respect to					
	Unit costs		World market price		Capacity utilization[1]	
	1 year	Long-run	1 year	Long-run	1 year	Long-run
Agricultural products	X	X	X	X	X	X
Forestry products	0.000	0.000	0.360	1.000	0.000	0.000
Fish products	0.000	0.000	0.365	1.000	0.000	0.000
Mining products	0.117	0.580	0.077	0.420	0.500	0.250
Food products	0.401	0.401	0.599	0.599	0.130	0.130
Beverages and tobacco	0.609	1.000	0.000	0.000	0.000	0.000
Textiles and wearing apparels	0.034	0.064	0.498	0.936	0.400	0.700
Wood and wood products	0.541	0.671	0.265	0.329	0.400	0.500
Paper and paper products	0.340	0.897	0.039	0.103	2.800	7.400
Industrial chemicals	0.399	1.000	0.000	0.000	0.000	0.000
Petrol	0.515	0.684	0.238	0.316	0.000	0.000
Other fuels	0.848	1.000	0.000	0.000	0.000	0.000
Other chemicals and mineral	0.394	0.485	0.419	0.515	0.600	0.600
Iron, steel and other metals	0.717	0.780	0.202	0.220	0.300	0.500
Machinery and metal products	0.242	0.400	0.364	0.600	0.000	0.000
Ships and oil platforms	0.000	0.000	0.488	1.000	0.000	0.000

X means that the export price of this commodity is exogenous.

[1] Due to the U-shape of the cost-curves in some industries this effect is calculated when capacity utilization increases from 0.95 to 0.96.

Table A.4: Determinants of export prices (continued).

| Commodity | Elasticities with respect to | | | | | |
| | Unit costs | | World market price | | Capacity utilization [1] | |
	1 year	Long-run	1 year	Long-run	1 year	Long-run
Printing and publishing	0.640	0.414	0.906	0.586	0.000	0.000
Electricity	X	X	X	X	X	X
Wholesale and retail trade	0.517	1.000	0.000	0.000	0.300	0.600
Crude and natural gas	X	X	X	X	X	X
Oil drilling	X	X	X	X	X	X
Ocean transport	X	X	X	X	X	X
Domestic transport	0.185	1.000	0.000	0.000	0.000	0.000
Banking and insurance	0.662	1.000	0.000	0.000	0.000	0.000
Housing services						
Other services	0.225	1.000	0.000	0.000	0.400	1.900
Government fees	1.000	1.000	0.000	0.000	0.000	0.000
Non-competing imports	X	X	X	X	X	X
Second-hand ships and platforms	X	X	X	X	X	X
Other exports related to oil activities	X	X	X	X	X	X
Tourism	E	E	E	E	E	E

X means that the export price of this commodity is exogenous.

E means that the export price of Tourism is determined as a weighted average of domestic consumer prices.

[1] Due to the U-shape of the cost-curves in some industries this effect is calculated when capacity utilization increases from 0.95 to 0.96.

Table A.5: Determinants of employment, wage earners.

| Commodity | Share of total employment in 1984 (%) | Elasticities with respect to | | | | | |
| | | Production | | Capital stock | | Time | |
		1 year	Long-run	1 year	Long-run	1 year	Long-run
Agriculture	5.5	X	X	X	X	X	X
Forestry	0.5	X	X	X	X	X	X
Fishing	0.3	X	X	X	X	X	X
Mining	0.4	0.370	0.740	0.000	0.000	-0.023	-0.056
Food, beverages and tobacco	3.2	0.363	0.462	-0.267	-0.340	0.000	0.000
Textiles and wearing apparels	0.9	0.429	0.549	-0.208	-0.266	-0.016	-0.020
Wood and wood products	1.8	0.263	1.000	-0.174	-0.398	-0.006	-0.014
Paper and paper products	0.8	0.195	0.353	-0.115	-0.208	-0.015	-0.027
Industrial chemicals	0.5	0.195	0.353	-0.115	-0.208	-0.015	-0.027
Refined oil products	0.1	X	X	X	X	X	X
Other chemical and mineral products	1.8	0.690	0.980	-0.504	-0.716	0.000	0.000
Iron, steel and other metals	1.4	0.422	1.000	-0.275	-0.652	-0.006	-0.014
Machinery and metal products	4.4	0.626	1.000	-0.328	-0.524	-0.003	-0.005

X means that employment in this industry is exogenous.

Table A.5: Determinants of employment, wage earners (*continued*).

Commodity	Share of total employment in 1984 (%)	Production		Capital stock		Time	
		1 year	Long-run	1 year	Long-run	1 year	Long-run
Ships and oil platforms	2.2	0.431	0.907	0.000	0.000	0.000	0.000
Printing and publishing	2.1	0.291	0.600	0.000	0.000	0.000	0.000
Electricity	1.0	X	X	X	X	X	X
Wholesale and retail trade	13.4	0.570	0.850	−0.150	−0.230	0.000	0.000
Production of oil and gas	0.6	X	X	X	X	X	X
Oil drilling	0.2	X	X	X	X	X	X
Ocean transport	1.5	X	X	X	X	X	X
Domestic transport	8.3	0.064	1.391	0.000	0.000	0.000	0.000
Banking and insurance	2.5	0.671	0.913	0.000	0.000	0.000	0.000
Housing services	0.2	0.070	0.583	0.000	0.000	0.000	0.000
Other services	13.8	0.319	0.822	0.000	0.000	0.004	0.019
Government	23.7	X	X	X	X	X	X

Elasticities with respect to

X means that employment in this industry is exogenous.

Table A.6: Determinants of gross investment.

Commodity	Share of total investment in 1984 (%)	Rel. factor prices		Production		Gross profits		Credit supply	Time	Lagged capital stock
		1 year	Long-run	1 year	Long-run	1 year	Long-run			
Agriculture	3.4	0	0	0.000	0.000	0.023	0.056	0.000	0	−0.076
Forestry	0.4	0	0	0.071	0.071	0.022	0.091	0.000	0	−0.004
Fishing	0.9	−41	−41	0.021	0.021	0.178	0.178	1.756	0	−0.205
Mining	0.3	−137	−137	0.238	0.238	0.508	0.508	0.000	0	−0.058
Food, beverages and tobacco	1.8	0	0	0.043	0.067	0.000	0.000	0.000	0	0.000
Textiles and wearing apparels	0.2	0	0	0.022	0.022	0.000	0.000	0.009	0	0.000
Wood and wood products	0.6	0	0	0.055	0.115	0.155	0.155	0.000	0	−0.105
Paper and paper products	0.4	0	0	0.000	0.000	0.118	0.590	0.000	0	−0.008
Industrial chemicals	0.5	0	0	0.000	0.000	0.121	2.298	0.000	0	−0.120
Refined oil products	0.1	X	X	X	X	X	X	X	X	X
Other chemical and mineral products	0.9	0	0	0.000	0.067	0.000	0.000	0.000	0	−0.030
Iron, steel and other metals	1.1	0	0	0.000	0.000	0.190	0.375	0.000	0	−0.035
Machinery and metal products	1.6	−63	−317	0.086	0.086	0.000	0.000	0.000	0	−0.043

X means that gross investment in this industry is exogenous.

Table A.6: Determinants of gross investment (continued).

Commodity	Share of total investment in 1984 (%)	Rel. factor prices		Production		Gross profits		Credit supply	Time	Lagged capital stock
		1 year	Long-run	1 year	Long-run	1 year	Long-run			
Ships and oil platforms	0.6	−134	−134	0.004	0.004	0.000	0.000	0.000	0	−0.003
Printing and publishing	0.6	−53	−130	0.167	0.167	0.217	0.217	0.000	0	−0.128
Electricity	7.0	X	X	X	X	X	X	X	X	X
Construction	1.8	−79	−392	0.053	0.053	0.000	0.000	0.038	0	−0.138
Wholesale and retail trade	3.47	−919	−2340	0.063	0.190	0.047	0.117	0.000	−192	−0.470
Production of oil and gas	25.4	X	X	X	X	X	X	X	X	X
Oil drilling	0.8	X	X	X	X	X	X	X	X	X
Ocean transport	2.9	X	X	X	X	X	X	X	X	X
Domestic transport	7.4	−31	−77	0.486	0.486	0.000	0.000	0.070	−271	−0.242
Banking and insurance	3.4	0	0	0.000	0.235	0.133	0.679	0.000	0	−0.493
Housing services	14.4	E	E	E	E	E	E	E	E	E
Other private services	4.5	−236	−1180	0.101	0.101	0.000	0.000	0.053	0	0.000
Government	11.7	X	X	X	X	X	X	X	X	X

X means that gross investment in this industry is exogenous.
E means that there is a special investment model/equation for Housing services.

Table A.7: Determinants of relative energy input.

Sector	Relative price elasticities	
	1 year	Long-run
Agriculture	−0.550	−1.113
Forestry	0.000	0.000
Fishing	0.000	0.000
Mining	−0.168	−1.135
Food, beverages and tobacco	−0.399	−1.239
Textiles and wearing apparels	−0.761	−0.899
Wood and wood products	−0.650	−1.072
Paper and paper products	−0.491	−0.491
Industrial chemicals	−0.062	−1.372
Refined petroleum products	0.000	0.000
Other chemicals and mineral prod.	−0.222	−0.716
Iron, steel and other metals	−0.006	−0.014
Machinery and metal products	−0.634	−1.062
New ships and oil platforms	−0.049	−0.230
Printing and publishing	−0.686	−1.472
Electricity	0.000	0.000
Construction	−1.261	−2.759
Wholesale and retail trade	0.000	0.000
Production of oil and natural gas	0.000	0.000
Oil drilling	0.000	0.000
Ocean transport	0.000	0.000
Domestic transport	−0.522	−1.075
Banking and insurance	0.000	0.000
Housing services	0.000	0.000
Other private services	−0.403	−1.092
Government		
− Defence	−0.835	−0.999
− Public administration	−0.585	−0.887
− Education	−0.506	−1.317
− Health services	−0.509	−0.705

Table A.8: Determinants of consumption demand by category.

Consumption category	Budget share 1984 (%)	Direct price elasticity	Expenditure elasticity
Food	20.2	−0.30	0.45
Beverages and tobacco	6.3	−0.40	0.75
Clothing and footwear	7.4	−0.54	1.00
Electricity	5.2	−0.63	1.09
Fuel	1.1	−0.24	1.09
Petrol and car maintenance	5.1	−0.81	1.60
Furniture, etc.	4.5	−0.64	1.25
Purchases of cars	5.5	−0.73	1.42
Other consumer durables	1.7	−0.73	1.45
Household equipment	1.8	−0.51	1.00
Goods for recreation and entertainment	4.2	−0.71	1.40
Other goods	3.1	−0.47	0.90
Rents(Housing services)	11.1	−0.60	1.09
Public transport services	4.7	−0.60	1.16
Public entertainmnet	2.2	−0.38	0.75
Various household services	1.4	−0.26	0.50
Other services	6.9	−0.72	1.40
Tourism abroad	6.3	−0.82	1.60
Medical care and health services	4.3	X	X

X means that consumption of Medical care and Health services is exogenous as it is mainly financed by the government.

Appendix B　A Simplified equation system and a summary of the main dimensions of MODAG A

5.1　A simplified equation system

Below we have attempted to indicate the main structure of MODAG A by a set of equations which gives a very simplified representation of the model. The main simplifications consist in suppressions of

(i) the input-output structure, both for prices and quantities,

(ii) the disaggregation by commodity, industry, final demand categories, kind of taxes and by socioeconomic groups,

(iii) the differentiation between domestic and export prices, and between import prices and competitive prices on the export markets,

(iv) the explicit functional forms, and

(v) the dynamic structure (expectation formation, adjustments to desired or optimal levels, etc.)

In addition, the division between exogenous (marked by an asterisk) and the endogenous variables in the equation system below is more clear-cut than in the actual model. Some of the detailed model variables included in the aggregated exogenous or endogenous variables of the simplified equation system may belong to the other category. This is of special importance for regulated and negotiated prices and resource based production (and exports) which are all exogenous in the actual model.

Prices

$$P = f_P(UVC, PK^*, CAP)(1 + t_i^*) , \qquad (\text{B.1})$$

$$UVC = w^* N/X . \qquad (\text{B.2})$$

(B.1) is the price equation, stating that the price of Norwegian production is a function of variable unit costs UVC, the competitive world market price PK and the capacity utilization index CAP. t_i is the net indirect tax rate. (B.2) defines variable unit costs as variable costs, here represented by wage costs per man-year w and labour input in man-years N, per unit of production X.

Factor demand (labour and capital)

$$N = f_N(X, CAP, t).\qquad(B.3)$$

Labour demand (employment) is a function of production X, capacity utilization CAP, and technical change t. Capacity utilization is defined by

$$CAP = f_{CAP}(X/K_{-1}).\qquad(B.4)$$

Thus (B.3) and (B.4) imply that N is a function of X and K_{-1}.

$$K = f_K(p^J/w^*, X, t).\qquad(B.5)$$

Demand for capital (desired capital stock) is a function of production X, technical change t, and relative factor prices p^J/w, where p^J is the user cost of capital, which depends on the rate of interest r, prices P, depreciation rates, tax rules, etc. For simplicity we write

$$p^J = f_Q(r^*, P).\qquad(B.6)$$

Private investment demand

By definition

$$J = K - K_{-1} + D,\qquad(B.7)$$

where D is depreciation given by

$$D = f(K),\qquad(B.8)$$

and J is gross private investment.

Private consumption

$$C = f\big((YH - TD)/P, KREDH^*/P\big),\qquad(B.9)$$
$$YH = w^*N + YU^* + hYR,\qquad(B.10)$$
$$YR = PX/(1 + t_i^*) - w^*N,\qquad(B.11)$$
$$TD = f_T(YH).\qquad(B.12)$$

Private consumption C is a function of real disposable income $(YH - TD)/P$ and real credit supply to households $KREDH^*/P$. Income for households is, according to (B.10), defined as wage income $wN +$ transfers from the government and net interest income $YU+$ profits going to households $h\,YR$. Profits (operating surplus) YR is according to (B.11) defined as factor income $PX/(1+t_i)$ less wage income wN. Direct personal taxes TD is a function of household income.

Exports

$$A = f_A(P/PK^*, V^*). \tag{B.13}$$

In (B.13) export demand is written as a function of relative prices P/PK and a growth indicator for the world market V.

Imports

$$B = f_B(P/PK^*)(cC + gG^* + jJ + aA). \tag{B.14}$$

c, g, j and a are import coefficients relative to the average import-coefficient (given by f_B as a function of relative prices). C (private consumption), G (government consumption and investment), J (private investment) and A (export) represent final demand categories.

Domestic production

GDP (domestic production) X is defined by the commodity balance equation

$$X = C + G^* + J + A - B. \tag{B.15}$$

The model above has 15 equations between the
   (i) 15 endogenous variables: X, C, J, A, B, K, D, CAP, N, P, P^J, UVC, YR, YH, TD, and the
   (ii) 8 exogenous variables: G, YU, t_i, $KREDH$, r, w, PK and V.

5.2   Summary of the main dimensions

Table B.1 gives a list of variables and equations in MODAG A, categorizing the variables as exogenous or endogenous and the equations as stochastic or non-stochastic. At any point in time a number of lagged or predetermined values of endogenous variables enters the model as "exogenous" variables. These are left out of table B.1. MODAG A is mainly built for the Ministry of Finance for policy purposes and not for forecasting purposes by an independent agency. Of the exogenous variables, 155 are economic policy variables. To some extent some of the financial variables may also be caracterized as policy variables. A few exogenous variables in the group "Other" are also heavily policy influenced or a representation of "external forces" of the economy. Among the 218 "other" exogenous variables, 75 are zero almost by definition or by assumption.

Table B.1: Number of variables and equations in MODAG A.

VARIABLES		
Exogenous		439
Government expenditures	28	
Direct and indirect tax rates	127	
World market demand and prices	57	
Financial variables	9	
Other	218	
Endogenous		1225
Total		1664
EQUATIONS		
Stochastic		183
domestic and export prices	49	
import shares and exports	26	
consumer demand	19	
investment and inventories	39	
labour demand	24	
energy demand	26	
Non-stochastic and identities	1042	
Total		1225

Related to the MODAG A model described in this paper, there exists a separate recursive accounting model with nearly 1400 equations that is solved after the main model. The purpose of this model is mainly to transform the model results into the form of complete "national accounts" for the future years for which the model is solved.

References

Armington, P. [1969], "A Theory of Demand for Products Distinguished by Place of Production", *IMF Staff Papers, 16,* 159–178.

Aukrust, O. [1970], "PRIM I. A Model of the Price and Income Distribution Mechanism of an Open Economy", *The Review of Income and Wealth, 16,* 51–78 (also as Articles from the Central Bureau of Statistics, No. 117, Oslo).

Aukrust, O. [1977], "Inflation on the Open Economy: A Norwegian Model", in *Worldwide Inflation: Theory and Recent Experience,* ed. Krause and Salant. Washington, D.C.: Brookings, 109–166 (also as Articles from the Central Bureau of Statistics, No. 96, Oslo).

Aukrust, O. [1978], "Econometric Methods in Short-Term Planning", in *Econometric Contributions to Public Policy,* ed. Stone and Petterson. London: Macmillan Press Ltd., 64–83 (also as Articles from the Central Bureau of Statistics, No. 117, Oslo).

Bergan, R. and Ø. Olsen [1985], "Eksporttilpasning i MODAG A", Reports from the Central Bureau of Statistics, No. 85/29, Oslo.

Bergan, R., Å. Cappelen and M. Jensen [1985], "A Disaggregated Study of Investment Behaviour in Norway", paper to ECE seminar on the Interrelationships between Structural Change and Investment Policies, Kiev, Sept. Mimeo, Central Bureau of Statistics, Oslo.

Bergland, H. and Å. Cappelen [1981], "Produktivitet og sysselsetting i industrien", Reports from the Central Bureau of Statistics, No. 81/23, Oslo.

Biørn, E. [1983], "Gross Capital, Net Capital, Capital Service Price and Depreciation", Reports from the Central Bureau of Statistics, No. 83/27, Oslo.

Biørn, E. [1984], "Inflation, Depreciation, and the Neutrality of the Corporate Income Tax", *Scandinavian Journal of Economics, 86,* 214–228.

Bjerkholt, O. [1983], "Experiences in Using Input-Output Techniques for Price Calculations", in *International use of Input-output Analysis*, ed. Stäglin. Gottingen: Vandenhoeck and Ruprecht(also as Articles from the Central Bureau of Statistics, No. 141, Oslo).

Bjerkholt, O. and S. Longva [1980], "MODIS IV. A Model for Economic Analysis and National Planning", Social Economic Studies from the Central Bureau of Statistics, No. 43, Oslo.

Bojer, H. [1966], "Notat om sammenhengen mellom Richard Stones lineære utgiftsfunksjoner og Ragnar Frisch' 'Complete Scheme for Computing all Direct and Cross Demand Elasticities in a Model with many sectors'", Memorandum from the Institute of Economics, University of Oslo, Oslo.

Bruno, M. [1979], "Price and Output Adjustment: Micro foundations and aggregation", *Journal of Monetary Economics, 5*, 187–212.

Bye, T. and P. Frenger [1984], "Energy Substitution in EMOD-MODAG", Mimeo, Central Bureau of Statistics, Oslo.

Cappelen, Å [1980], "Inntektsfordeling og konsum 1962–1978", Articles from the Central Bureau of Statistics, No. 123, Oslo.

Cappelen, Å. and S. Longva [1984], "The effects of income settlements in Norway analysed by the model MODAG A", paper presented at the Fourth International Symposium on Forecasting, London, July. Mimeo, Central Bureau of Statistics, Oslo.

Cappelen, Å., E. Garaas and S. Longva [1981], "MODAG. En modell for makroøkonomiske analyser", Reports from the Central Bureau of Statistics, No. 81/30, Oslo.

Drèze, J.H. and F. Modigliani [1981], "The trade-off between real wages and employment in an open economy (Belgium)", *European Economic Review, 150*, 1–40.

Edgreen, G., K.O. Faxen and C.E. Odhner [1973], *Wage Formation and the Economy.* London: Allen and Unwin.

Eriksen, T. and J.F. Qvigstad [1983], "Finmod — en finanspolitisk modell", *Sosialøkonomen, 1.*

Frenger, P. [1985], "Consumer Demand for Energy in EMOD-MODAG", Mimeo, Central Bureau of Statistics, April, Oslo.

Frisch, R. [1961], "A Survey of Types of Economic Forecasting and Programming and a Brief Description of The Oslo Channel Model", Memorandum from the Institute of Economics, University of Oslo.

Johansen, K.E. and H. Strand [1981], "Macroeconomic Models for Medium and Long-Term Planning", Articles from the Central Bureau of Statistics, No. 128, Oslo.

Johansen, L. [1974], *A Multi-Sectoral Study of Economic Growth* (enlarged Edition). Amsterdam: North-Holland Publishing Company.

Larsen, K.A. and P. Schreiner [1985], "On the Introduction and Application of the MSG Model in the Norwegian Planning System", in *Production, Multi-Sectoral Growth and Planning*, ed. Førsund, Hoel and Longva. Amsterdam: North-Holland Publishing Company, 241–269.

Longva, S., L. Lorentsen and Ø. Olsen [1985], "The Multi-Sectoral Growth Model MSG-4. Formal Structure and Empirical Characteristics", in *Production, Multi-Sectoral Growth and Planning*, ed. Førsund, Hoel and Longva. Amsterdam: North-Holland Publishing Company, 187–240.

Persson, J. [1982], "Analyse av lagertilpassingen i norsk økonomi", Working Paper from the Ministry of Finance, No. 4, Oslo.

Ringstad, V. [1974], "Prisutvikling og prisadferd i 1960-årene. En presentasjon og analyse av nasjonalregnskapets prisdata 1961–1969", Social Economic Studies from the Central Bureau of Statistics, No. 23, Oslo.

Sevaldson, P. [1964], "An Industry Model of Production and Consumption in Norway", *The Review of Income and Wealth, 10.*

Stølen, N.M. [1983], "Importandeler og relative priser. En MODAG-rapport", Reports from the Central Bureau of Statistics, No. 83/33, Oslo.

Tveitereid, S. and J. Lædre [1981], "Markedsindikatorer for norsk eksport", Reports from the Central Bureau of Statistics, No. 81/35, Oslo.

Utredningsutvalget [1966a, 1966b], "Innstilling I og II fra utredningsutvalget for inntektsoppgjørene 1966", Statsministerens kontor, Oslo.

Macroeconomic Medium-Term Models in the Nordic Countries
O. Bjerkholt and J. Rosted (Editors)
© *Elsevier Science Publishers B.V. (North-Holland), 1987*

The Effects of Fiscal Policy in MODAG A

by

Roar Bergan
Central Bureau of Statistics,
Oslo, Norway

Fiscal policy is the terrain of macroeconomics where the gulf between perceptions of the general public and economists' doctrines is the widest.

—James Tobin (1980)

The theoretical debate on the effectiveness of Keynesian stabilization policies has been going on now for several decades. New trends in macroeconomic theory have come to downgrade the importance of fiscal policy as a means of raising output and employment. Despite this debate, most macroeconometric models seem to produce Keynesian results when expansionary fiscal policy is applied. In a much cited review of eleven econometric models of the United States, Fromm and Klein [1973] concluded that "there is relatively uniform agreement about the pattern and magnitude of fiscal policy impacts". Judging from more recent surveys by Chan-Lee and Kato [1984], Lybeck et al. [1984] and Wallis et al. [1984], macroeconomic models still have substantial fiscal policy multipliers, at least in the short and medium run. With respect to the long-run effects, the results are more ambiguous, ranging from highly positive to highly negative multipliers.

This paper discusses fiscal policy within an annual macroeconometric model of the Norwegian economy called MODAG A. In section 2, traditional multiplier experiments are conducted to illustrate some important properties of the model. However, without appropriate adjustment of the exogenous variables, such experiments will be of limited interest for policy analysis. Some possible objections to the relevance of the calculations are therefore raised in section 3.

1.   Main features of MODAG A

(The Norwegian) models, in which the major final demand aggregates are predicted exogenously, and in which coefficients are not estimated econometrically, are completely different from the other models surveyed; no comparable work exists elsewhere.
—Jean Waelbroeck (1975)

The MODAG-model was developed for the Ministry of Finance as a supplementary tool to the disaggregated national budgeting model MODIS IV. MODIS has been a central feature of the Norwegian short-term planning process for more than twenty years. However, besides assuring consistency it primarily plays the role of a system for gathering information. This is rather different from the ordinary use of macroeconomic models throughout the world. The first version of MODAG was just an aggregated copy of MODIS, considerably simplified with respect to the description of government policy variables and incorporating little of economic theory besides an input-output framework and a consumption function. However, work was soon begun on building a more elaborate version of MODAG, called MODAG A, for short to medium-run policy analysis. Since a comprehensive presentation of MODAG A already has been given in this volume by Cappelen and Longva [1984], I will only summarize the main features of the model.

Size: MODAG A, vintage 1984, has 33 sectors of production and 41 commodities, of which 34 are produced domestically.

Prices: Product prices are generally a function of variable unit costs, a price index for competing goods and the rate of capacity utilization. The price index for competing goods has normally estimated weights in the equations for domestic product prices according to the degree of exposure to foreign competition, and it is also a dominating factor in the development of export prices. Unit cost considerations dominate the setting of domestic prices on sheltered goods, but in addition they also influence export prices, especially when exports are clearly a secondary market. The rate of capacity utilization, reflecting the market situation, is present mainly in some of the equations for export prices. Import prices and the exchange are still exogenous.

Production and inventories: The volume side of the model is Keynesian in inspiration in that most quantities are demand determined. Variations in demand will always be met by variations in production or inventories at a given price. It is furthermore assumed that separate demand curves can be identified for Norwegian products both on domestic and foreign markets.

Household consumption: Total private consumption is determined as a function of real disposable income and consumer credits. The demand for the separate consumer goods are then derived according to Stone's Linear Expenditure System.

Private investment: Equations for investment in 20 private industries have been included in MODAG A. The basic model is that of the neoclassical approach to investment behaviour incorporating adjustment costs. Due to imperfect capital markets and rationing of credit, the speed of adjustment is assumed to be dependent on the operating surplus, which reflects internally generated funds, and on the credit supply to companies. During the process of estimation, this general model produced somewhat differing results for different industries. In manufacturing, output generally proved to be the most significant explanatory variable, but for the most export-oriented manufacturing sectors only the operating surplus seemed to have any influence on investment, implying rather a primitive behaviour in these sectors. For investment in housing, a completely different formulation was chosen — incorporating the central role of demographic factors, but allowing income, the interest rate and relative price effects to influence behaviour.

Exports: Exports of manufacturing products are determined by demand functions with indices for demand in the importing countries and for the relative price between Norwegian exports and the price of competing products abroad as arguments. Nonetheless, 65 percent of Norwegian exports are exogenous in MODAG A, including exports from the petroleum and ocean transport sectors.

Imports: Domestic demand for a particular good is allocated between Norwegian products and imports according to import-share functions dependent on the relative prices of the two competing goods.

Labour productivity: The demand for labour is determined by short-run production functions, which respond sluggishly to changes in production. At low rates of capacity utilization, increased production is assumed to lead to higher labour productivity in the short run, implying economics of scale in the short-run production function.

Government sector: Due to the fact that the model is used by the Ministry of Finance, the government sector is treated almost completely exogenously. There is a distinction in MODAG A between state and local governments, and both are divided into subsectors according to type of activity. The users of the model must provide numerical values for employment, expenditures on goods and services and investment for each of the seven government subsectors of the model. On the incomes side, revenues from personal income taxation are determined endogenously in tax functions. With respect to indirect taxes, changes in tax rates are given exogenously, making the tax yield endogenous.

2.   Dynamic multipliers of MODAG A

> *Dynamic multipliers seem to come out of an econometric model as a cheap by-product much as tallow is produced out of a meat slaughter-house. They do not seem to be developed and treated and scrutinized by the model builder with the kind of care that they deserve at the time the model is constructed.*
> –Arthur M. Okun (1975)

The numerical values of multipliers computed on different models will differ for several reasons. First, properties of the economy itself will have a substantial impact. Savings behaviour, tax rates, the size of foreign trade, the institutional framework for wage and price-setting and the functioning of financial markets are all factors of critical importance for the values and time structure of fiscal multipliers. This implies that we should not in general expect multipliers computed with different models to coincide. Second, since models are constructed for different purposes, their descriptions of a given economy differ. Third, the size and timing of the exogenous shocks are often not standardized.

Some features of the Norwegian economy that are important when judging the effectiveness of fiscal policy will be discussed in section 3. However, at the outset I would like to point to the importance of the large and rather special foreign trade sector in the Norwegian economy. By 1984 imports amounted to 39% of gross domestic product while exports reached

48% of GDP. The magnitude of Norwegian economy; imports opens up possibilities of large leakages when fiscal policy is applied. With respect to the export sectors, petroleum and ocean transport play a dominant role with 55% of total exports and 23% of GDP. Large profit margins in the petroleum sector cause it to be virtually unaffected by domestic wage and price movements. The same situation to some extent also holds for some of the traditional export sectors, at least in the short to medium run. Industries like ocean transport and some energy-intensive manufacturing are characterized by a low variable to fixed-costs ratio, high labour productivity and a high import-share of materials input.

The multipliers below are calculated as deviations from a reference scenario for the Norwegian economy from 1984 to 1993. The numerical value of a multiplier is generally dependent on the size and timing of the imposed exogenous shock. The most important mechanism behind these non-linearities is usually that some measure of labour-market tightness influences the wage-formation process. A Phillips-curve relationship is not however incorporated in MODAG A and the feedbacks from quantities to prices are weak. The inclusion of capacity utilization as an explanatory variable in some of the price equations and equations for labour demand, does not apparently alter this picture. The calculated multipliers are therefore probably only modestly affected by the size of the shock and the market situation in the control trajectory, although this should obviously be taken into account when interpreting the results. The actual significance of the measure of capacity utilization in the computations is hard to deduce without alternative simulations. Although the feedback effects from quantities to prices are weak, the distribution of factor income between wages and operating surplus, and accordingly the effects on consumption and investment, will depend on the rate of capacity utilization. As explained below, the nominal wage-price path in the reference scenario is also of importance in some of the simulations.

2.1 Real input multipliers

In this section the effects of five different government policies will be studied. The multipliers are normalized to give a real input shock of 1 billion Norwegian kroner from 1984 onwards. In section 2.3 we look at the consequences of two other policies: increases in the value-added tax and in payroll taxation.

The results below are generated by changing only the relevant government policy parameters, leaving all other exogenous variables unchanged

Table 2.1: Real gross domestic product multipliers for policies A–E. Increase in real-GDP to real change of fiscal policy parameters.

	1984	1985	1986	1987	1988	1989	1990	1993
Policy A	1.30	1.47	1.51	1.54	1.55	1.55	1.56	1.56
Policy B	0.89	0.99	1.04	1.04	1.04	1.03	1.02	0.99
Policy C	0.95	1.01	1.07	1.12	1.14	1.16	1.17	1.18
Policy D	0.48	0.74	0.78	0.80	0.80	0.80	0.79	0.76
Policy E	0.41	0.57	0.59	0.61	0.61	0.61	0.60	0.59

compared to the reference scenario. The results are thus not corrected for relationships lacking in the model or implausible effects. This may of course lead to unrealistic results, but it gives a good illustration of the properties of the model as it stands. The different policies studied are the following:

Policy A: A sustained increase in government employment in 1984, equivalent to a raise in wage-costs by 1 billion 1984-Nkr.

Policy B: A sustained increase in government purchases of goods and services for non-defense purposes by 1 billion Nkr in fixed 1984-prices in 1984.

Policy C: A sustained increase in government investment by 1 billion Nkr in fixed 1984-prices in 1984.

Policy D: A sustained reduction of income taxation in 1983 equivalent to 1 billion 1984-Nkr.

Policy E: A sustained increase in transfers to households in 1983, equivalent to 1 billion 1984-Nkr.

Under policies A, B, C and E, the 1 billion Nkr expenditure increase is allocated to the various expenditure items according to their weights in the base year (1984). Under policy D the tax-relief is distributed among socioeconomic groups according to their share of the total personal income-tax bill. This is important since savings behaviour and marginal tax-rates differ between the different types of households.

The real gross domestic product multipliers of the five policies are shown in table 2.1. It appears that the level of the multipliers varies significantly between the alternatives. The multiplier of increased government employment, policy A, is by 1993 2.6 times the value of the multiplier of policy E, increased transfers. With respect to the dynamic patterns, all multipliers except those for policies A and C peak after 4–5 years, although there are differences in both the increasing and decreasing phase. Before proceeding to a comparison of the policies, we shall take a closer look at the effects of each of them.

Policy A: Increased government employment

The increased government employment raises the gross product of government sectors by 1 billion 1984-Nkr throughout the simulation period. From table 2.2 it's seen that government consumption increases by just 0.99 billion, the reason being that government fees, which are endogenously determined in MODAG A, increase somewhat. Policy A affects the private sector initially through the consumption function. Increased government employment raises the real income of households and thereby private consumption. Most of the growth of real income is achieved already in 1984, but due to the appearance of lagged income in the consumption function, the effects on private consumption is not exhausted before 1985–86. The reason why private consumption does not peak is that the real wage of new government employees increases throughout the simulation period.

It appears from table 2.2 that prices are only modestly affected in MODAG A by the increased level of activity. Note that the average indices of the table are influenced both by changes in the individual price indices of the model and by changes in the composition of the totals. The price effects in 1984 are dominated by two factors: increased labour productivity and increased utilization of capacity. As explained above, increased production will in the short run lead to higher labour productivity and thereby a reduction in the unit costs of production. Since it is current and not normalized unit costs which enter the price equations, there is a tendency to lower prices, especially for goods sold on the home market. The capacity effect for these goods can be ignored in this scenario so the overall impression is a reduction of home prices, although the magnitude is very modest.

It is well known that the effects of increased capacity utilization on price behaviour is theoretically ambiguous. Concerning the export-price equations of MODAG A, the capacity utilization index enters nine of them including all cases with positive coefficients. This can be interpreted as Norwegian exporters having some sort of short-run market power, although the numerical significance of these capacity effects is rather modest. They are thus not strong enough to prevent a slight steady decrease in average export prices, leading to a very modest increase in exports.

Table 2.2: The effects of policy A, increased government employment.
(Wage costs increased by 1 billion 1984-Nkr.)

	1984	1985	1986	1987	1988	1989	1990	1993
Changes in constant prices (million Nkr)								
Private consumption	441	634	678	708	728	742	753	770
Govt consumption	990	986	984	984	984	983	983	983
Gross investment	57	141	157	159	151	140	129	107
Increase in stocks	−5	−6	−5	−5	−7	−7	−6	−7
Exports	−7	−14	−12	−9	−4	0	4	14
Imports	171	268	289	299	303	306	307	311
GDP	1304	1474	1513	1537	1549	1553	1556	1556
Excl. oil, ocean trans and govt	303	472	512	535	547	551	554	554
Manufacturing	33	51	59	62	64	65	65	67
Changes in price indices (%)								
Private consumption	−0.01	−0.01	−0.02	−0.02	−0.03	−0.03	−0.02	−0.02
Gross investment	−0.01	−0.01	−0.02	−0.03	−0.03	−0.03	−0.03	−0.02
Exports	0.00	0.00	0.00	−0.01	−0.01	−0.01	−0.01	−0.01
GDP	−0.01	−0.01	0.00	0.00	0.01	0.01	0.02	0.01
Changes in current prices (million Nkr)								
Wage costs	1045	1162	1263	1358	1452	1548	1650	1992
Operating surplus	143	196	173	149	130	118	110	112
Manufacturing	26	59	33	20	14	12	10	12
Export surplus	−171	−297	−330	−357	−379	−399	−420	−488
Govt budget surplus	−460	−416	−429	−453	−481	−510	−543	−658
Changes in employment, wage earners (1000 man-years)								
Total	7.37	7.70	7.87	7.96	8.00	8.01	8.02	8.01
Excl. oil, ocean trans and govt	0.37	0.70	0.87	0.96	1.00	1.01	1.02	1.01
Manufacturing	0.07	0.14	0.17	0.18	0.18	0.17	0.15	0.13

Private investment in MODAG A is generally a function of production, relative factor prices, gross operating surplus, credit supply to firms, lagged capital stock and a trend. Because of the small price effects and no exogenous adjustment of interest rates or credit supply, the main force behind changes in private gross investments in the present scenario is increased production. Since the initial demand increase stems from private consumption, output is primarily raised in the production of services, construction and in some manufacturing sectors producing consumption goods. These are also the industries where the capital stock is expanded.

When an accelerator effect dominates the investment equations, one should expect that gross investment first increases and then falls off when the increase in production stops. A new and higher level of investment should be reached, reflecting the depreciation of the higher capital stock. Table 2.2 shows that this picture is also obtained in the present simulation. The increase in gross investment reaches a peak in 1986–87 when most of the growth in output is obtained, and it falls off in the following years to reach a level in 1993 107 million Nkr higher than in the base run.

Since relative prices are almost unaffected, import shares are not influenced and imports grows proportionally to the increased domestic demand. By 1993 imports are raised by 311 million Nkr in fixed 1984-prices, leading to a reduction of the export-surplus of 490 million.

Of the total increase in employment of 8010 man-years, approximately 7000 man-years are absorbed by the government sectors. The development of employment in the private sector illustrates how the equations for labour demand and private capital formation interact. Initially the raise in output leads to increased productivity of labour and a less than proportional increase in labour demand. From 1985 on this gain of productivity slowly disappears and labour demand grows. However, as private investment is growing and the firms are thereby building up production capacity, productivity is again increasing and a dampening of labour demand occurs during the last years of the simulation period. By 1993, the private sector employment has increased by about 1000 man-years, of which just 130 are in manufacturing.

The observed growth in wage-costs under policy A is primarily a reflection of the increased employment in the government sectors. By 1993 wage-costs in the private sector have increased by 240 million Nkr, implying that the distribution of factor income between wages and operating surplus is virtually unchanged.

Although policy A consists of a growth in government wage-costs of 1 billion 1984-Nkr, the government budget balance is only worsened by

460 million Nkr in 1984. This is of course due to higher incomes from direct and indirect taxation. From 1984 to 1985 household saving is reduced, leading to a growth in government incomes from indirect taxation and a strengthening of the budget balance. From 1986 onwards the growth in wage-costs again dominates and by 1993 the budget deteriorates by 658 million Nkr or 440 million 1984-Nkr when deflated by the price index for domestic use of goods and services.

Policy B: Increased government purchases of goods and services

The increased purchases of goods and services for non-defense purposes raises government consumption by 0.97 billion Nkr. Again the endogenously determined government fees ensures that a 1 billion increase is not reached. The initial impact on the private sector of the economy is in this case a direct stimulus to domestic production. In 1984 the gross product of the private sector increases by 885 million Nkr compared to the 304 million increase in the case of policy A.

Policy B increases total employment in 1993 by approximately 2600 man-years. This is of course substantially less than under policy A where government employment alone was raised by 7000 man-years. Again we see how the equations for investment and labour demand interact to reduce employment growth in manufacturing during the last part of the decade.

Looking at domestic demand, we see that the increase in private consumption is now just half as large as under policy A, while the opposite is true for private investment, reflecting the greater initial boost of production. The dynamic pattern of consumption and investment is now changed with a marked dampening of consumption and a stronger decline in gross investment during the last years.

The price effects in table 2.3 indicate that the movements are now more distinct although still very small. Since the stimulus to domestic production is initially greater, both the effects of changed capacity utilization and changed labour productivity are now greater than they were when government employment was increased. This leads to a further reduction in the growth of prices of domestic goods. However, the reduction is not as large as the reduction in the average index for consumption goods suggests, since this index also incorporates substitution effects in private consumption.

A closer look at the individual price indices for goods delivered to the domestic market reveals that the capacity utilization effects on prices initially dominate the productivity effects in all cases where the rate of capacity utilization enters the price equation — mainly in some of the manu-

Table 2.3: The effects of policy B, increased government purchase of goods and services by 1 billion Nkr in fixed 1984-prices.

	1984	1985	1986	1987	1988	1989	1990	1993
Changes in constant prices (million Nkr)								
Private consumption	188	290	342	370	383	386	386	374
Govt consumption	973	970	969	968	968	968	968	969
Gross investment	250	334	336	305	270	238	213	169
Increase in stocks	−19	−4	−5	−8	−13	−9	−9	−9
Exports	−28	−44	−34	−22	−10	−2	7	29
Imports	478	556	573	570	561	554	547	537
GDP	885	990	1035	1044	1037	1028	1019	995
Excl. oil, ocean								
trans and govt	878	982	1028	1036	1030	1020	1011	987
Manufacturing	147	152	163	165	166	166	167	171
Changes in price indices (%)								
Private consumption	−0.02	−0.03	−0.05	−0.06	−0.06	−0.06	−0.06	−0.05
Gross investment	−0.05	−0.05	−0.06	−0.08	−0.09	−0.08	−0.07	−0.06
Exports	0.01	0.00	−0.01	−0.01	−0.02	−0.02	−0.03	−0.03
GDP	−0.02	−0.03	−0.04	−0.05	−0.05	−0.05	−0.04	0.01
Changes in current prices (million Nkr)								
Wage costs	226	340	410	454	487	516	546	652
Operating surplus	426	338	275	195	140	111	91	83
Manufacturing	114	167	94	58	43	43	41	55
Export surplus	−486	−642	−666	−689	−708	−730	−755	−849
Govt budget surplus	−664	−625	−622	−643	−673	−707	−746	−888
Changes in employ- ment, wage earners (1000 man-years)								
Total	1.56	2.23	2.55	2.66	2.69	2.68	2.67	2.63
Excl. oil, ocean								
trans and govt	1.56	2.23	2.55	2.66	2.69	2.68	2.67	2.63
Manufacturing	0.34	0.46	0.50	0.50	0.48	0.45	0.42	0.35

facturing sectors. The reduction in average price growth in 1984 thus stems from productivity gains in the sectors producing services and in the construction sector. As new capacity is built up and output growth increases, the overall reduction in the growth of domestic prices is strengthened until 1988, after which it is reduced in line with the reduction in GDP-growth.

For export prices the increased capacity utilization in 1984 leads to a modest increase in the average price on exports. Over the years, however, the reduction in unit costs dominates, giving a modest reduction in the growth of export prices and consequently a somewhat higher volume of exports.

Imports are now increased by almost 75 percent more than in the case of policy A. In 1993 imports are raised by 537 million 1984-Nkr, which is substantial compared to the GDP increase of 995 million. The growth of imports leads to a reduction of the export-surplus of 849 million Nkr in 1993.

The deterioration of the government budget is also more severe under policy B because less of the income growth is allocated to households and is therefore not captured by the personal income tax. Since the incomes of firms are growing, some corrections in the exogenous estimates of corporate tax revenues should have been made, but the significance of this for the government budget surplus is probably small.

Policy C: Increased government investment

For private consumption and private investment multipliers, the results of policies B and C are rather similar. The steady increase in government consumption, which is observed in table 2.4, is of course a reflection of the depreciation of the addition to the government capital stock. The development of government consumption is also the reason why GDP-growth is not peaking as it does under policy B. However, the gross product of the private sector of the economy does peak in 1989, somewhat later than in the previous case.

With respect to price effects, the most striking feature in table 2.4 is that the growth in the average price of investment goods is now reduced when compared to policy B. This reflects the fact that a larger part of the increased domestic demand is now allocated to sectors where the rate of capacity utilization does not enter the price equation for goods delivered to the domestic market. The development in the construction sector is at the centre of the issue. While GDP in 1984 is only 60 million Nkr higher under policy C than under policy B, the gross product in the construction sector is almost a quarter of a billion Nkr higher. Through the equation for labour demand in this sector a reduction in unit costs is induced, and thus a reduction in the output price of the construction good.

It may seem surprising that policy C is less import-demanding than policy B. The marginal import-propensity for investment goods are generally believed to be higher than for other demand categories. The explanation for this is that the composition of government investment differs from that of private investment in that it contains more buildings and constructions at the expense of machinery and other import-intensive equipment.

Despite the fact that the gross product of the private sector increases more when government investment is increased than when government purchases of goods and services are increased, policy C gives a smaller effect on employment. This again is a reflection of the different allocation of the gross product among industries. Output is now growing less in the labour-intensive production of services and more in construction and manufacturing.

Policy D: Reduction of personal income taxes

The tax-reduction of policy D is carried out by changing the constant-terms of the tax-functions for the three socioeconomic groups of the model, using the consumer price index of the reference scenario to inflate the amount that is given in tax-relief. The tax-functions of MODAG A is a considerable simplification compared to the actual Norwegian tax system. Personal income taxes are classified into seven different kinds and for each kind and socioeconomic group a linear approximation to the actual tax system is implemented. The relevant average and marginal tax-rates are computed in a pre-model to MODAG A which is based on actual tax rates, income distribution and the taking account of income growth and inflation. This means that one should ideally recalculate the tax-rates when doing impact calculations on the model, but this has not been done in the present case as the changes, when compared to the reference path, are so small.

Tax-reductions under policy D can be interpreted as a direct deduction in the calculated tax amounts under the present tax-regime, leaving the marginal tax rates unchanged. Another way of reducing taxes is to reduce the tax-rates of the original system. This could be done such that the real value of of the tax-bill computed on the tax-base of the reference scenario is reduced by the requested amount (see Fromm and Taubman [1967]). This alternative would be more expansive, since increased incomes then would be taxed at lower marginal rates. Our choice does not, however,

Table 2.4 The effects of policy C, increased government investment by 1 billion Nkr in fixed 1984-prices.

	1984	1985	1986	1987	1988	1989	1990	1993
Changes in constant prices (million Nkr)								
Private consumption	178	250	303	341	359	366	368	358
Govt consumption	−5	3	12	21	31	41	51	84
Gross investment	1233	1272	1281	1288	1278	1264	1243	1189
Increase in stocks	−23	5	5	0	−8	−4	−4	−3
Exports	−19	−43	−35	−29	−19	−12	−1	32
Imports	419	482	494	500	497	497	492	480
GDP	946	1006	1071	1121	1143	1159	1166	1178
Excl. oil, ocean trans and govt	936	985	1040	1080	1091	1097	1093	1073
Manufacturing	180	165	183	194	198	202	205	214
Changes in price indices (%)								
Private consumption	−0.01	−0.02	−0.03	−0.04	−0.05	−0.05	−0.05	−0.05
Gross investment	−0.12	−0.09	−0.10	−0.15	−0.17	−0.16	−0.15	−0.12
Exports	0.01	0.01	0.01	0.00	−0.01	−0.01	−0.02	−0.02
GDP	−0.03	−0.03	−0.04	−0.05	−0.06	−0.06	−0.06	−0.06
Changes in current prices (million Nkr)								
Wage costs	228	332	398	444	476	503	528	606
Operating surplus	426	373	324	250	200	181	166	162
Manufacturing	151	258	123	63	44	48	51	77
Export surplus	−412	−527	−555	−592	−619	−647	−672	−743
Govt budget surplus	−638	−622	−618	−632	−661	−694	−735	−877
Changes in employment, wage earners (1000 man-years)								
Total	1.59	2.18	2.47	2.59	2.62	2.60	2.56	2.43
Excl. oil, ocean trans and govt	1.59	2.18	2.47	2.59	2.62	2.60	2.56	2.43
Manufacturing	0.47	0.59	0.64	0.65	0.64	0.61	0.58	0.47

Table 2.5: The effects of policy D, reduced personal income taxation by 1 billion
1984-Nkr.

	1984	1985	1986	1987	1988	1989	1990	1993
Changes in constant prices (million Nkr)								
Private consumption	702	986	1029	1052	1063	1066	1066	1055
Govt consumption	−15	−23	−24	−24	−24	−24	−24	−24
Gross investment	90	222	240	236	218	196	177	139
Increase in stocks	−9	−9	−7	−8	−10	−9	−9	−9
Exports	−12	−22	−19	−12	−4	2	8	22
Imports	272	417	439	444	441	436	430	423
GDP	484	738	781	800	801	795	787	761
Excl. oil, ocean trans and govt	482	736	779	797	799	793	785	758
Manufacturing	52	80	89	93	93	93	92	92
Changes in price indices (%)								
Private consumption	−0.01	−0.02	−0.03	−0.04	−0.04	−0.04	−0.04	−0.03
Gross investment	−0.01	−0.01	−0.03	−0.04	−0.04	−0.04	−0.04	−0.02
Exports	0.01	0.00	0.00	−0.01	−0.01	−0.02	−0.02	−0.02
GDP	−0.01	−0.01	−0.02	−0.03	−0.03	−0.03	−0.03	−0.03
Changes in current prices (million Nkr)								
Wage costs	82	162	209	238	258	274	288	336
Operating surplus	229	305	263	218	184	163	149	146
Manufacturing	42	92	51	30	20	16	14	17
Export surplus	−272	−462	−502	−531	−553	−572	−593	−665
Govt budget surplus	−772	−678	−688	−711	−743	−778	−817	−962
Changes in employment, wage earners (1000 man-years)								
Total	0.59	1.10	1.34	1.44	1.47	1.47	1.45	1.40
Excl. oil, ocean trans and govt	0.59	1.10	1.34	1.44	1.47	1.47	1.45	1.40
Manufacturing	0.12	0.22	0.26	0.27	0.26	0.24	0.22	0.17

influence the rate of inflation by affecting the labour supply, since employment is completely demand-determined and wage-rates are exogenous in
MODAG A.

The impacts of policy D travel the same channels as for policy A. Real
disposable income of households is increased, private consumption stimulated and investment increased because of the accelerator effects. The main
difference between the two scenarios is that the direct effect on GDP and
employment of increased government employment is now missing. Looking
at the private sector of the economy, the initial stimulus is larger under
the present policy because of the effects of the tax-system. While real
incomes are now fully increased by the reduced tax-amount, some of the
increased government wage-costs under policy A are immediately captured
by the government through payroll and personal income taxes. This is
reflected in the larger reduction in the government budget surplus when
income taxes are reduced. Comparing tables 2.2 and 2.5, the changes in
the different items seem by and large to be proportional to the difference
in private consumption growth.

Policy E: Increased transfers to households

Policy E can be analysed along the same lines as policies A and D. Three
parts of the model are of vital importance in explaining the differences
between these three policies: the tax functions, the consumption function
and the equation for investment in dwellings.

In MODAG A, government transfers to households are classified into
8 groups and the transfer amounts are all given exogenously. For impact
calculations the important thing to note is that the different types of transfers are allocated to the three socioeconomic groups in different proportions.
Since marginal tax and savings-rates vary between types of households, it is
important which transfers are increased. The calculations in this paper are
conducted by increasing pensions and family allowances, implying that a
large part of the government expenditure growth will end up as incomes for
pensioners with low marginal tax rates and a lower propensity to consume
than wage-earners.

Comparing policies A and E one should remember that the initial
expenditure increase is larger under policy E, since payroll taxes are cap-
turing some of the increase under policy A. The difference in real disposable
income for households is even greater due to the lower tax rates of pensioners, who now share a larger part of the income growth. On the other
hand, the lower marginal propensities to consume of pensioners lead to a

Table 2.6 The effects of policy E increased transfers to households of 1 billion
1984-Nkr.

	1984	1985	1986	1987	1988	1989	1990	1993
Changes in constant prices (million Nkr)								
Private consumption	596	796	817	835	845	850	851	849
Govt consumption	−13	−18	−19	−19	−19	−19	−19	−19
Gross investment	76	141	150	146	134	120	108	86
Increase in stocks	−7	−6	−6	−7	−8	−7	−7	−7
Exports	−10	−17	−14	−9	−3	2	6	17
Imports	231	325	337	341	340	338	335	333
GDP	411	570	592	606	610	608	604	593
Excl. oil, ocean trans and govt	409	568	590	604	608	606	602	591
Manufacturing	44	60	65	68	68	69	69	70
Changes in price indices (%)								
Private consumption	−0.01	−0.02	−0.02	−0.03	−0.03	−0.03	−0.03	−0.03
Gross investment	−0.01	−0.01	−0.02	−0.03	−0.03	−0.03	−0.02	−0.02
Exports	0.00	0.00	0.00	−0.01	−0.01	−0.01	−0.01	−0.01
GDP	−0.00	−0.01	−0.02	−0.02	−0.02	−0.02	−0.02	−0.02
Changes in current prices (million Nkr)								
Wage costs	69	125	157	177	192	205	217	258
Operating surplus	194	229	197	167	143	129	120	121
Manufacturing	36	65	37	23	15	13	11	11
Export surplus	−231	−362	−386	−408	−426	−443	−461	−524
Govt budget surplus	−686	−579	−601	−624	−652	−683	−716	−843
Changes in employment, wage earners (1000 man-years)								
Total	0.50	0.85	1.01	1.07	1.10	1.10	1.10	1.08
Excl. oil, ocean trans and govt	0.50	0.85	1.01	1.07	1.10	1.10	1.10	1.08
Manufacturing	0.10	0.16	0.19	0.19	0.18	0.17	0.16	0.13

smaller impact on private consumption of a given growth in household income. From tables 2.2 and 2.6 it appears that the net effect of policy A on private consumption in 1984 is stronger than that of policy E, counted per million of government budget deterioration. Comparing policies D and E the same way, confirms that increased transfers, the way they are carried out here, is a less efficient way of raising private consumption.

Despite the stronger growth in private consumption and private sector production in scenario E, gross investment is virtually equal in scenarios A and E. This is due to developments in the dwellings sector. While investment in the present case is increased in most industries, it is considerably reduced in the dwellings sector as compared to scenario A. Again the difference in the distribution of real income growth provides the key to the solution. The relationship for gross investment in the dwellings sector contains a real income variable for households, excluding pensioners. Since real income for wage-earners and the self-employed is lower than in scenario A, the growth of investment in the dwellings sector is also reduced.

2.2   Summary and comparison of policies A-E

Knowing the essential Keynesian features of MODAG A, the results of the five policies analysed above are of little surprise: fiscal policy has lasting effects on output and employment. The numerical values of the multipliers are, however, rather modest. The long-run GDP-multipliers are probably below 1 in most cases. Table 2.7 displays the effects of the five policies by 1993. Judging from the ability to raise output and employment, policy A is by far the most efficient. The increase in employment is more than three times that of any of the other policies. This is of course the result of policy A's direct effect on GDP and employment without leakages through imports, saving and taxation. The effects on the balance of trade and the government budget also seems to be in favour of a policy of raising government employment.

Usually one will not only be concerned with the total effect on GDP and domestic use of goods and services when analysing the costs and benefits of a policy, but also with their specific effects. Central objectives of many governments in the early eighties seem to have been to increase private sector investment and output. With respect to these goals, policy A is less attractive, since output and employment in the private sector of the economy are only modestly affected. Further, as for the increased transfers of policy E, demand growth is highly biased towards consumption while the effect on investment is relatively small.

Table 2.7: The effects of policies A–E by 1993. (Deviations from the reference scenario.)

	Policy A	Policy B	Policy C	Policy D	Policy E
Changes in constant prices (Million Nkr)					
Private consumption	770	374	358	1055	849
Govt. consumption	983	969	84	−24	−19
Gross investment	107	169	1189	139	86
Increase in stocks	−7	−9	−3	−9	−7
Exports	14	29	32	22	17
Imports	311	537	480	423	333
GDP	1556	995	1178	761	593
Exclusive oil, ocean transp. and govt.	554	987	1073	758	591
Manufacturing	67	171	214	92	70
Changes in price indices (%)					
Private consumption	−0.02	−0.05	−0.05	−0.03	−0.03
Gross investment	−0.02	−0.06	−0.12	−0.02	−0.02
Exports	−0.01	−0.03	−0.02	−0.02	−0.01
GDP	0.01	−0.04	−0.06	−0.03	−0.02
Changes in current prices (Million Nkr)					
Wage costs	1992	652	606	336	258
Operating surplus	112	83	162	146	121
Manufacturing	12	55	77	17	11
Export surplus	−488	−849	−743	−665	−524
Govt. budget surplus	−658	−888	−877	−962	−843
Changes in employment, wage earners, 1000 man-years					
Total	8.01	2.63	2.43	1.40	1.08
Exclusive oil, ocean transp. and govt.	1.01	2.63	2.43	1.40	1.08
Manufacturing	0.13	0.35	0.47	0.17	0.13

Because of the small price responses, the effects of the different policies on the balance of trade are mainly due to increased imports. Measured in terms of the GDP-increase, the import-leakages are substantial, by 1993 amounting to 56 percent in the cases of reduced taxes and increased transfer payments. If the reduction of the export-surplus is measured in terms of the deterioration of the government budget, the effect is even larger — almost 95 percent when government purchases are increased. When comparing the policies, it should be remembered that increased imports usually are considered to be less severe if they are for investment rather than consumption purposes.

The policies of section 2.1 were normalized to give a real input shock of 1 billion 1984-Nkr in 1984. The budget effect of the policies are different, however, and from the point of view of the government other normalization procedures may seem more reasonable. One possibility is to give the shock in current values (see Klein and Burmeister [1974]). In this case the budget effects would still differ and a better alternative may be to use the fiscal policy instruments to neutralize the endogenous feedback effects, deteriorating the budget by a given amount. Looking at table 2.7, it seems rather implausible, however, that this procedure would change any of the policy conclusions.

One should finally keep in mind that the policies in this section were simulated by a proportional adjustment of the various incomes and expenditure-items and that a different allocation would have produced different results. The significance of this can only be revealed by a more disaggregate analysis.

2.3   Effects of VAT and payroll taxation

This section deals with the consequences of increasing the value added tax and payroll taxation. In contrast to the policies studied in section 2.1, price changes will now play a crucial role in the results obtained. Both the value added tax and the payroll taxation are *ad valorem* taxes, respectively on commodity flows and the use of labour. We have the in the present case chosen to implement the policies by increasing the relevant tax rates:

Policy F: Value added tax rates increased by 5 percent from 1984 onwards, equivalent to a rise in the VAT-rate form 20 to 21 percent.

Policy G: The tax rates for employers' contributions to the social security schemes increased by 5 percent from 1984 onwards.

By making proportional adjustments to the tax rates of the reference scenario, the policies in this section are not directly comparable with those of section 2.1. Since the tax bases are increasing, the real Nkr value of the heavier taxation will now increase over the simulation. It is possible to change the tax rates in such a way that a constant Nkr real input shock is obtained (see, e.g., Fromm and Taubman [1967]). This requires, however, that one keep track of the tax-base in the reference scenario. The detailed treatment of indirect taxation in MODAG A has prevented us from doing this here.

Policy F: Increased value added tax

To understand how the increased valued added tax works in MODAG A, it is useful to take a closer look at the fundamental value concepts and the price equations of the model. The quantities of commodities flows are measured in unit prices of the base year, presently taken to be 1984. The most important concept for evaluating these flows is (approximate) basic values, which is preferred to purchasers' value or producers' value because trade margins and commodity tax rates may vary between receiving sectors of the same commodity. With respect to domestic prices, the behavioural price equations of the model explain for each commodity the basic value price index of the commodity. In addition to these behavioural price equations, indices for the market prices of the various demand categories are also included. These equations are similar in structure, and to illustrate their properties we shall look at the price indicies for private consumption.

Private consumption is subdivided into 19 groups of goods and services, called private consumption activities. Each activity is evaluated in purchaser's value and receives the different commodities of the model in fixed proportions that are determined by the input-output structure of the base year. The substitution in consumption is thus a substitution between the consumption activities. The price index of consumption activity j is of the following form:

$$PC_j = \sum_i (1 + \tau_{CMij} TM_i)(1 + \tau_{CVij} TV_i)\Lambda_{Cij}\big((1 - \varphi_{Cij}DI_i)BH_i \tag{2.1}$$
$$+ \varphi_{Cij}DI_i BI_i\big).$$

Here BH_i and BI_i are the basic value price indices on domestic and imported deliveries of commodity i, respectively, while DI_i is an exogenously determined index of changes in the import-share of the commodity. DI_i equals 1 in the base year. The τ's, Λ's and φ's are coefficients calculated from the national accounts of the base year of the model. All commodity taxes are treated as *ad valorem* taxes in MODAG A and they are taken care of by the first two parentheses of (2.1). We have distinguished between the value added tax, represented by the first parenthesis, and other (net) commodity taxes. Despite the fact that the VAT-rate in Norway is 20 percent, the actual rates accrued on the individual commodity flows in the model will for several reasons differ from this general rate. The base year VAT-rates, τ_{CMij}, will thus in general differ both between commodities and receiving activities.

Although the model contains very detailed information on the tax rates of the base year of the model, the treatment of changes in these rates is considerably simplified for simulation purposes. For each commodity only one exogenous index, TM_i, of changes in the VAT-rates is included.

The simulations in this subsection have been carried out by increasing the TM_i's by 5 percent from 1984 onwards, equivalent to a 1 percentage point increase in the VAT-rate. It appears from (2.1) that to the extent the domestic (basic value) price indices, the BH_i's, are not changed, taxes are completely passed on to consumers. However, the BH_i's will normally change as both input prices, productivity and capacity utilization change when the VAT-rate is increased. Although most of the increased VAT on input of materials is refundable, and thus according to the model not taken into account in the price calculations, there will be some direct price-increasing effects on input prices of the VAT-change. Together with the reduction in productivity arising from lower levels of output, this will tend to increase the BH's. Lower output will in the short run also lower capacity utilization, which will apply a downward pressure on prices. It appears that the net effect of these changes vary both between commodities and between the prices charged on the domestic and foreign markets. In a number of cases, more than 100 percent of the changes are passed on.

The consequences of increasing the value added tax is displayed in table 2.8. The initial impact is to raise market prices, particularly on consumption goods. As wage rates are exogenous, this price increase lead to a reduction in the real income of households, approximately 0.75 percent in 1984, reducing private consumption substantially. By 1993 consumption is down 2252 million Nkr compared to the reference scenario. The reduction in consumption creates negative effects on investment. These effects are strengthened by the increased user cost of capital as investment prices increases and by the reduced real value of the operating surplus. The contractive effect is also illustrated by the reduction in private sector employment — 3150 man-years by 1993.

The development of exports deserves an explanation. As there is no VAT on exports, there will be no direct effect on export prices of the increase in the VAT-rate. The reduction in domestic demand, however, will reduce the output of sectors producing for the foreign market. This decrease in the rate of capacity utilization will for some commodities lead to a reduction of the export price and thereby exports will increase. Although the average price on exports is increasing already the first year, the relatively high price-elasticities on commodities with reduced export-prices ensure that total exports are slightly higher than in the reference scenario for the first three years. Over the years, the rates of capacity utilization returns to normal levels and the input price increase will also appear in the export prices.

Table 2.8 also shows that to the extent that compensating income claims can be avoided, increased VAT has positive effects on the export surplus and on the government budget balance.

Policy G: Increased payroll taxation

In Norway the employer's contribution to the social security scheme is geographically differentiated with rates differing from 6 to 16.8 percent of the employee's compensation. The average rate for the economy as a whole in 1964 was 15.73 percent.

The exogenous wage-rates in MODAG A are rates of paid-out wages per man-year in each sector of production. Wage costs per man-year in sector j, WC_j is given by:

$$WC_j = (1 + \tau_{Fj}TF_j)W_j .\qquad (2.2)$$

Here τ_{Fj} is the base year average rate of the employer's contribution to social security in sector j, TF_j is an exogenous index of changes in the base-year rate, while W_j is the exogenous wage-rate. In the simulation below, the TF_j's are increased by 5 percent from 1984 onwards.

From (2.2) it appears that from the producer's point of view, increased payroll taxation works much like an increase in the wage-rate. The big difference between the two cases is of course that with an increased payroll taxation the increased labour cost is income for the government and not for households, resulting in an unambiguous contractive effect on the domestic economy. Table 2.9 shows how private consumption, investment and employment are gradually reduced compared to the reference scenario. Comparing tables 2.8 and 2.9, we see that under policy G investment is relatively more squeezed than consumption. Further, the increase in wage-costs reduces exports already in the first year. The reason why export prices appear to be only modestly affected by the increased taxation, is that several are treated exogenously. Excluding only oil and gas exports makes the average increase in export prices 0.24 percent in 1993. In the same year the volume of exports is down 326 million Nkr, but the reduction in imports assures that there is still an improvement in the foreign balance

Table 2.8: The effects of policy F, value added tax rates increased by 5 percent.

	1984	1985	1986	1987	1988	1989	1990	1993
Changes in constant prices (million Nkr)								
Private consumption	−1079	−1609	−1763	−1889	−1986	−2065	−2126	−2252
Govt consumption	20	35	39	43	45	47	48	51
Gross investment	−165	−394	−490	−519	−514	−488	−458	−380
Increase in stocks	16	17	17	19	23	22	22	24
Exports	8	21	6	−15	−29	−63	−86	−151
Imports	−414	−670	−753	−802	−833	−855	−870	−910
GDP	−786	−1260	−1438	−1559	−1638	−1691	−1728	−1798
Excl. oil, ocean trans and govt	−784	−1256	−1434	−1555	−1634	−1686	−1724	−1793
Manufacturing	−93	−147	−182	−204	−218	−228	−236	−260
Changes in price indices (%)								
Private consumption	0.61	0.67	0.70	0.73	0.75	0.76	0.76	0.75
Gross investment	0.28	0.31	0.33	0.38	0.40	0.39	0.38	0.36
Exports	0.01	0.02	0.04	0.05	0.07	0.08	0.09	0.09
GDP	0.40	0.44	0.46	0.49	0.51	0.51	0.51	0.50
Changes in current prices (million Nkr)								
Wage costs	−141	−281	−382	−457	−517	−567	−614	−757
Operating surplus	−565	−647	−569	−472	−402	−360	−332	−328
Manufacturing	−100	−189	−111	−66	−47	−43	−39	−37
Export surplus	442	786	908	1012	1101	1184	1267	1524
Govt budget surplus	1218	1168	1169	1229	1307	1399	1500	1849
Changes in employment, wage earners (1000 man-years)								
Total	−1.01	−1.90	−2.44	−2.75	−2.93	−3.02	−3.08	−3.15
Excl. oil, ocean trans and govt	−1.01	−1.90	−2.44	−2.75	−2.93	−3.02	−3.08	−3.15
Manufacturing	−0.22	−0.39	−0.50	−0.56	−0.56	−0.54	−0.51	−0.42

Table 2.9 The effects of policy G payroll tax rates increased by 5 percent.

	1984	1985	1986	1987	1988	1989	1990	1993
Changes in constant prices (million Nkr)								
Private consumption	−271	−474	−623	−753	−850	−918	−969	−1054
Govt consumption	7	14	19	24	27	29	31	33
Gross investment	−90	−229	−318	−388	−411	−398	−377	−317
Increase in stocks	20	1	15	11	14	7	11	11
Exports	−38	−42	−108	−144	−178	−206	−237	−326
Imports	−85	−177	−245	−312	−350	−370	−378	−389
GDP	−287	−552	−769	−938	−1048	−1116	−1163	−1264
Excl. oil, ocean trans and govt	−286	−551	−767	−935	−1045	−1113	−1159	−1259
Manufacturing	−72	−136	−205	−247	−274	−293	−308	−358
Changes in price indices (%)								
Private consumption	0.09	0.17	0.23	0.28	0.31	0.33	0.34	0.35
Gross investment	0.16	0.23	0.29	0.34	0.36	0.37	0.36	0.36
Exports	0.03	0.06	0.07	0.08	0.10	0.11	0.12	0.13
GDP	0.20	0.27	0.32	0.36	0.39	0.40	0.41	0.42
Changes in current prices (million Nkr)								
Wage costs	1492	1543	1587	1647	1734	1846	1980	2478
Operating surplus	−946	−812	−790	−737	−687	−666	−662	−737
Manufacturing	−221	−229	−206	−189	−187	−201	−214	−259
Export surplus	111	289	326	412	479	531	575	689
Govt budget surplus	914	935	957	991	1047	1122	1210	1528
Changes in employment, wage earners (1000 man-years)								
Total	−0.46	−1.02	−1.54	−1.94	−2.19	−2.33	−2.41	−2.55
Excl. oil, ocean trans and govt	−0.46	−1.02	−1.54	−1.94	−2.19	−2.33	−2.41	−2.55
Manufacturing	−0.19	−0.40	−0.61	−0.72	−0.77	−0.77	−0.75	−0.71

— although much smaller than in table 2.8. Despite that the reduction in GDP is smaller in the present case, the changed composition of demand leads the gross product of the manufacturing sectors to be lower than when the VAT-rate is increased.

2.4   Balanced budget multipliers

This section reports the multiplier effects of an increase in government expenditures financed by increased taxation. In the simplest possible Keynesian textbook-models this balanced budget multiplier is shown to be unity, but even small refinements of the model makes this neat result invalid. Especially the incorporation of a financial sector makes it difficult to deduce analytical propositions of the size of the balanced budget multiplier.

The multipliers below are calculated by combining some of the policies of section 2.1:

Policy H: Increased government employment by 1 billion 1984-Nkr (policy A), financed by increased personal income taxation (policy D).

Policy I: Increased government purchases of goods and services by 1 billion 1984-Nkr (policy B), also financed by increased personal income taxation.

To keep the government budget balance unchanged on average in the simulation period, proportional adjustments in the changes in the tax amounts of policy D have been made, i.e., again the intercepts of the tax functions are used to change the burden of taxation. The results of the two experiments are shown in tables 2.10 and 2.11.

With respect to policy H, increased government employment, we find that the GDP-multiplier is slightly above 1, which is not surprising as the model now stands. The increased government employment directly increases GDP by 1 billion. The increased wage incomes of households are, however, exposed to higher taxation so their disposable income is approximately unchanged and private consumption, the vehicle of expansion under policy A, stays almost as in the reference scenario. The reasons why private consumption changes somewhat are partly that we have allowed the increased government employment to receive a somewhat higher real wage over the years, and partly that there is a reshuffling of real income between socioeconomic groups. All the increased wage-income is distributed to wage-earners with relatively high marginal propensities to consume, while a proportional adjustment of taxes for all three socioeconomic groups are made. Policy H therefore implies a redistribution of income between households that increases private consumption. This highlights that the effects

Table 2.10: The effects of policy H, increased government employment financed by increased taxation of households. Wage costs increased by 1 billion 1984-NKr.

	1984	1985	1986	1987	1988	1989	1990	1993
Changes in constant prices (million Nkr)								
Private consumption	−16	−6	9	24	37	49	61	85
Govt consumption	1000	1000	1000	1000	999	999	999	998
Gross investment	−2	−3	1	5	9	11	13	16
Increase in stocks	0	0	−0	−0	−0	−0	−1	−1
Exports	0	0	−0	−1	−1	−1	−1	−1
Imports	−6	−3	4	11	17	22	27	37
GDP	989	994	1006	1017	1028	1036	1044	1061
Excl. oil, ocean trans and govt	−11	−6	6	17	27	36	44	61
Manufacturing	−1	−1	1	2	3	4	5	7
Changes in price indices (%)								
Private consumption	0.00	0.00	0.00	0.00	0.00	0.00	0.00	0.00
Gross investment	0.00	0.00	−0.00	−0.00	−0.00	−0.00	−0.00	−0.00
Exports	−0.00	0.00	0.00	0.00	0.00	0.00	0.00	−0.00
GDP	−0.00	0.00	0.01	0.02	0.03	0.03	0.03	0.03
Changes in current prices (million Nkr)								
Wage costs	992	1056	1127	1203	1284	1370	1462	1774
Operating surplus	−5	−3	3	8	11	12	14	17
Manufacturing	−1	−1	−0	1	1	2	3	4
Export surplus	6	4	−4	−12	−20	−27	−35	−56
Govt budget surplus	41	24	18	9	2	−4	−13	−33
Changes in employment, wage earners (1000 man-years)								
Total	6.99	6.99	7.00	7.02	7.04	7.06	7.07	7.10
Excl. oil, ocean trans and govt	−0.01	−0.01	0.00	0.02	0.04	0.06	0.07	0.10
Manufacturing	−0.00	−0.00	0.00	0.00	0.01	0.01	0.01	0.02

Table 2.11: The effects of policy I, increased government purchase of goods and services by 1 billion 1984-NKr financed by increased taxation of households.

	1984	1985	1986	1987	1988	1989	1990	1993
Changes in constant prices (million Nkr)								
Private consumption	−451	−607	−595	−586	−583	−582	−582	−586
Govt consumption	987	990	990	990	990	990	990	991
Gross investment	168	133	119	92	74	61	53	41
Increase in stocks	−11	4	2	−1	−4	−1	−1	−1
Exports	−18	−23	−17	−11	−5	−3	1	9
Imports	230	177	174	166	160	158	156	152
GDP	445	320	325	318	311	308	305	302
Excl. oil, ocean trans and govt	440	314	320	313	306	302	300	297
Manufacturing	100	79	82	82	82	83	84	87
Changes in price indices (%)								
Private consumption	−0.01	−0.02	−0.02	−0.02	−0.02	−0.02	−0.02	−0.002
Gross investment	−0.04	−0.03	−0.03	−0.05	−0.05	−0.05	−0.04	−0.04
Exports	0.00	−0.00	−0.00	−0.01	−0.01	−0.01	−0.01	−0.01
GDP	−0.02	−0.02	−0.02	−0.03	−0.03	−0.02	−0.02	−0.02
Changes in current prices (million Nkr)								
Wage costs	152	193	221	238	253	268	285	346
Operating surplus	217	60	35	−5	−29	−39	−46	−50
Manufacturing	74	82	45	28	23	26	27	40
Export surplus	−239	−222	−210	−207	−206	−211	−218	−244
Govt budget surplus	38	−8	5	5	4	2	−2	−13
Changes in employ- ment, wage earners (1000 man-years)								
Total	1.03	1.23	1.33	1.36	1.36	1.36	1.35	1.36
Excl. oil, ocean trans and govt	1.03	1.23	1.33	1.36	1.36	1.36	1.35	1.36
Manufacturing	0.23	0.26	0.27	0.27	0.25	0.24	0.23	0.20

of the balanced budget experiment are essentially dependent on the way the tax increase is implemented.

The main problem with using MODAG A to analyse the effects of policy H is the lack of modelling of the wage-formation process. Policy H implies an after-tax real-wage cut for wage-earners as compared to the reference scenario. This could easily stimulate wage-inflation and tend to bring the GDP-multiplier below 1, since reduced exports and private investment would create negative multiplier effects.

By policy I, an increased government expenditure financed by taxation of households, the balanced budget multiplier is brought down to 0.30 by 1993. This is due to two factors: an import-leakage which was avoided when government employment was increased, and a major reduction of household income. The increased expenditures will initially stimulate private sector production and imports. Due to the labour demand functions, most of the increased factor income in 1984, however, will end up as operating surplus; this occurs in sectors where operating surplus only modestly affects the consumption-motivating income of households. At the same time, the burden of financing the increased government expenditures is placed entirely on households, leading to a reduction of their real incomes that squeezes consumption. Tendencies to after-tax real-wage resistance could also in this case change the multiplier results.

3.   Some critical remarks

The computations in section 2 could be criticised in several respects:

(1) There are important mechanisms in the Norwegian economy that are not accounted for by the relationships in MODAG A.

(2) The chosen specifications of some blocks of the model is inappropriate.

(3) Given the specifications of the model, some parameter-choices are unfortunate.

Mainly due to their intensive use by government agencies, Norwegian macroeconomic models have traditionally been very open in the sense that few behavioural relationships have been incorporated and consequently many areas of the Norwegian economy have been handled outside the model. Although mechanical multiplier experiments, conducted by changing only a few policy variables, will in these situations give important information on the properties of the model itself, they give little information on the real-world effects of the policies. A careful scrutiny of possible feedback-effects on the exogenous variables of the model should then be carried out to make the computations realistic. When policy alternatives are studied in a particular situation, exogenous corrections in the behavioural equations of the model should also be considered. Although MODAG A is substantially more closed than its "big brother" MODIS IV, there are still important lacunae which call for exogenous corrections in the simulations above if they are to be taken seriously. The most obvious candidates for further improvements are a wage-formation block and the modelling of the financial sector, both areas of ongoing work.

3.1   Feedbacks from wages

With respect to the policies of section 2, the wage-effects have two aspects: the policies will affect real-wages differently and they will affect the labour-market situation differently.

Standard macroeconomic modelling indicates that a wage-increase may be the result of a tighter labour market. As shown by Stølen [1986], the macroeconomic consequences in Norway of such an increase will be highly dependent on government policy responses regarding transfers and regulated prices. An isolated wage-rate increase will in MODAG A have the initial effect of raising household income, and thereby consumption, increasing private investment and improving the government budget balance. The effects of changed relative factor prices on investment and of increased government wage-costs on the budget balance are thus dominated by the output and tax-increase of private consumption growth. The employment effects after 10 years are negative, but rather small.

In the simulations in section 2.1, employment is increased by 1100 to 8000 man-years. Due to part-time work, the increase in the number of employed may be somewhat higher; as a maximum estimate from 1400 to 10000 persons. Of this increase, some must be expected to come from people previously not seeking work, i.e., not registered as unemployed initially. Assuming, as has been done in previous work by the Ministry of Finance (Eriksen et al. [1981]), that this applies to 50 percent of the increased employment, we are left with a reduction in unemployment of from 750 persons in the case of policy E, to 5000 persons in the case of policy A. This means that unemployment is reduced by less than 0.25%-points from a level of 2–2.5 percent along the reference path. To my knowledge, none of the empirical investigations of the Phillips-curve-relationship in Norway (see, e.g., OECD [1975, 1978], Isachsen and Raaum [1983], Hersoug [1983]) or Stølen [1985]) suggests that this reduction could have any substantial influence on the growth of money wages. Even if such effects are at work, it is difficult to see how they could alter the main policy conclusions. It should also be remembered that a wage increase could lower the estimated reduction in unemployment by increasing labour supply, at least for female workers.

The real-wage effect applies especially to policy D of reduced taxation and the simulations in 2.3. While policies A through C work via increased activity level in the government sector, the initial effect of policy D is an after-tax real-wage increase for workers. Knowing the central position of real-wage calculations in the wage-negotiations in Norway, it seems plausible that a real-wage increase brought about by reduced taxes, may influence the nominal wage-rates. If there is such a real-wage effect working, it could tend to make policy D relatively more attractive than it appears in section 2.1. The importance of this will of course depend on the actual degree of real-wage resistance. For the contractive policies of section 2.3 it is even more likely that the nominal wage-rates will be affected. While unions may dispute the relevance of bringing changes in personal taxation into negotiations, there is convincing evidence that real-wage cuts brought about rising prices is an accepted argument for wage claims.

3.2   Financial implications

The most striking differences between macroeconomic models are usually found in the description of the financial markets. When a financial sector is lacking, the interpretation of fiscal policy analysis should be that an accommodating monetary policy is being followed. Looking at MODAG A, some financial variables do appear: an interest rate in the investment demand equations, credit supply variables in the consumption function and some of the investment equations and interest payments as a part of household incomes. All these variables are determined exogenously by the user of the model and an accommodating monetary policy at least must mean that they are not affected.

The financial markets in Norway have in the post-war area been among the most heavily regulated in the western world. The government has intended to control the size and sources of credit supply and the allocation of credit between purposes as well as interest rates. The result of this process, in Norway known as "credit-budgeting", has been sustained disequilibrium in credit markets. For short-run policy-analysis, the main tools of the Ministry of FinanceMinistry of Finance, Norway have been the MODIS-model run in tandem with KRØSUS, a model of the credit flows of the Norwegian economy. KRØSUS has been used to assure consistency between the credit flows and wealth accumulation of the private sector and the estimates for private consumption and sectorial investment from MODIS. One aspect of the credit regulations has been the establishing of state banks giving subsidized loans to purposes given priority such as education, housing and investment in primary industries and manufacturing. Another aspect has been a heavy regulation of the capital flows to and from abroad.

Despite the regulations, market forces have been at work, leading credit flows into new channels of financial intermediation and resulting in occasionally large discrepancies between the goals of the credit-budget and the realized figures.

As the credit markets in Norway are being gradually deregulated, the need to incorporate an explicit financial sector in MODAG A is growing. Within this work, a careful reconsideration of the way financial variables now enter the model should also be made, especially the use of a nominal interest rate in the investment functions and the broad measures of credit to households and companies.

The financial variables of MODAG A have somewhat different interpretations. With respect to the credit variables in the investment equations, some are obviously government policy variables in that they represent lending ceilings for state banks. The more general variables pertaining to credit to companies and households must, however, be thought of as reflecting rationing of lending from private financial institutions and can thereby only indirectly be controlled by the government. Finally, the interest-variable in the investment relationships indicates that the rationing has not been completely effective for all kinds of business activity.

What happens if an accommodating monetary policy is not being followed? An exhaustive answer to this question lies outside the scope of this paper, but some comments on the importance of possible feedback effects in MODAG A seems appropriate. It appears that a policy leading to higher interest rates and a squeeze of credit supply to households and companies could have substantial effects in the model. A simple impact calculation of an increase of all interest-magnitudes in the model by 10 percent has been carried out. This amounts to a 1.3 percentage-point increase in 1984 and a 1 percentage-point increase in 1993 of the nominal interest rate of the investment equations. The calculation shows that this increase has a major depressing effect on the economy by reducing private investments by 0.65 billion Nkr and GDP by 1 billion Nkr in 1993, when compared to the reference scenario. A 1 percent reduction of credit supply to households and companies (see Stølen [1986]) will reduce GDP by 0.23 billion Nkr by 1993. Comparing these figures to the multipliers of section 2.1, demonstrates the importance of the assumption of an accommodating monetary policy for the numerical values of the multipliers.

It should also be mentioned that there could be effects working in the other direction: increased wealth of households may have a direct effect on private consumption and a general raising of interest rates may, via intertemporal substitution in consumption, have a similar effect.

Another source of uncertainty is the development of the exchange rate. Several outcomes are possible here (see Penati [1983]), but considering the Norwegian regulations of capital flows, it seems plausible that a downward pressure on the exchange rate of an expansionary fiscal policy may predominate. A depreciating exchange rate will have conflicting effects in MODAG A in that real incomes of households, and thereby consumption is reduced while exports are stimulated and import-demand dampened. As shown by Stølen [1987], the net result of these effects on GDP is slightly negative, and accordingly the multipliers of section 2.1 will decrease if a depreciation of the exchange rate occurs.

3.3   Export behaviour

Another field for future research is the modelling of supply behaviour in some of the export-oriented manufacturing sectors such as the production of metals, industrial chemicals and paper and paper products. Today output in these sectors are completely demand determined while the supply behaviour mainly enters through the investment and price setting equations. In the short run, when there is incomplete information leading to sluggish responses, this may be a realistic description of these sectors. However, in the long run, the small open economy assumptions of export-prices determined at the world markets and the volumes of export determined by supply, seem more plausible. So far, empirical investigations along the lines of this model have not been successful (see Bergan and Olsen [1985]) and the present model formulation at this point is obviously at variance with current thinking on export behaviour in Norway.

References

Bergan, R. and Ø. Olsen [1985], "Eksporttilpasning i MODAG A", Reports from the Central Bureau of Statistics, no. 85/29, Oslo.

Cappelen, Å. and S. Longva [1987], "MODAG A. A Medium-Term Macroeconomic model of the Norwegian Economy", in this volume.

Chan-Lee, J.H. and H. Kato [1984], "A Comparison of Simulation Properties of National Econometric Models", *OECD Economic Studies, 2/84.*

Eriksen, T., J.F. Qvigstad and A. Rødseth [1981], "Finanspolitiske indikatorer og en finanspolitisk modell", Working Paper no. 2 from the Ministry of Finance, Oslo.

Fromm, G. and L.R. Klein [1973], "A Comparison of Eleven Econometric Models of the United States", *American Economic Review, 63.*

Fromm, G. and L.R. Klein (ed.) [1975], *The Brookings Model: Perspective and Recent Developments.* Amsterdam: North-Holland.

Fromm, G. and P. Taubman [1967], *Policy Simulation with an Econometric Model.* Amsterdam: North-Holland.

Hersoug, T. [1983], "Tarifftillegg, lønnsglidning og samlet lønnsøkning i Norge 1946–81", Memorandum from Institute of Economics, University of Oslo.

Isachsen, A.J. and O. Raaum [1983], "Solidarisk lønnspolitikk – Hvor effektiv er den egentlig?", *Sosialøkonomen, 3.*

Klein, L.R., and E. Burmeister (ed.) [1976], *Econometric Model Performance.* Philadelphia: University of Pennsylvania Press.

Lybeck et al. [1984], "A Comparison of the Dynamic Properties of Five Nordic Macroeconometric Models", *Scandinavian Journal of Economics, 86.*

OECD [1975], "Economic Survey. Norway", Paris.

OECD [1978], "Economic Survey. Norway", Paris.

Okun, A.M. [1975], "Uses of models for policy formulation", in *The Brookings Model: Perspectives and Recent Developments,* ed. Fromm and Klein .

Penati, A. [1983], "Expansionary Fiscal policy and the Exchange Rate", *IMF Staff Papers, 3.*

Stølen, N.M. [1985], "Faktorer bak lønnsveksten", *Økonomiske Analyser, 9.*

Stølen, N.M. [1987], "Effects of changes in wages and exchange rates analysed by the model MODAG A", in this volume.

Tobin, J. [1980], "Stabilization Policy Ten Years Later", *Brookings Papers on Economic Activity, 1.*

Waelbroeck, J. [1975], "A survey of short-run model research outside the United States", in *The Brookings Model: Perspective and Recent Developments*, ed. Fromm and Klein .

Wallis, K.F., M.J. Andrews, D.N.F. Bell, P.G. Fisher and J.D. Whitley (eds.) [1984], *Models of the U.K. Economy.* Oxford: Oxford University Press.

Macroeconomic Medium-Term Models in the Nordic Countries
O. Bjerkholt and J. Rosted (Editors)
© *Elsevier Science Publishers B. V. (North-Holland), 1987*

Analysing the Effects of Changes in Wages and Exchange Rates with MODAG A

by

Nils Martin Stølen
Central Bureau of Statistics,
Oslo, Norway

1. Introduction

As is the case for the other Nordic countries, the Norwegian economy can be characterized as small and open. In 1985 exports and imports amounted to close to 50 and 40 per cent, respectively, of the gross domestic product. Because of the openness of the economy the level of domestic activity is highly dependent on fluctuations in the world market. At the same time an increase in domestic costs which is stronger than that experienced among our competitors abroad may lead to losses in Norwegian market shares, both on domestic and export markets. From 1980 to 1985 unit labour costs in Norwegian manufacturing industries increased by about 11 per cent relative to our trading partners. In the same period employment in these industries decreased by close to 40 thousand man-years while employment in the service industries increased by more than 110 thousand man-years. The reduction in employment in manufacturing was especially strong in 1982 and 1983. This has created a fear that the balance of payments may be too dependent on the oil and gas revenues, which account for more than one-third of Norwegian export income. A sudden fall in these revenues, which indeed happened in the beginning of 1986, may therefore cause severe problems if they stay at a low level for several years. As a consequence of this it has been proposed that a lower increase in wage rates or a devaluation is necessary to improve profitability and production in the exposed industries and thereby the balance of payments. To achieve these goals the Norwegian currency has in fact been adjusted several times in recent years, and in May 1986 there was a devaluation of 12 per cent.

In this paper we shall discuss the effects of changes in wage and exchange rates by using the macroeconomic model MODAG A. This model is described in Cappelen and Longva [in this volume], and its first version was developed for use by The Technical Calculation Committee for Income Settlements in the spring of 1983.[1]

For studying the effects of changes in wage and exchange rates, a macroeconomic model like MODAG A may be considered only to be a tool. The model is not capable of giving us the exact results for several reasons:

- Several important economic behavioural mechanisms are not represented in the model in a satisfactory way. An obvious weakness of the present version of the model is the weak influence of the supply side, both on the commodity and the labour markets. Apart from the resource-based industries, production is determined from the demand side while the producers are assumed to be active in price-setting. However, the exposed industries may in the medium term face given prices from the world market. In the labour market neither supply of labour nor wage formation is incorporated in the version of the model presented in this paper, and the financial markets are not modelled yet.

- Some of the estimated relationships incorporated in the model are uncertain and may even be misspecified.

---

[1] See Cappelen and Longva [1984] for a more detailed description of the historical background regarding the use of income policy in Norway. To make it possible for the central authorities to carry out an income policy it is of decisive importance that the parties involved have the same information about the actual situation in the economy and a common view of the economic consequences of the possible outcomes of an income settlement. To achieve these goals The Technical Calculation Committee for Income Settlements (also called the Aukrust Committee after its chairman until 1985) was appointed by the government in 1965 and has been in existence since. A main task for the Aukrust Committee has been to present conditional forecasts for the price and income development for alternative outcomes of the income settlements, i.e., changes in wage rates and agricultural prices, but from 1983 the committee is also requested to make estimates for employment effects.

The reports from The Technical Calculation Committee for Income Settlements are published in the series Norges Offentlig Utredninger (Norway's Public Reports) NOU. See NOU [1983] for a presentation of the work carried out in connection with the income settlements in 1983.

– The model contains a lot of exogenous variables which are entirely or partly under the control of the central government and several of these variables may be changed as a result of changes in wage and exchange rates.

Rather than a total description of how changes in wage and exchange rates influence the Norwegian economy, the main emphasis in this paper is on explaining the results from the model calculations.[2] However, we have supplemented the model calculations by commenting on the missing effects, and we have also presented the effects of changes in government regulated prices, credit market variables and transfers as a consequence of changes in wage and exchange rates.

Our point of departure for the calculations has been a reference scenario for the Norwegian economy derived by means of MODAG A. On the basis of this scenario we have calculated multipliers which represent the impacts of a 1 percent change in wage rates, government regulated prices, credit market variables, transfers and exchange rates on important model determined (endogenous) variables. Both the effects on the endogenous variables and the change in exogenous variables are measured as deviations from the reference scenario.

2.   Effects of changes in wage rates

2.1   Institutional background

Even though a considerable part of the wage increases is the result of wage drift,[3] national income settlements in Norway either directly or indirectly affect most wage and salary earners. About two-thirds of all wage and salary earners belong to a union. Negotiations take place for most groups of income earners simultaneously. Wage agreements between the Norwegian Federation of Trade Unions (LO) and the Norwegian Employers' Confederation (NAF) are made at approximately the same time as agricultural prices and subsidies are fixed through negotiations between the government and the agricultural organizations. Wage adjustments in the public sector

---

[2] A more total calculation is carried out by the Aukrust Committee (see NOU, [1983]) and by the Ministry of Finance (Lunde [1984]) in connection with the Revised National Budget (St. meld. nr. 88 [1983–84]).

[3] Wage drift is defined as the difference between the total yearly increase in wage rates and the increase obtained in the central income settlements.

are also part of the income settlement, and pensions and other government transfers are regulated in accordance with the changes in wage rates.

During the past decade changes in wage rates for employees in different industries have been fairly parallel. Although some compensation has been given to the groups with the lowest income in the central agreements, stronger wage drifts for the high-income groups have tended to maintain the wage differentials between industries. When looking at the effects of changes in wages we have therefore found it relevant and a reasonable approximation to change the wage rates for all industries by the same percentage.

Even though it is technically easy to analyse the impacts of a change in wage rates in a model like MODAG A, where wage rates are exogenous, the practical relevance of treating wage rates as exogenous variables can be discussed since wage rates are endogenous in the real world. From economic theory it can be concluded that wage formation is a rather complicated process where the position of power of the different parties in in the labour market may influence the result.[4] But the market forces are also of importance as they partly may influence the parties involved at the same time as they have an independent impact through wage drift and changes in prices.

To analyse wage and price formation in a small open economy Odd Aukrust has developed a model called the Scandinavian model of inflation (see Aukrust [1970, 1977]). In this model wage rates in the long run are assumed to depend on the change in product prices and productivity in industries exposed to foreign competition, while wage rates in the sheltered industries are assumed to follow the development in the exposed industries. In the short run, however, the wage rates may to a certain extent fluctuate around this main course. If the wage increases for some years are stronger than these allowed by the main course this may cause an increase in unemployment, and the forces in the labour market may then reduce the wage increases in the next periods.

If equilibrium in the labour market is restored fairly quickly there is no need to worry about the impact of higher wage rates on unemployment. The labour market can then be left to itself without any interference from the central authorities. However, observations from most OECD-countries indicate that the Phillips-curve may become rather flat even at a moderate

---

[4] See Lindbeck and Snower [1985] for an overview of the economic theories for wage formation.

level of unemployment.[5] One reason for this is that trade unions may be reluctant to accept a cut in real wages even if unemployment is high. It may therefore take many years before equilibrium is restored. Due to a balance of payments restriction the central authorities may also be unable to decrease unemployment by a more expansive economic policy.

In such a situation it seems to be a reasonable policy to try to shift the Phillips-curve downwards and thereby get lower nominal wage increases. An analysis of how much the unemployment and the balance of payments may be improved is then necessary to get the trade unions and the general public to accept this, i.e., to change their behaviour.

Unemployment in Norway has stayed at a low level for most years since the second world war. Even the peak of 3.3 percent reached in 1983 was rather low compared to unemployment rates experienced in most other western countries. The aim for incomes policy in Norway has been to prevent too high wage increases and to reach a feasible solution without having to use unemployment as a regulator. Due to the rise in the revenues from sale of crude oil and natural gas it has been rather easy to keep unemployment in Norway at a low level without being too much concerned with the balance of payments. The stronger wage increases in the last decade than those allowed by the increase in competitive prices and productivity in exposed industries may be considered to have been a necessary development in order to channel the oil revenues into the economy. However, as mentioned in the introduction it has been argued that Norway has become too dependent on these revenues, and the fall in oil prices in 1986 has made the need for an income policy even greater than before.

When looking at the total effects of a change in wage and exchange rates it is necessary to take the resulting increase in government controlled variables into consideration. In this chapter we have therefore also presented the effects of a change in government regulated prices, government transfers and nominal credit market variables.

2.2   Effects on endogenous variables in MODAG A

2.2.1   Prices

As discussed by Cappelen and Longva [1987] it is convenient to make a distinction between the price part and the quantity part in the description of MODAG A. Although MODAG A is formally a simultaneous model in prices and quantities, the main effects in the model go from the price part

---

[5] See Coe [1985] for a survey over the Phillips-curves in the OECD countries.

to the quantity part. In discussing the effects of changes in wages and exchange rates we will therefore ignore the effects going from the quantity part to the price part.

An increase in wage rates and government regulated prices will lead to an increase in variable unit costs for the producers. As a result of this the producers will raise their prices, both on the domestic market and on the export market. In the sheltered industries the higher costs will almost entirely be passed on into higher prices. This will only partly be the case in the exposed industries, which also have to consider the prices on competing foreign products. The profitability of the exposed industries will therefore decrease as a result of higher wage rates and government-regulated prices.

The impacts of changes in wage rates and government regulated prices (agricultural prices and electricity prices) are presented in tables 2.1 and 2.2. The effects on the consumer price index are distributed over a period of time; almost the total price effect of a wage increase has been realized by the fifth year. Compared to other countries the direct effect of wages on consumer prices is rather small in Norway. The reason for this is that government regulated prices and especially import prices weigh heavily in the consumer price index. As seen from tables 2.1 and 2.2 the elasticity of consumer prices with respect to a combined change of wage rates and government regulated prices after 10 years is estimated to be 0.58. This result is very close to the estimate of the same elasticity in the report from the first Aukrust Committee (see Utredningsutvalget [1966]) and confirms one of the "stylized facts" about the behaviour of the Norwegian economy. The impact on investment prices seems to be of the same magnitude as the impact on consumer prices, but the effect on investment prices appears earlier. Because export prices are very much dependent on the prices of competing products and because wage costs only constitute a small part of the total variable costs in the most important exporting industries, the impact on export prices of higher wages rates is much smaller than the effect on consumer prices.

2.2.2   Import shares

Apart from electricity, ships and oil-drilling platforms the commodity imports in MODAG A are determined endogenously. The determination of imports, however, is different for different groups of commodities. For so-called non-competitive imports (commodities of which, by definition there is no comparable Norwegian production), imports are determined directly from the commodity balance equations. This is also the case for imports

Table 2.1: Effects of a 1 percent increase in wage rates.

	1984	1985	1986	1987	1988	1990	1993
Changes in constant prices (%):							
Private consumption	0.28	0.26	0.19	0.14	0.11	0.09	0.09
Gross investments*	−0.01	−0.05	−0.23	−0.36	−0.41	−0.37	−0.27
Manufacturing	0.07	−0.34	−0.77	−1.02	−1.01	−0.79	−0.63
Exports**	−0.09	−0.09	−0.19	−0.23	−0.26	−0.29	−0.34
Imports	0.15	0.14	0.11	0.07	0.06	0.05	0.06
GDP*	0.09	0.05	−0.03	−0.09	−0.12	−0.14	−0.15
Manufacturing	−0.05	−0.14	−0.27	−0.34	−0.38	−0.42	−0.46
Changes in price indices (%):							
Private consumption	0.12	0.21	0.28	0.34	0.38	0.42	0.44
Gross investments	0.21	0.31	0.37	0.42	0.45	0.46	0.47
Exports**	0.08	0.14	0.16	0.19	0.21	0.25	0.29
GDP	0.27	0.36	0.42	0.47	0.51	0.53	0.54
Changes in current prices Million Nkr.							
Wage costs	2168	2336	2454	2583	2742	3158	3969
Operating surplus	−1012	−765	−790	−748	−702	−680	−755
Manufacturing	−268	−220	−240	−241	−248	−287	−341
Export surplus	−215	−178	−174	−115	−79	−68	−120
Govt. budget surplus	319	563	510	489	490	542	655
Changes in employment, wage earners, 1000 man-years							
Total	0.16	−0.02	−0.48	−0.86	−1.11	−1.29	−1.34
Manufacturing	−0.10	−0.31	−0.54	−0.68	−0.74	−0.74	−0.70
Changes in employment, wage earners (%)							
Total*	0.01	−0.00	−0.04	−0.06	−0.08	−.09	−0.09
Manufacturing	−0.03	−0.09	−0.16	−0.20	−0.22	−0.22	−0.21

* In private industries exclusive oil and ocean transport.
** Exclusive oil, natural gas and services.

Table 2.2: Effects of a 1 percent increase in government regulated prices.

	1984	1985	1986	1987	1988	1990	1993
Changes in constant prices (%):							
Private consumption	−0.06	−0.09	−0.11	−0.12	−0.13	−0.14	−0.16
Gross investments*	0.16	0.16	0.10	0.03	0.01	0.05	0.04
Manufacturing	−0.02	−0.28	−0.57	−0.74	−0.67	−0.30	−0.18
Exports**	−0.00	0.01	−0.02	−0.04	−0.06	−0.04	−0.04
Imports	0.02	0.00	−0.02	−0.03	−0.04	−0.04	−0.04
GDP*	−0.01	−0.03	−0.05	−0.07	−0.08	−0.09	−0.10
Manufacturing	−0.05	−0.14	−0.27	−0.34	−0.38	−0.42	−0.11
Changes in price indices (%):							
Private consumption	0.10	0.12	0.13	0.13	0.14	0.14	0.14
Gross investments	0.00	0.00	0.01	0.01	0.01	0.02	0.02
Exports**	0.01	0.03	0.05	0.07	0.09	0.10	0.10
GDP	0.05	0.07	0.08	0.09	0.10	0.10	0.10
Changes in current prices Million Nkr.							
Wage costs	−3	−10	−23	−39	−53	−69	−111
Operating surplus	138	174	191	229	273	334	368
Manufacturing	−109	−93	−72	−45	−20	−6	−28
Export surplus	−15	51	88	153	198	224	271
Govt. budget surplus	76	82	72	55	46	47	17
Changes in employment, wage earners, 1000 man-years							
Total	−0.01	−0.05	−0.13	−0.21	−0.27	−0.32	−0.43
Manufacturing	0.01	0.01	0.00	0.00	0.01	0.02	−0.01
Changes in employment, wage earners (%)							
Total*	−0.00	−0.00	−0.01	−0.02	−0.02	−0.03	−0.03
Manufacturing	0.00	0.00	0.00	0.00	0.00	0.01	0.00

* In private industries exclusive oil and ocean transport
** Exclusive oil, natural gas and services

of commodities which are directly based on natural resources (primary industry products, crude oil and gas). In MODAG A the production of these commodities are stipulated exogenously and imports are thereby residually determined. Tourism abroad is determined in the consumption model.

For the remaining commodities imports are determined by import shares, and for manufacturing goods these import shares are specified and estimated as a function of the ratio between the domestic and the corresponding import price.[6] The import shares in MODAG A are assumed to be independent of the demand for domestic products. This means that the income elasticity for imports is equal to 1 for a given composition of demand. A central parameter in the import model is the elasticity of substitution. For most of the commodities this parameter is estimated to have a value between 1 and 1.5. For those commodities and services where the import shares are still exogenous, estimation results indicated no significant connection between changes in import shares and relative prices. The imports of these commodities are also rather small.

In MODAG A higher wage rates and regulated prices lead to a rise in domestic prices. As import prices are exogenous in the model, this will lead to a rise in the import shares too, and about one half of this change will take place during the first year for a given change in relative prices. Higher import shares means that production will decrease for a given domestic demand.

The assumption of constant import prices can of course be discussed. Some empirical work indicates that import prices are affected but this is not incorporated in the model yet. If an increase in domestic prices indeed leads to an increase in import prices this means that the losses in market shares in this paper is overstated. On the other hand, if the import prices also increase this means that the effects on consumer prices are understated. This will cause a lower growth in private consumption and imports than presented in tables 2.1 and 2.2.

2.2.3   Exports

Exports of resource-based products such as crude oil and natural gas, electricity, fish and agricultural products, etc. are assumed to be supply determined and are exogenously given in the model. The same is true for exports of ocean transport services. For most other export products, demand relations, which determine exports as a function of the demand level

---

[6] The import share model is documented in more detail in Stølen [1983b].

on the world markets and of the ratio between the Norwegian export price and an exogenously given competitive price, have been introduced.[7]

Because increased costs will partly be passed on in higher export prices, both higher wages and government regulated prices will lead to lower exports and production in the exporting industries. The long run price elasticity for the most important exported commodities is estimated to have a value between −1 and −2. As we can se from tables 2.1 and 2.2 the effects on exports are distributed over a period of time and only one half of the total effect has appeared during the third year. The rather slow adaptation of exports to an increase in domestic costs is to a large degree caused by long lags both in the export price and volume equations.

In percent the effect on total exports is rather small because about two-thirds of the Norwegian exports are exogenous in the model. We have therefore chosen to present the percentage effect on exports exclusive of oil, natural gas and services. This elasticity is also rather small because wage increases have only a small effect on export prices. One reason for this is that many of the export manufacturing industries are energy intensive, and wage costs constitute only a small part of total costs. The influence on exports of wage cost changes are therefore likely to be much smaller in Norway than in most other industrialized small open economies. The rise in wage rates will however cause a fall in the profitability of the exporting industries, and because of the small effects from a change in investments and capacity on supply of products (the so-called supply-side effects), the decrease in exports that results from higher wage rates may be understated in MODAG A.

2.2.4   Private consumption

An increase in wage rates will in the first years stimulate private consumption because the marginal propensity to consume out of wage incomes is larger than the marginal propensity to consume out of operating surplus (profits). This effect on private consumption of an increase in wage rates is probably larger in Norway than in most other countries because import prices and government regulated prices weigh heavily in the consumer price index. However, the positive effect on private consumption declines over time, and after the seventh year the elasticity seems to stabilize at 0.09. The decreasing elasticity is caused by a loss in market shares both on the domestic market and the export market. This tends to reduce employment and

---

[7] The export model is documented in more detail in Bergan and Olsen [1985].

Table 2.3: Effects of a 1 percent increase in government transfers.

	1984	1985	1986	1987	1988	1990	1993
Changes in constant prices (%):							
Private consumption	0.17	0.22	0.24	0.24	0.24	0.25	0.25
Gross investments*	0.07	0.14	0.15	0.15	0.15	0.13	0.12
Manufacturing	0.09	0.13	0.14	0.15	0.15	0.13	0.10
Imports	0.08	0.11	0.12	0.12	0.12	0.13	0.11
GDP*	0.09	0.12	0.13	0.13	0.13	0.14	0.14
Manufacturing	0.04	0.06	0.07	0.07	0.07	0.07	0.07
Changes in current prices, Million Nkr.							
Wage costs	−41	78	102	119	135	162	210
Operating surplus	115	145	132	119	135	104	116
Manufacturing	21	42	24	16	12	11	11
Export surplus	−137	−226	−251	−277	−300	−348	−432
Govt. budget surplus	−482	−449	−487	−526	−569	−667	−848
Changes in employment, wage earners,1000 man-years							
Total	0.30	0.53	0.65	0.72	0.77	0.82	0.88
Manufacturing	0.06	0.10	0.12	0.13	0.13	0.12	0.11
Changes in employment, wage earners (%)							
Total*	0.02	0.04	0.05	0.05	0.06	0.06	0.06
Manufacturing	0.02	0.03	0.04	0.04	0.04	0.04	0.03

* In private industries exclusive oil and ocean transport.

income in the exposed industries. At the same time lower investments will reduce employment and income in the building and construction industries and the industries producing machinery and other investment equipment.

Higher government regulated prices will obviously lead to a decrease in real disposable income and consumption. From tables 2.3 and 2.4 we can see that an increase in transfer payments and a more expansive credit policy will work in the opposite direction. The total effects of a simultaneous increase in wage rates and government controlled variables are further discussed in section 2.3.

2.2.5 Production and employment

Due to reduced market shares increased wage rates lead to lower production and employment in the exposed manufacturing industries. As pointed out

Table 2.4: Effects of a 1 percent increase in nominal credit variables.

	1984	1985	1986	1987	1988	1990	1993
Changes in constant prices (%):							
Private consumption	0.11	0.14	0.13	0.12	0.12	0.12	0.11
Gross investments*	0.13	0.14	0.13	0.12	0.11	0.09	0.07
Manufacturing	0.09	0.11	0.10	0.07	0.10	0.08	0.06
Imports	0.06	0.08	0.07	0.07	0.07	0.06	0.05
GDP*	0.07	0.08	0.07	0.05	0.07	0.07	0.06
Manufacturing	0.05	0.06	0.05	0.07	0.05	0.04	0.04
Changes in current prices, Million Nkr.							
Wage costs	34	56	62	65	68	75	90
Operating surplus	88	92	63	47	37	24	18
Manufacturing	19	29	13	6	3	0	−3
Export surplus	−111	−161	−152	−155	−162	−175	−205
Govt. budget surplus	88	123	117	118	122	132	154
Changes in employment, wage earners, 1000 man-years							
Total	0.24	0.38	0.40	0.39	0.39	0.38	0.37
Manufacturing	0.06	0.08	0.09	0.08	0.08	0.07	0.05
Changes in employment, wage earners (%)							
Total*	0.02	0.03	0.03	0.03	0.03	0.03	0.03
Manufacturing	0.02	0.03	0.03	0.02	0.02	0.02	0.02

* In private industries exclusive oil and ocean transport.

above this market share effect seems to be smaller in Norway than in most other countries but the effect on exports may have been understated in MODAG A.

On the other hand, in the short-run increased consumption demand stimulates production and employment in the sheltered industries. The net effect of higher wages on gross national product and total employment is therefore very small in MODAG A, especially in the short run. This is also the case in the Central Bureau of Statistics' quarterly model KVARTS (see Biørn, Jensen and Reymert [1985]).

Due to the long lags in the market share relations and the decrease in real investments the effects on national product and employment tend to be more negative in the long run than in the short run. As a result of the change in the composition of production against the more labour-intensive sheltered industries and increasing returns to scale in the production functions the negative percentage effect on employment is smaller than the effect on production. In the long run a rise in wage rates by 1 percent may cause a decrease in employment by 0.09 percent or about 1,300 man-years. About one-half of the decrease in employment will take place in the manufacturing industries.

A rise in government-regulated prices means both lower real disposable income and lower market shares and will cause a fall both in the national product and in total employment. An increase in transfer payments and credit variables will work in the opposite direction. The total effect of higher wage rates is therefore dependent on how much transfers, regulated prices, credit and other government controlled variables are changed. This will be further discussed in section 2.3.

2.2.6 Investments

Investments in the production of oil and natural gas, electricity supply, shipping and in the public sectors are exogenously given in the model. Together the investments in these sectors constituted more than 50 percent of total investments in gross real capital in 1984.

For most of the other industries output is the main explanatory variable of investments.[8] However, in primary industries and in the most export-oriented industries, operating surplus seems to be of great importance. Rather than the level of investments it is assumed that operating surplus and credit supply primarily affect the speed of adjustment. This aspect is strengthened by imperfect capital markets and the existence of credit rationing during the period from which the data for estimation is taken. Relative factor prices seem to have some effect in labour intensive sectors.

Gross investments in dwellings are determined by lagged real disposable incomes for wage earners and the self employed, the relative price between new houses and other consumer goods and the nominal rate of interest in commercial banks.

As can be seen from table 2.1, higher wage rates result in a substantial decrease in the operating surplus. This effect will tend to reduce investments. In section 2.2.5 it was pointed out that production will decrease in the exposed industries as a result of higher wage rates. This effect will also contribute to lower investments in the exposed industries. In the sheltered

---

[8] The investment relations are documented in Bergan, Cappelen and Jensen [1985].

industries the positive effect of greater production seems to outweigh the negative effect of a smaller operating surplus in the short run. In the long run, however, production seems to decline in the sheltered industries too, and investments will also decrease in these sectors. Because of a rise in disposable income in households, investments in houses will increase. In addition, higher wage rates result in a substitution from labour to capital in some industries.

The overall result of higher wage rates on total investments seems to be negative. In the short run the total result is very small as some effects imply higher investments, while others work in the opposite direction. As a result of losses in market shares for exposed industries the negative effect on total investments seems to be larger in the long run. The fall in investments seems to reach a bottom after five years as capital is adapted to the new level of production.

In MODAG A prices of agricultural products are assumed to be controlled by the central government. A rise in these prices will therefore lead to a higher operating surplus and higher investments in these industries. After some years this positive effect on total investments of a rise in government regulated prices will be balanced by a decline in investments in the other industries as a result of a rise in electricity prices, lower private consumption and a loss in market shares. An increase in transfer payments and a more expansive credit policy will cause an increase in investments.

2.2.7 Export surplus

Both because of higher consumption demand and because of reduced market shares for import competing industries imports increase as a result of higher wage rates. Due to the fall in investments and the reduced positive effect on private consumption, the increase in imports seems to be smaller in the long run than in the short run. As pointed out in section 2.2.3 exports will decrease as a result of an increase in wage rates. The resulting effect on the export surplus is negative, but the effect is smaller in the long run because of the declining growth in imports. Higher export prices also tend to reduce the fall in the export surplus.

Higher government regulated prices cause imports to decrease in the long run because the real income effect via private consumption outweigh the effect of a loss of market shares. As the reduction in imports is stronger than the reduction in exports and as export prices get higher, an increase in agricultural prices and electricity prices results in a higher export surplus. An increase in transfer payments and credit variables will stimulate domestic demand and imports and lead to a fall in the export surplus.

2.3 A simultaneous change in wage rates and government controlled variables

Because of the simultaneity of income settlements as pointed out in section 2.1, it will be of interest to study the result of a parallel increase in incomes for wage-earners, pensioners, farmers and fishermen. This is also done by the Ministry of Finance (Lunde [1984]) in connection with the Revised National Budget 1984 (St. meld. nr. 88 [1983–84]). A problem in carrying out such a calculation is that it is very difficult to know exactly to what degree and how fast the central authorities will adjust the variables under their control. The central authorities may have many goals which they are trying to fullfil and the different goals may be in conflict with each other.

One of the frequent goals of the central authorities is to influence the development of the income distribution. The aim of the calculations presented in this section is to illustrate the effects of a change in wage rates when the income distribution is constant. Apart from a parallel increase in government transfers and wage rates, economic policy is assumed to be unchanged in these calculations, i.e., the real levels of government consumption and investments and government regulated prices and credit variables are kept constant.

To maintain the real values of government regulated prices and nominal credit variables in the calculations presented below we have assumed that these variables increase in accordance with the expected long run increase in the consumer price index. Because of lags in the price equations this may overstate the increase in government regulated prices and nominal credit variables in the short run.

Because of progressive income taxes, higher wage rates mean higher average tax rates in the short run. In the longer run it seems more realistic that the real tax rates are kept unchanged. This is not done in the calculations presented below, and the presented effects may therefore be too contractive in the long run. Nominal interest rates are also included in the relations for user costs of capital and the demand for housing. As inflation increases in the short run constant nominal interest rates mean that the effects may be too expansionary. In the long run, however, when prices again change in accordance with the reference scenario, this weakness is of no importance.

Given the assumptions discussed above we have in table 2.5 presented the effects of a 1 percent increase in wage rates combined with an increase in government transfers of 1 percent and an increase in government regulated prices and nominal credit variables of 0.5 percent as this increase seems to be in accordance with the resulting effect on the consumption price index in the long run. Real disposable income for households will increase as a result of this and thereby cause higher private consumption. The higher prices for Norwegian commodities lead to a fall in market shares both on the export and the domestic markets. In the short run the effects on total production and employment are dominated by the positive income effects, and for the same reason total investments seem to increase. However, in the longer run the losses in market shares will cause lower production and employment in the exposed industries and together with lower profitability the fall in production will cause investments in these industries to decrease. As a consequence, the initially positive effect on private consumption, production and employment in the sheltered industries will also be reduced. In the long run it seems that the positive income effect for households on private consumption and thus on total production and employment is slightly less than the negative market share effect. However, taking the uncertainty of the estimated equations into account, the impact on total employment in the model may be characterized as negligible.

The connection between changes in wages and employment seems to be somewhat smaller in MODAG A than in similar macroeconomic models in almost every comparable country. In most of the models in the United Kingdom[9] and the other Nordic countries[10] an increase in wage rates by 1 percent is estimated to reduce employment by 0.2–0.3 percent. In the Treasury-model of The United Kingdom the elasticity is, however, as small as −0.06.

The tendency to larger negative effects on employment in the macroeconomic models in other countries may be due to:

– A large share of Norwegian exports is very little influenced by changes in wage rates. About two-thirds of the Norwegian exports are exogenous in MODAG A, and crude oil, natural gas and ocean transport constitute a large part of this. As the rest of the exporting industries are rather capital, energy, and import intensive wage costs constitute

---

[9] See M.S. Andrews et al. [1984] for a survey of the connection between changes in wage rates and employment in the macroeconomic models of the United Kingdom.

[10] See Lauritzen, Jansson and Sourama's contributions in this volume for a presentation of the impacts of a change in wage rates in the macroeconomic models in Denmark, Sweden and Finland, respectively.

only a small part of the total costs in these industries.

- An increase in wage rates seems to have a stronger effect on real incomes in households and thereby private consumption in MODAG A than in most of the models in other countries. This is probably due to a larger effect of an increase in transfers in MODAG A and a greater difference between the marginal propensity to consume out of wage incomes than out of operating surplus than in the other models. Compared to the models in The United Kingdom the effects on consumer prices of an increase in wages are smaller in MODAG A as the Norwegian economy is more open.

- Supply-side effects seem to be incorporated in the other models to a somewhat larger degree than in MODAG A as exports and imports are dependent on the operating surplus in the exposed industries. The only supply-side effects in the version of MODAG A presented in this paper are effects from changes in productivity and capacity utilization on product prices.

- The demand effects of an increase in investments are, however, modelled in MODAG A, and compared to the other models more of the investments in sheltered industries and in dwellings seem to be endogenous. These relations work in a positive direction regarding employment, especially in the short run, as investments in these sectors are dominated by the positive income effects.

- The demand elasticity of employment with respect to output is less than 1 in MODAG A, even in the long run. Even though this result is not in accordance with the textbooks, an elasticity less than 1 seems to be quite common in most empirical work.[11]

Both the real-income effects, which tend to increase domestic demand and imports, and the loss in market shares both on the domestic market and the export market, will have a negative impact on the export surplus. Due to the fall in investments and the reduced effect on private consumption the increase in imports and the fall in export surplus become smaller over time. After 10 years the effect on the export surplus is more negative again as exports decline more than imports because of long lags in the price and demand equations for exports. The fall in the export surplus of about 500 millions Nkr after 10 years constitutes about 0.09 percent of GDP.

---

[11] See Bergland and Cappelen [1981] and Stølen [1983a] for a more detailed discussion of this subject and an overview of the literature in this field. Drèze and Modigliani report a short-run output elasticity of employment of 0.3 for Belgium.

Table 2.5: Effects of a 1 percent increase in wage rates combined with an increase in government transfers of 1 percent and an increase in government regulated prices and nominal credit variables of 0.5 percent.

	1984	1985	1986	1987	1988	1990	1993
Changes in constant prices (%):							
Private consumption	0.48	0.51	0.43	0.38	0.36	0.33	0.32
Gross investments*	0.21	0.24	0.04	−0.14	−0.20	−0.17	−0.10
Manufacturing	0.20	−0.31	−0.87	−1.19	−1.15	−0.77	−0.59
Exports**	−0.09	−0.09	−0.20	−0.25	−0.29	−0.31	−0.36
Imports	0.27	0.29	0.26	0.21	0.21	0.20	0.18
GDP*	0.21	0.20	0.11	0.04	0.01	−0.01	−0.03
Manufacturing	0.01	−0.06	−0.20	−0.28	−0.33	−0.38	−0.43
Changes in price indices (%):							
Private consumption	0.17	0.26	0.34	0.39	0.43	0.47	0.49
Gross investments	0.20	0.30	0.37	0.41	0.44	0.46	0.47
Exports**	0.09	0.16	0.19	0.23	0.26	0.30	0.34
GDP	0.29	0.39	0.45	0.51	0.55	0.57	0.57
Changes in current prices, Million Nkr.							
Wage costs	2225	2437	2522	2715	2885	3323	4168
Operating surplus	−784	−487	−531	−491	−412	−397	−446
Manufacturing	−292	−210	−246	−119	−245	−275	−346
Export surplus	−415	−459	−457	−367	−361	−392	−519
Govt. budget surplus	−81	217	118	50	5	−36	−108
Changes in employment, wage earners, 1000 man-years							
Total	0.58	0.68	0.31	−0.05	−0.28	−0.44	−0.49
Manufacturing	−0.01	−0.16	−0.46	−0.60	−0.57	−0.57	−0.57
Changes in employment, wage earners (%)							
Total*	0.04	0.06	0.02	−0.00	−0.02	−0.03	−0.03
Manufacturing	−0.00	−0.05	−0.10	−0.15	−0.17	−0.17	−0.17

* In private industries exclusive oil and ocean transport
** Exclusive oil, natural gas and services

2.4   Balance-of-payments constraint

For countries with a deficit or only a small surplus on the balance of payments a reduction in the export surplus following higher wage rates may force the government to make the economic policy more contractive. If the effects of a more contractive policy are included, higher wage rates will have a more negative effect on employment than what follows from the direct elasticities in tables 2.1 and 2.5.

In 1985 Norway had a balance of payments surplus of 26.6 billion Nkr, about 5.7 percent of GDP, but as a result of the fall in oil revenues Norway may experience a large deficit in 1986. Because of the fall in the oil revenues it has been argued that the balance of payments is too dependent on these incomes, and if they stay low for several years this may cause severe problems. As a consequence of this it has been argued that lower wage increases are necessary to increase profitability and production in traditionally exposed industries (especially manufacturing).

If domestic costs continue to grow faster than among our competitors abroad it may be necessary to lower demand to maintain the balance of payments. As can be seen from the analysis in Bergan [in this volume] the impacts on employment for a given change in the balance of payments induced by a change in fiscal policy are highly dependent on how this change takes place.

The elasticity of employment from a change in wage rates may be larger when wage rates are assumed to increase less than they do in the reference scenario compared with a situation when they increase more. The reason for this is that the government may carry out a change in policy which has only a small effect on employment when the aim is to improve the balance of payments, while a change in policy which has a large effect on employment is carried out when there is unemployment and the balance of payments leaves room for a more expansionary policy.

To get a "neutral" elasticity we have in table 2.6 chosen to present the effect on employment of a parallel change in private consumption, government employment, government purchases of commodities and services and government investments. To illustrate that the elasticities may be dependent on the choice of fiscal policy we have however presented the isolated elasticities of a change in income taxes and government expenditures respectively.

From the table it can be seen that the elasticity between employment and wage rates under the assumption of a parallel increase in all incomes is estimated to be -0.16 in the long run when the balance of payments is

Table 2.6: Elasticities of total employment keeping the balance of payments constant.

Government Policy	Wage rates		Real wage rates		Wage rates and government controlled variables		Real wage rates and government controlled variables	
	1 year	10 years	1 year	10 years	1 year	10 years	1 year	10 years
A parallel decrease in government expenditures	−0.30	−0.19	−0.34	−0.34	−0.61	−0.32	−0.60	−0.62
Increased income taxes	−0.00	−0.04	−0.00	−0.08	−0.02	−0.09	−0.03	−0.17
A parallel decrease in government expenditures and private consumption	−0.10	−0.09	−0.11	−0.16	−0.22	−0.16	−0.22	−0.32

maintained by a parallel decrease in private consumption and government expenditures. This means than an increase in wage growth by 1 percentage point above the reference scenario may lead to a decrease in employment of about 3,000 man-years in the long run. The effect in the short run is even larger mainly because a change in government employment has a large direct effect on employment while the effect on the balance of payments is more sluggish. Too much attention should not be given to this point as the balance of payments is a more binding constraint in the long run than in the short run.

The corresponding long-run elasticity in the Danish model ADAM is estimated to be about -0.4 (see Lauritzen [1987]). As it is not clear how the fiscal policy is changed to maintain the balance of payments in that paper, it is, however, difficult to make a direct comparison. For the Swedish model AMMA Jansson and Olofsson [1987] reports a long run employment elasticity of -0.3 when the balance of payments is maintained by a decrease in private consumption. The corresponding elasticity in MODAG A is estimated to be close to -0.1.

The results for the real wage elasticities of employment, keeping the balance of payment constant by parallel decrease in government expenditures and private consumption, may be compared to estimates for similarly defined elasticities reported by Drèze and Modigliani [1981]. Their results for Belgium are in the order of -0.1 to -0.2 in the short run and, according to our estimates, -0.3 to -0.5 in the long run, keeping capacity constant.

The estimates are remarkably similar, and the reasons why the elasticities for Norway are a bit smaller than those for Belgium (in absolute values) in the long run is probably the same as those outlined in section 2.3. In addition the difference between the short run and long run output elasticities of employment seems to be larger in Belgium than in Norway.

When capacity is changed Drèze and Modigliani report an elasticity about -2. The extra effects of a change in capacity are in their calculations assumed to take place through scrapping of real capital and appear as pure supply side effects as production is decreased through a fall in exports and an increase in imports. In MODAG A no comparable elasticity exists because the effect of a change in capacity on production supply is not yet included in the model. There is, however, a small supply effect in MODAG A as prices on domestic produced products are assumed to be dependent on productivity and in some industries on the utilization of capacity. The demand effect via investments is also incorporated in the model.

Attempts to estimate a supply model for exports of the three staple commodities: paper and paper products, industrial chemicals and metals were not successful. Although the "supply-side-effects" may be of some importance in Norway too, it does not seem likely that these effects are as large as reported by Drèze and Modigliani. In the Swedish and Danish models, supply side effects are incorporated in the same way as they were done by Drèze and Modigliani, but the elasticities between employment and real wages are only reported to be as large as −0.75 and −0.86 (−1.5 in ADAM when only endogenous employment is taken into account), respectively. As a consequence of the aspects mentioned in section 2.3 it is likely that the employment elasticity in MODAG A would be smaller than in AMMA and ADAM even if the supply-side effects were incorporated in the model.

3.   Effects of changes in exchange rates

3.1   Institutional background

As the Norwegian economy may be characterized as small and open it may be reasonable to assume that no change in foreign prices, measured in foreign currency, will take place due to a change in the Norwegian exchange rates exchange rates. In the calculations presented in this chapter we have therefore assumed that a devaluation of the Norwegian kroner (Nkr) will lead to a similar increase in import prices and foreign competitive prices measured in Nkr. Although the Norwegian economy is small and open this assumption may be discussed, but we have done little empirical work on this subject. The figures presented in the tables below should therefore be interpreted as a result of a change in world market prices of 1 percent instead of a devaluation of 1 percent. It is also a matter of discussion how fast a change in exchange rates will influence import prices. In this paper we have assumed that import prices will be changed immediately, but since some contracts may be made in Nkr this may be unrealistic.

In addition to the direct effects caused by higher prices on foreign products, wage rates may increase if the wage earners demand compensation for the devaluation. As wage rates are exogenous in MODAG A we have to make an assumption outside the model about how much they will change when we want to look at the total effect of a devaluation. This is further discussed in section 3.3. If wage rates are compensated it is not unrealistic to assume that transfer payments and some of the regulated prices are changed too. This will then cause the same effects as those outlined in section 2.

3.2   Effects on endogenous variables in MODAG A

3.2.1   Prices, import shares, exports and private consumption

Both the variable unit costs and the competitive price index influence the prices of Norwegian products. The relative importance of the two factors is dependent on the size of the market share and on the homogeneity of the Norwegian and foreign products. The change in the competitive prices index is important in the determination of export prices and of domestic prices of commodities produced and marketed domestically under strong foreign competition. As higher import prices also mean higher costs, a devaluation results in an increase of the prices of Norwegian products measured in Nkr.

When wage rates are held constant, the rise in the prices of Norwegian products tends to be smaller than the rise in competitive prices. As a result import shares will fall while exports will increase. If import prices are decreased measured in foreign currency as a result of devaluation this means that the fall in import shares is overestimated in the model. When wage rates are kept constant the increase in costs will not be as large as the increase in product prices, and the exposed industries will experience higher profitability.

The impacts of changes in world market prices are presented in table 3.1. The effect of higher import prices on the consumer price index is distributed over a period of time, but most of the effect has appeared after only two years.

Because export prices are highly dependent on the prices of competing products measured in foreign currency the impact on export prices measured in Nkr of a devaluation is rather large.[12] This is partly also the case for the price of investment products, and in addition to the effect caused by the price increase on competing products, investment prices are also increased as a result of higher input costs in the industries producing investment commodities.

As about two-thirds of Norwegian exports are exogenous in MODAG A we have chosen to present the percentage effect on exports of commodities exclusive oil and natural gas. This elasticity is also rather small because the prices of some of the most important ordinary export commodities are highly dependent on competitive prices. As the supply-side effects caused by a higher operating surplus are small in the model the increase in exports

---

[12] The export prices of crude oil and natural gas and the prices of services from ocean transport measured in Nkr are assumed to increase by 1 percent as a result of a devaluation by 1 percent.

may have been underestimated. Due to lags and the effects of increased capacity utilization in the first year in the export price equations the effect on exports in the second year is smaller than in the first. In the long run the lags in the export demand equations cause the effect on exports to be larger again.

When wages are kept constant, a devaluation results in lower private consumption due to a fall in private real disposable income. The effect on private consumption is lower in the first year than in the second as a result of the lag in the consumption function and lags in the price equations. Almost the whole effect of a devaluation on private consumption has appeared after the second year.

3.2.2   Production and employment

As in the case of changes in wage rates a devaluation has two primary effects on production and employment. These effects will, however, work in the opposite direction compared to the increase in wage rates. Due to higher market shares a devaluation of Nkr will lead to higher production in the exposed industries. On the other hand lower consumption demand results in lower production and employment in the sheltered industries when wage rates are kept constant. The net effect of a devaluation on gross national product is therefore also very small but negative in MODAG A. Due to the lag in the consumption function the effects seem to be less negative in the first year than in the second. The effect on production is smaller again after 10 years because the effect of declining investment demand almost disappears. A devaluation seems to have no significant effect on employment. Although there is a small decrease in production, employment is unchanged due to increasing returns to scale in some industries.

3.2.3   Investments

A devaluation results in a substantial increase in the operating surplus, also in real terms. This effect will tend to increase the investments. In section 3.2.2 it was pointed out that production will increase in the exposed industries, and this effect will also contribute to higher investments in these industries. On the other hand lower disposable income for households will result in lower production and investments in the sheltered industries and also lower investments in new houses.

Because of the lags in the price equations, the consumption function and investments in houses, the decline in investments will be smaller in the first year than in the second. After seven years the decline will decrease again as capital is adjusted to the new level of production in the sheltered industries while it is not adjusted yet in the exposed industries.

3.2.4   Export surplus

When wage rates are kept constant imports will decrease as a result of a devaluation both because of lower consumption and investment demand and because of reduced import shares. As exports increase because of a relatively lower price on Norwegian export products this will lead to an improvement of the export surplus. Prices of both exports and imports rise as a result of the devaluation. As import prices in foreign currency are assumed to be kept constant, import prices measured in Norwegian currency also increase by the same percent as Nkr is devalued. This is also the case for the exogenous export prices. For most manufactured products export prices will be reduced measured in foreign currency, but increased measured in Norwegian currency. Because the prices of so many of the important export commodities in MODAG A are assumed to be given in foreign currency, the average export price rises by 0.93 percent after 10 years as a result of a devaluation of 1 percent. Because of an export surplus in the reference scenario the price effects almost seem to balance.

In addition to the export surplus the balance of payments is dependent on the surplus in the balance of interests and transfers. The deficit in this account was about 14.5 billion Nkr in 1985, and a devaluation will therefore lead to a smaller improvement in the balance of payments than in the export surplus alone.

3.3   Indirect effects caused by wage compensation

As discussed in section 3.2 a devaluation will result in higher import prices. This price increase will also cause a rise in domestic prices and improved profitability in the exposed sectors, while the increase in consumer prices will cause a fall in private real disposable income. Both these factors may cause an increase in wage rates. As they are exogenous in MODAG A we have to make an assumption outside the model about how much they will change when we want to look at the total effect of a devaluation.

As discussed in section 2.2.5 an increase in wage rates has only a minor effect on total production and employment in MODAG A. In section 3.2.2 we saw that a devaluation also seems to have only minor direct effects. We can therefore conclude that the total effect of a devaluation on total

Table 3.1: Effects of a 1 percent increase in world market prices.

	1984	1985	1986	1987	1988	1990	1993
Changes in constant prices (%):							
Private consumption	−0.25	−0.36	−0.39	−0.41	−0.42	−0.42	−0.40
Gross investments*	−0.09	−0.33	−0.44	−0.44	−0.41	−0.27	−0.09
Manufacturing	0.17	−0.04	−0.16	−0.23	−0.21	0.13	0.47
Exports**	0.21	0.03	0.11	0.12	0.14	0.15	0.22
Imports	−0.23	−0.32	−0.37	−0.37	−0.38	−0.36	−0.29
GDP*	−0.02	−0.09	−0.11	−0.12	−0.12	−0.10	−0.04
Manufacturing	0.19	0.19	0.20	0.19	0.19	0.23	0.32
Changes in price indices (%):							
Private consumption	0.31	0.38	0.41	0.43	0.45	0.47	0.46
Gross investments	0.47	0.56	0.59	0.61	0.61	0.59	0.55
Exports**	0.69	0.86	0.84	0.85	0.85	0.85	0.81
GDP	0.29	0.40	0.41	0.42	0.43	0.44	0.44
Changes in current prices, Million Nkr.							
Wage costs	25	10	4	−5	−10	4	68
Operating surplus	696	1095	1181	1286	1403	1796	2532
Manufacturing	131	442	484	536	586	700	803
Export surplus	592	883	1004	1098	1200	1456	2063
Govt. budget surplus	−41	−120	−135	−143	−143	−117	−53
Changes in employment, wage earners, 1000 man-years							
Total	0.15	0.03	−0.03	−0.09	−0.11	−0.04	0.21
Manufacturing	0.29	0.43	0.51	0.52	0.53	0.57	0.66
Changes in employment, wage earners (%)							
Total*	0.01	0.00	0.00	−0.01	−0.01	0.00	0.01
Manufacturing	0.09	0.13	0.15	0.15	0.16	0.17	0.20

* In private industries exclusive oil and ocean transport
** Exclusive oil, natural gas and services

production and employment is rather small irrespective of how large the wage compensation may be.

While an increase in wage rates causes lower production and employment in exposed industries and higher production and employment in sheltered industries, a devaluation works in the opposite direction. The degree of wage compensation may therefore influence the distribution of production and employment between industries, and this will also be of importance for the change in the export surplus.

Empirical investigations carried out recently at the Central Bureau of Statistics (see Stølen [1985]) indicate that a rise in the world market prices results after a few years in an equivalent increase in wage rates, both because of better profitability in the exposed sectors (which can be considered as wage leaders in Norway) and because of a rise in the consumer price index. This is in accordance with the Scandinavian model of inflation presented in Aukrust [1977]. If this is the case the positive short-run effect on competitiveness and employment in the exposed sectors, and the balance of payments will vanish after some years.

4.   Summary

From the model-calculations presented in this paper it can be seen that a change in wage and exchange rates has two main effects which will work in opposite directions regarding total production and employment:

I. A decrease in wage rates or a devaluation will improve competitiveness for the exposed sectors and result in larger production, employment and investments in these industries.

II. On the other hand a decrease in wage rates or a devaluation will decrease the household's real disposable income and result in larger private consumption, production, employment and investments in the sheltered industries.

In the case of a change in wage rates when the change in government controlled variables also is taken into account, the income effect seems to dominate the market share effect in the short run, while the opposite seems to be the case in the long run. Because of the missing equations in the model and the uncertainty in those equations which are already incorporated, the effects on total production and employment, both in the short and long run, of a change in wage rates may be considered as negligible. Even if we succeed in incorporating the supply-side effects, there is no reason to believe that the real income effect will be very much dominated by the competitiveness effect.

An increase in wage rates will, however, cause a deterioration in the balance of payments. If the central government feels that the balance of payments should not deteriorate, it may carry out a more contractive economic policy as a response. This will obviously reduce employment. The effect on employment of a contractive policy will depend on how the tightening is to be carried out.

A devaluation will have a positive effect on production and employment in the exposed industries and on the balance of payments in the short run. The effects on total production and employment seem to be negligible as the positive effects in the export industries are balanced by lower production and employment in the sheltered industries. In the long run it seems, however, that wage rates will be fully compensated as a result of a devaluation. A devaluation will then have no effect on competitiveness in the exposed industries, employment or balance of payments.

References

Andrews, M.J., D.N.F. Bell, P.G. Fisher, K.F. Wallis and J.D. Whitely [1984], "Models of the UK Economy and the Real Wage-Employment Debate", Discussion Paper No. 3, ESRC Macroeconomic Modelling Bureau.

Aukrust, O. [1970], "PRIM I. A Model of the Price and Income Distribution Mechanism of an Open Economy", *The Review of Income and Wealth*, *16*, 51–78.

Aukrust, O. [1977], "Inflation in an Open Economy: A Norwegian Model", in *Worldwide Inflation: Theory and Recent Experience*, ed. Krause and Salant. Washington D.C.: Brookings Institution, 109–166.

Bergan, R., Å. Cappelen and M. Jensen [1985], "Investment behaviour in Norway", paper presented at the Seminar on connections between structural changes and investment policy. Kiev, September 23–27.

Bergan, R. and Ø. Olsen [1985], "Eksporttilpasning i MODAG A", Rapporter No. 85/29 from The Central Bureau of Statistics, Oslo.

Bergan, R. [1987], "The effects of fiscal policy i MODAG A", in this volume.

Bergland, H. and Å. Cappelen [1981], "Produktivitet og sysselsetting i industrien", Rapporter No. 81/23 from The Central Bureau of Statistics, Oslo.

Biørn, E., M. Jensen and M. Reymert [1985], "KVARTS - A Quarterly Model of the Norwegian Economy", Discussion paper No. 13 from The Central Bureau of Statistics, Oslo.

Cappelen, Å, and S. Longva [1984], "The Effects of Income Settlements Analysed by the Model MODAG A", paper presented at the International Institute of Forecasters, Fourth International Symposium on Forecasting, London, July 8–11, 1984.

Cappelen, Å and S. Longva [1987], "MODAG A: A Medium Term Annual Macroeconomic Model of the Norwegian Economy", in this volume.

Coe, D.T. [1985], "Nominal Wages, the NAIRU and Wage Flexibility", OECD Economic Studies No. 5, 87–126.

Drèze, J.H. and F. Modigliani [1981], "The trade-off between real wages and employment in an open economy (Belgium)", *European Economic Review, 15,* 1–40.

Jansson, L. and T. Olofsson [1987], "An aggregate model for medium-term analysis (AMMA)", in this volume.

Lauritzen, F. [1987], "Real wage, exchange rate and employment in the Danish economy", in this volume.

Lindbeck, A. and D.J. Snower [1985], "Explanations of Unemployment", *Oxford Review of Economic Policy, 1,* 34–59.

Lunde, G. [1984], "Virkninger av lavere lønnsvekst — Beregninger med MODAG A", unpublished note dated May 16, The Ministry of Finance, Oslo.

NOU [1983], "Om grunnlaget for inntektsoppgjørene 1983", Norges offentlige utredninger No. 23, Oslo.

Rødseth, A. [1985], "Dynamics of Wages and Trade in a Fixed-Exchange-Rate-Economy", *Scandinavian Journal of Economics, 87*, 120–136.

Sourama, H. [1987], "KESSU III: The effects of wage increases and fiscal policy", in this volume.

St. meld. Nr. 88 [1983–84], "Revidert Nasjonalbudsjett 1984", Ministry of Finance, Oslo.

Stølen, N.M. [1983a], "Etterspørsel etter arbeidskraft i norske industrinæringer", Rapporter No. 83/29 from The Central Bureau of Statistics, Oslo.

Stølen, N.M. [1983b], "Importandeler og relative priser. En MODAG-rapport", Rapporter No. 83/33 from The Central Bureau of Statistics, Oslo.

Stølen, N.M. [1985], "Faktorer bak lønnsveksten", Økonomiske analyser No. 9 from The Central Bureau of Statistics, Oslo.

Utredningsutvalget [1966], "Innstilling II fra Utredningsutvalget for inntektsoppgjørene 1966", The Prime Minister's Office, Oslo.

Macroeconomic Medium-Term Models in the Nordic Countries
O. Bjerkholt and J. Rosted (Editors)
© *Elsevier Science Publishers B.V. (North-Holland), 1987*

An Econometric Model
for
Medium-Term Analysis (EMMA)

by

Thomas Olofsson

Ministry of Finance,
Stockhom, Sweden

1. Introduction

Medium-Term Surveys have been carried out since the early fifties at the
Ministry of Finance in Sweden. A major aim of these surveys has been to
assess the potential supply of the economy in a medium-term perspective
and how it can accommodate different demand developments. Furthermore, different policy strategies to accomplish overall policy goals, such as
full employment, price stability, high economic growth and external balance, have been analyzed. The models used for medium-term analysis have
been strongly influenced by these purposes.

EMMA (Econometric Model for Medium-Term Analysis)[1] is an input-
output model used primarily for answering such questions as how much will
be produced in various industries and what the demand will be for different
final uses. However, the model can also be used to set levels of private or

---

[1] EMMA was initially developed by Carl Johan Åberg for the 1970 Medium-Term
Survey (MS 70). See Åberg, C. J., *Plan och prognos, LU 70*, Bilaga 9, SOU 1971:70.
The model has subsequently been further developed and revised at the Ministry of
Finance. The present documentation is based on an earlier presentation of EMMA
in Bilaga 17, LU 84, SOU 1984:7.

government consumption and price and wage growth rates consistent with external balance and full employment at some future point in time (the projection year). EMMA includes estimated equations of exports, imports, prices and distribution of total consumption.

EMMA is formulated entirely in real terms. It has no money or asset markets, so problems connected with things like budget deficits or inflation cannot be satisfactorily dealt with in the model. The model is static, implying that adjustment over time cannot be studied. The model is not particularly suitable for policy simulations or comparative static analyses. The model can be solved for a base year and for one or more projection years.

In section 2 the input-output equations are presented. The determination of final demand is also briefly dealt with, but discussed in more detail in sections 3, 4, 5 and 6. The determination of prices and the labour market are treated in sections 7 and 8 respectively. A brief summary completes the paper. The Appendix contains lists of industries, private consumption items and government purposes.

2.   The Model

The present model overview describes an open economy with 24 industries. Production also takes place in central and local government sectors. Industries, households and government sectors demand goods and services from domestic and foreign industries either as intermediate goods or for final demand.

In the overall balance-of-resource equation gross outputs at purchasers' prices from 23 industries equal the sum of demand for domestically produced intermediate input investment, consumption and exports. Formally we write this as

$$q = \Omega q + c + i + g + x - m \,, \qquad (2.1)$$

where q is the 23×1 vector of gross production in industries, while Ω is the 23×23 input-output matrix, the elements, ω_{ij}, of which denote the amount of commodity i needed to produce one unit of commodity j, c is private consumption, i is private investments, g is government net demand (demand less sales of goods and services) for investment and consumption purposes, x is exports and m is imports. These latter variables are, of course, also 23×1 vectors. (Sector 24, foreign tourist services, is not included in the overall balance equation).

Total final demand we denote by the vector d, i.e.,

$$d = c + i + g + x - m. \tag{2.2}$$

How is d determined? We first write final demand (2.2) in more detail as

$$d = \xi c^v + \phi i^d + \varphi g^i + r g^c + x - m. \tag{2.3}$$

The distribution of private consumption over 11 different consumption items is determined by relative prices and total consumption expenditure. The demand for commodity items, c^v, is transformed by the 23×11 matrix, ξ, to demand for deliveries from the 23 industries. Private investments, including investment in stock, are exogenously determined for all industrial sectors. ϕ is a 23×23 matrix transforming investment demand, i^d, to demand for deliveries. Central and local government (exogenous) investment demand, g^i, for 8 and 7 different purposes, respectively (i.e., a total of 15 items) are transformed by a 23×15 matrix, φ. The same applies to government (exogenous) net consumption, g^c, and the corresponding matrix, r. Exports are estimated as functions of world market demand and relative prices for each of the 23 industries. The import demands are also estimated as functions of relative prices, domestic demand and variables reflecting domestic import competing conditions.

Value added at purchasers' values for an industry, y_j, is defined as

$$y_j = q_j \left(1 - \sum_{i=1}^{23} \omega_{ij} \right). \tag{2.4}$$

The sum of final demand for deliveries from industries equals total value added produced in industries. To obtain total GDP we must add value added produced in the government sector and the balance of foreign tourist services $(x_{24} - m_{24})$. This gives us

$$GDP = \sum_{i=1}^{23} y_i + \sum_{j=1}^{15} g_j^{va} + x_{24} - m_{24}. \tag{2.5}$$

Now, the matrices Ω, ξ, ϕ, φ and r are all exogenous. For the projection year these matrices are set according to historical values, informed guesses or subject to trend projections. The values of the elements in the input-output matrix Ω are crucial for the solution of the model. Other important exogenous variables are labour productivities, the average wage rate, the world market price level, import prices, and total real private and government consumption for the projection year.

Given these exogenous variables and transformation matrices, it is possible to solve the model for the vector q, i.e., the level of production in the 23 industries, and as we shall see, the prices of domestic products, export prices, unemployment and the current account.

3.   Private consumption

The model used for estimation of private consumption is the linear expenditure system[2] with habit formation, originally formulated by Stone [1954]. We begin with a general linear formulation of demand equations, i.e.,

$$p_i q_i = \beta_i C + \sum_{j=1}^{n} \beta_{ij} p_j \qquad i = 1, \ldots, n, \tag{3.1}$$

where q_i is quantity demanded of commodity i, p_i is the price of commodity i, C is total nominal expenditure, $\sum_i p_i q_i$, and the β's are constants.

We now impose three theoretical restrictions, namely: adding up, homogeneity of degree zero and symmetry.[3]   The only form of (3.1) that satisfies these restrictions is the linear expenditure system,

$$p_i q_i = p_i \gamma_i + \beta_i \left(C - \sum_k p_k \gamma_k \right), \quad \sum_k \beta_k = 1 \qquad i = 1, \ldots, n, \tag{3.2}$$

where the γ's are constants. As is well known, these restrictions are not necessary — at an aggregate level — for any theoretical reason. They are introduced for the purpose of increasing the degrees of freedom.

To get an idea of the implications of the restrictions imposed, let us note that the expenditure function associated with (3.2) is

$$e(u, p) = \sum_k p_k \gamma_k + u \prod_k p_k^{\beta_k}, \tag{3.3}$$

---

[2] For an overview of this system, see Deaton and Muellbauer [1980].

[3] The additivity requirement implies that the weighted average of income elasticities of demand is unity, the weights being the relative shares of each good in total expenditure. Homogeneity of degree zero means that a proportional change in prices and income leaves demand unchanged. Symmetry implies that the cross-price derivatives of the Hicksian (compensated) demand functions are symmetric.

where $e(u, p)$ is the minimum expenditure needed to reach a given utility level u at prices p and Π is the multiplication operator. We know that the expenditure function must be concave in p. This requires that all β_i are nonnegative and C no less than $\sum_k p_k \gamma_k$ so that $q_i \geq \gamma_i$, for all i. If this does not hold, (3.2) cannot be derived from constrained utility maximization.

The parameters γ_i are often interpreted as minimum required quantities. The expenditures $p_i \gamma_i$ are made first, leaving a "residual" to be allocated between commodities in fixed proportions β_i. This is reflected in the expenditure function as a fixed-cost element $\sum_k p_k \gamma_k$.

EMMA uses a version of (3.2) where the parameter γ_i is equal to $\alpha_i c_{i,t-1}$, whereby the "required" quantities γ_i can be interpreted as a habitual factor in demand. The parameter α_i is a measure of the strength of the habitual factor and t denotes time. Demand functions are estimated for 11 commodity items, such as clothing, housing services, energy, food, etc. Goods in each commodity group are assumed to have zero cross-price elasticities, so that the demand for each good in the group can be obtained by a constant distribution vector. The system of consumption equations in EMMA can now be written as

$$c_j^v = \alpha_j^v c_{j,t-1}^v + \frac{\beta_j^v}{p_j^v} \left(C - \sum_{k=1}^{11} p_k^v \alpha_k^v c_{k,t-1}^v \right) \qquad j = 1, \ldots, 11 \,,$$
$$\sum_j \beta_j^v = 1 \,,$$

(3.4)

where c_j^v is consumption demand for commodity group j, α_j^v is the habitual factor, β_j^v is the marginal expenditures propensity and p_j^v is the price of commodity j.[4]

Prices of the commodities are determined by the price block described below. The total volume of consumption expenditure, $\sum_j c_j^v$, i.e., the value of expenditures in the prices of a base year, is determined exogenously.[5] Thus, our submodel calculates demand for commodity groups, given real total consumption expenditures and prices.

---

[4] In EMMA, (3.4) is estimated as a per capita relation. This implies that the resulting demand must be multiplied by the size of the population. In this presentation we simply include this multiplicative factor in the matrix, Ξ, defined above.

[5] In applications of aggregate models such as EMMA, volume variables such as q are really volume variables measured in the constant prices of a base year. This implies that price variables are normalized to be unity in the base year.

The calculations are made according to the following procedure. The real value of total expenditures is exogenously determined for the projection year. But in (3.4) we need nominal expenditures, C, for the latter year (in current prices). These are obtained by multiplying exogenous real expenditures by a price level P. The price level, P, for the projection year is obtained from the price block. Since a lagged consumption variable is an argument in equation (3.4), we must calculate this variable for each consecutive year between the base year and the projection year in order to obtain the consumption distribution of the projection year. Assuming constant growth rates of the variables, prices and real aggregate consumption are calculated by interpolation for each consecutive year. Applying (3.4) we can determine demand for each commodity group year per year.

Finally, it is necessary to transform demand for each group of commodities to demand for deliveries from our 23 industries. We have

$$c = \xi c^v . \tag{3.5}$$

4.   Private investments

Private investment demand by investing industry (including investment in stocks), i^d, is exogenously determined for each of 23 industries and transformed to demand for deliveries by

$$i = \phi i^d . \tag{4.1}$$

5.   Government

Total government net demand for deliveries from industries is the sum of government investment, and net consumption not produced within the government sector itself. Net consumption is total demand for deliveries less sales of goods and services. We begin with the consumption component.

First, a base level of consumption for different purposes is calculated as to a "minimal" level, based on decisions already made and basic social requirements, g^{b_1}. To this one may add an amount of consumption, g^{b_2}, designed for special purposes, e.g., increases in childcare facilities. These are vectors representing demand for deliveries for eight purposes (final uses) such as defense, education, health services, etc., at both central and local government levels. As local government does not include defense there are 8 plus 7, i.e., 15, different government expenditure items in total.

Second, there is leeway for an incremental demand of deliveries above the basic requirements. Formally, we represent this by the total amount of expenditures above the basic level, G, and a constant 15×1 vector, γ^u, specifying in what proportions an increment in total demand for deliveries are distributed among different purposes. The product, $\gamma^u G$, is then a vector of "extra" demand for different purposes above the base level. We can thus write gross demand (including sales), g^d as

$$g^d = g^b + \gamma^u G \qquad j = 1, \ldots, 15, \tag{5.1}$$

where g^b is the sum of g^{b_1} and g^{b_2}.

The sale of goods and services, g_j^s, is determined as an exogenous proportion of demand for deliveries and wage costs less capital depreciation, $\delta_j g_j^s$. Formally, we write this for each type of final use as

$$g_j^s = \frac{P_j}{1 - \delta_j} \left(g_j^d + w_j L_j^g \right) \qquad j = 1, \ldots, 15, \tag{5.2}$$

where P is the exogenously calculated share of public sales, δ the rate of physical depreciation of capital, w the wage level (including employers' fees and indirect taxes) and L_j^g the employment level in government production for purpose j.

Thus, government net consumption demand for consumption purposes, g^c, can now simply be written as the difference $g^d - g^s$.

Next, government investment demand is an exogenously given vector, g^i, describing demand for deliveries for each final use exemplified above. This demand is transformed to demand for deliveries. We can now express total government net demand for deliveries, as

$$g = \varphi g^i + r(g^d - g^s). \tag{5.3}$$

Equation (5.3) describes total government demand for goods and services produced in the 23 industries. It gives us the vector g that is needed in the balance-of-resource equation (2.1).

We noted in section 2 that we must include value added produced in the government sector to obtain GDP. Value added produced for final use j in the government sector, g_j^{va}, is equal to wage expenditures (including indirect taxes). To obtain gross value added one must add capital depreciation, $\delta_j \left(g_j^{va} + g_j^d \right)$. This gives us for each type of purpose j,

$$g_j^{va} = \frac{1}{1 - \delta_j} \left(\delta_j g_j^d + w_j L_j^g \right) \qquad j = 1, \ldots, 15 \,,$$

where δ_j is the rate of physical depreciation of capital.

Finally, the total amount of government consumption, g^{tc} is defined as the sum of value added in the government sector and net demand for deliveries, g^c. Formally, we can write this as

$$g^{tc} = \sum_{j=1}^{15} \left(g_j^{va} + g_j^c \right) \,. \qquad (5.4)$$

6.   The current account

The current account, ca, is the difference between the export value of goods and services, $p^x \cdot x$, and the import value of goods and services, $p^m \cdot m$, plus the net foreign transfers, T^f (interest payments included). We write this as

$$ca = p^x \cdot x - p^m \cdot m + T^f \,, \qquad (6.1)$$

where p^x and p^m are price vectors and x and m the export and import vectors, respectively.

Exports are assumed to be a function of world demand (depending on world income) and relative prices, i.e., firms are facing a negatively sloped demand curve with an intercept depending on world income. The general model applied to estimation of exports for the 23 industries is described by the following equations.[6]

$$\ln x_i = \ln x_i^c + \ln x_i^w + \sum_{r=0}^{1} \alpha_{ir}^x \ln \left(p_i^x / p_i^w \right)_{t-r}$$
$$+ \sum_{r=1}^{2} \beta_{ir}^x \ln(1 - \pi_i)_{t-r}^{-1} \qquad i = 1, \ldots, 23 \,, \qquad (6.2)$$

---

[6] The export and import functions are derived and estimated by the National Institute of Economic Research. See "Export och import av varor", LU 84, Bilaga 14, SOU 1984:7.

where x^w is world market demand (depending primarily on world income and determined outside the model), x^c is a correction factor due to changes such as trade-liberalization or protectionism, p^w is the world price level and the last variable is an (exogenously determined) profit variable equal to 1 over 1 minus the gross share of capital in value added, π.

Exports are thus a function of the world market demand and Sweden's competitive position. In the basic industries such as steel, mining and engineering, the profit variable is used as a proxy for supply conditions. For some of the goods-producing industries, conditions outside the model other than the world market demand are of greater importance. This applies, for instance, to agriculture and sheltered food industries. In these cases exports are entirely exogenously determined. Thus, we note that for many industries some or all of the explanatory variables are excluded from the estimated equation.

Domestic demand (depending on income) and relative prices are the main determinants of imports. The general model can be written as

$$\ln m_i = \ln m_i^c + \ln m_i^y + \sum_{r=0}^{2} \alpha_{ir}^m \ln(p_i^{gh}/p_i^m)_{t-r}$$
$$+ \sum_{r=0}^{1} \beta_{ir}^m \ln(1 - \pi_i)_{t-r}^{-1} + \sum_{r=0}^{1} \gamma_{ir}^m \ln CU_{i,t-r} \quad i = 1, \dots, 23, \tag{6.3}$$

where m^c is a correction factor, m^y is a demand factor (indicator constructed as a weighted sum of the contents of imports in the input deliveries to the 23 industries and demand for private and government consumption, investment and export), p^m is the import price, p^{gh} is the domestic price, CU is the (exogenously determined) capacity utilization and π is the rate of profits as defined above. Equation (6.3) is estimated for most, but not all, of the 23 industrial sectors.

The variables linked to the supply side of import competing industries, the capacity utilization and the profit variable, are included in the import function of 7 industries. Further, in forestry, the rubber products industry and in the textile and clothing sector, the import volumes are entirely exogenously determined. The same also applies to the balance of foreign tourist service, i.e., the net of x_{24} - m_{24} is determined outside the model.

The balance of transfers (including interest payments) remains to be determined. The transfers are divided into five groups, for which separate exogenous assessments are made in current prices. These groups are foreign aid, private transfers, interest payments (including a correction entry), other transfers and a residual (excluding capital gains).[7]

7.   Prices and wages

Relative prices are included in the equations for the distribution of consumption and for the current account. Consequently, we need the price vector p^v and the consumer price P in the consumption function, the vectors p^x and p^w in the export function and the vectors p^m and p^{qh} in the import function. The world market prices, p_i^w, and the import prices, p_i^m, are exogenously set for each sector.

The theoretical foundations of the model used for estimating export prices, p^x, and product prices at purchasers' values, p^q, (the latter needed for the calculation of domestic prices, p^{gh}, used as arguments in the import function) are presented in Forslund and Lindh [1984].[8] Let us here just give a brief outline of the model.

The theoretical framework is an aggregate micro based model of the firm, designed for studies of price adjustments to supply and demand shocks. The market is assumed to be characterized by monopolistic competition. Thus, the firm is confronted with a negatively sloped demand curve. This assumption makes it possible to study market structures between the extremes of pure monopoly and perfect competition. Other crucial assumptions in the model are constant demand elasticities and firms' expectations concerning competitors' prices being based on the same sources. Further, the model is a partial one. This could be rationalized by the fact that wage formation in Sweden is quite centralized.

The equations for export prices and product prices are as follows.

$$\ln p_i^x = \alpha_i^0 + \alpha_i^1 \ln w_i + \alpha_i^2 \ln p_i^z + \alpha_i^3 \ln p_i^w \quad i = 1, \ldots, 23 \qquad (7.1)$$
$$\ln p_i^q = \beta_i^0 + \beta_i^1 \ln w_i + \beta_i^2 \ln p_i^z + \beta_i^3 \ln p_i^w \quad i = 1, \ldots, 23, \qquad (7.2)$$

where all the α_i's and β_i's are elasticities, p_i^z are the prices of intermediate goods and w_i is the hourly wage — all for sector i.[9]

An implication of the model is that the sum of the coefficients α^1, α^2, and α^3 in (7.1) must equal one. This implies that if the price elasticity

---

[7]   See Markowski (1984).

[8]   Their model is basically an application of Bruno [1979].

[9]   The world price level is constructed as a weighted index of product prices from our competing countries. Alternatively, the import price index has been used as a proxy for the world price level.

of demand approaches infinity, the coefficient of the world price level, α^3, approaches one, and the sum of the coefficients of w_j and p_j^z approaches zero. In this case the sector is a pure price taker. Finally, the relative size of α^1 and α^2 should reflect their respective cost shares in gross production. Similar considerations apply to (7.2).[10]

Equations (7.1) and (7.2) are then used in the equation for the domestic prices, p^{qh}. By definition, the value of total output must equal the sum of the value of domestically sold output (at domestic prices) and the value of export, i.e.,

$$p_i^q q_i = p_i^{qh}(q_i - x_i) + p_i^x x_i \qquad i = 1, \ldots, 23.$$ (7.3)

Thus, domestic prices can be written as

$$p_i^{qh} = (p_i^q q_i - p_i^x x_i)/(q_i - x_i) \qquad i = 1, \ldots, 23.$$ (7.4)

However, for these calculations to be possible we need the vectors w and p^z. First, we obtain the hourly wage rate by industry, w_j, by multiplying the (exogenous) average wage per hour, $\bar{w}$, by a vector, λ,

$$w = \lambda \bar{w}$$ (7.5)

where w is a 39×1 vector. The first 24 elements refer to the industrial sectors (including foreign tourist services) and the last 15 refer to government production. These latter wage levels are used in the calculation of government value-added.

Second, by definition the value of total deliveries of intermediate goods to sector j is identical to the sum of the value of domestically produced intermediate goods (at domestic prices) and the import value of intermediate goods. Hence, p_j^z is defined as

$$p_j^z = \sum_{i=1}^{23} \left(p_i^{qh}(\omega_{ij} - \omega_{ij}^m) + p_i^m \omega_{ij}^m \right) / \sum_{i=1}^{23} \omega_{ij} \quad j = 1, \ldots, 23,$$ (7.6)

where ω_{ij} are the elements of the input-output matrix Ω, and ω_{ij}^m are the elements of the import matrix, Ω^m. The latter is a matrix describing

---

[10] These hypothetical restrictions were not supported by the econometric results for 12 of 18 sectors, although the sum of the coefficients was close to one. In these cases the equations were reestimated without the theoretical restrictions.

the proportion of imports from sector i abroad needed in production in sector j.[11]

It is now possible to calculate the price vector facing the consumers, p, by weighing domestic and import prices with their respective shares of private consumption; namely,

$$p_i = p_i^{qh} \left(1 - \omega_{i,c}^m\right) + p_i^m \omega_{i,c}^m \qquad i = 1,\ldots,23, \qquad (7.7)$$

where $\omega_{i,c}^m$ is the import share in final private consumption.

As noted above, the distribution of consumption is estimated for commodity groups other than those of the industrial sectors. Thus the prices above have to be transformed to the appropriate consumption baskets, according to

$$p^v = p\xi \qquad (7.8)$$

The aggregate consumer price index, P, is defined by

$$\sum_i p_i^v c_i^v / \sum_i c_i^v . \qquad (7.9)$$

Finally, we see that the endogenous prices must be solved simultaneously with the entire model, since q, w and m are arguments in the price equations.

8.   Labour market

Total labour demand or employment, L, measured in hours, is the sum of employment in the industrial and government sectors, i.e.,

$$L = L^p + L^g . \qquad (8.1)$$

Employment in the industries L^p, is given by

$$L^p = \sum_{i=1}^{24} e_i y_i^f , \qquad (8.2)$$

where e_i is the labour requirement per unit of value-added, i.e., the inverse of labour productivity.

---

[11] Ω is exogenous in EMMA, although a priori the matrix should of course be dependent on relative prices.

Employment in the government sector, L^g, is determined in a manner similar to government consumption.

$$L^g = \sum_{j=1}^{15} L_j^b + \lambda \left(g^{b_2} + \gamma^u G \right) , \qquad (8.3)$$

where L_j^b is the employment level necessary to meet basic social requirements, λ is a vector transforming government expenditures to employment, g^{b_2}, γ^u, and G are defined in section 5 above.

The labour supply (in hours), L^s, is exogenously given from demographic data and assessments of participation rates. Finally, the unemployment (in hours) is given by

$$U = L^s - L . \qquad (8.4)$$

9.   Summary

As we have seen above, the model is solved for the vector q (gross output of industries) GDP, the consumption of 11 items, export and import for all industries, the current account, employment and unemployment, consumer, domestic, export and intermediate goods prices as well as a consumer price index.

At the same time a great number of variables are exogenously set, e.g., the input-output matrix, the labour productivities, the rate of wage increase, the real level of consumption, private investments and all government expenditures.

A major merit of EMMA is its ability to provide a framework for checking the consistency of different forecasts made in the Ministry of Finance in connection with the Medium-Term Surveys. The model also serves as an instrument for revising a particular projection.

EMMA can be used to set targets for the rate of wage increase and private or government consumption levels consistent with full employment and equilibrium in the current account at a future point of time. This is, in fact, the application for which EMMA has been used most frequently in the last Medium-Term Surveys. The model does not provide direct policy options in the usual sense to accomplish the goals of full employment and current account equilibrium, as certain important economic relationships are not included in the model, (e.g., models for wage formation, total private consumption or effects via the financial markets on investments and consumption). Another problem is that as the stock of capital is not included, capacity does not set any limits to production nor does production reach the limits of capacity-induced inflation.

Appendix 1   List of variables in EMMA

SECTOR	NAME
	Industries:
1	Agriculture and fishing
2	Forestry
3	Mining and quarrying
4	Sheltered food industry
5	Non-sheltered food industry
6	Beverage and tobacco industry
7	Textile and clothing industry
8	Wood, pulp and paper industry
9	Printing industry
10	Rubber products industry
11	Chemical industry
12	Petroleum and coal industry
13	Non-metallic mineral products industry
14	Basic metal industries
15	Engineering (excluding shipyards)
16	Shipyards
17	Other manufacturing industries
18	Electricity, gas, heating and water
19	Construction
20	Wholesale and retail trade
21	Transport and communication
22	Housing management
23	Private services
24	Foreign tourist services

SECTOR	NAME
	Government consumption and investment purposes:
	Central:
1	Defence
2	Judiciary
3	Education
4	Health service
5	Social welfare
6	Road administration
7	Other
14	Without purpose
	Local:
8	Judiciary
9	Education
10	Health service
11	Social welfare
12	Road administration
13	Other
15	Without purpose
	Consumption items:
1	Food
2	Beverage
3	Clothing
4	Culture goods and services
5	Hygiene and health care
6	Housing services
7	Transport and communications
8	Hobby articles
9	Furniture and interior design
10	Other goods and services
11	Energy

References

Bruno, M. [1979], "Price and Output Adjustment: Micro foundations and aggregation", *Journal of Monetary Economics, 187–211.*

Deaton, A. and Muellbauer [1980], *Economics and Consumer Behavior and Demand Analysis.* Cambridge: Cambridge University Press.

Forslund, A. and Lindh, Y. [1984], "Prisbildning på sektornivå", LU 84, Bilaga 16, SOU 1984:3.

Markowski, A. [1984], "Tjänestehandelns och transfereringarnas inkomst- och priskänslighet", LU 84, Bilaga 15, SOU 1984:7.

Ministry of Finance [1984], "An econometric Model for Medium-term Analysis (EMMA)", in *The 1984 Medium Term Survey of the Swedish Economy* (translation) of Appendix 17 in LU 84, SOU 1984:7.

Ministry of Finance [1976], "Långtidsutredningens modellsystem", LU 75, Bilaga 8, SOU 1976:42.

National Institute of Economic Research [1984], "Export och import av varor", LU 84, Bilaga 14, SOU 1984:7.

Stone, J.R.N. [1954], "Linear Expenditure Systems and Demand Analysis: an Application to the Pattern of British Demand", *Economic Journal, 64,* 511–527.

Åberg, C. J. [1971], "Plan och prognos — En studie i långtidsutrednings- arnas metodik", LU 70, Bilaga 9, SOU 1971:70.

Macroeconomic Medium-Term Models in the Nordic Countries
O. Bjerkholt and J. Rosted (Editors)
© Elsevier Science Publishers B. V. (North-Holland), 1987

An Aggregate Model
for
Medium-Term Analysis (AMMA)

by

Leif Jansson and Thomas Olofsson
Ministry of Finance,
Stockholm, Sweden

1. Introduction

AMMA — An Aggregate Model for Medium-Term Analysis — is one of the
two models used for medium-term prognoses at the Ministry of Finance in
Sweden.[1] AMMA is a medium-term model for analysing different policy
strategies and requirements for economic policy, given certain policy goals.
The model is dynamic, i.e., the solution of one period in the model depends
on the solutions in previous periods, and in this way describes a possible
path for the economy during the medium term. By making different assumptions regarding, for example, the development of wages, government
expenditures or the exchange rate, it is possible to trace the development
of GDP, unemployment and the balance of trade over time. The model
comprises five industries and a government sector. Private consumption,
exports, imports, employment, prices and wages are determined by econometrically estimated behavioural equations.

AMMA also contains a detailed description of financial revenues and
expenditures for institutional sectors. The financial part of the model,

---

[1] The dynamic version of AMMA was originally formulated by Leif Jansson and the
financial submodel, FIMO, by Thomas Nordström, both at the Ministry of Finance.
The model has been revised continuously since its creation and has also been used
in the annual Revised National Budget. We are grateful to Lars Heikensten for
comments on earlier drafts.

called FIMO, affects the real variables through household incomes, which in turn determine private consumption. Furthermore, the operating surplus of enterprises affects investments.

The next section gives a brief overview of the model and presents the input-output balance equation, from which can be solved the levels of production of five industries needed to meet final demand from the private, government and foreign sectors. In the following sections the labour market, private consumption and private investments are discussed and in section 6 the determination of the components of the balance of trade, exports and imports, is described. Section 7 completes the description of the model by covering wages and prices in the model. Sections 8 and 9 present the results of simulations of devaluations and wage decreases and fiscal multipliers, respectively.

2.   An overview of the model

AMMA is a model for an open economy with five industries producing goods and services. The private (industrial and household) and government sectors demand output from domestic and foreign industries, for intermediate deliveries and for final uses. In addition, central and local government also produce services.

In the input-output balance equation gross outputs from the five industries are set equal to the sum of demand for domestically produced products which are wanted for intermediate uses and for export, investment and consumption purposes. We have

$$q = \Omega q + c + i + g + x - m \,, \tag{2.1}$$

where q is a vector of gross production in five industries, Ω is a 5×5 input-output matrix whose elements, ω_{ij}, denote the units of commodity i needed to produce one unit of commodity j, c is private consumption, i is private investment, g is local and central government demand for investment and consumption purposes, x is export and m is import.

Value added at purchasers' values for industry j is defined as

$$y_j = q_j \left(1 - \sum_{i=1}^{5} \omega_{ij} \right) \qquad j = 1, \ldots, 5 \,. \tag{2.2}$$

Total deliveries for final demand from the industries, $d = c + i + g + x - m$, equal total value added in industry. GDP is the sum of value added in industry and value added produced in the (central and local) government sector, g^{va}. This gives us

$$GDP = \sum_{i=1}^{5} y_i + g^{va} \, . \tag{2.3}$$

In the model prices and wage rates are endogenously determined. In industry 2 — mining and manufacturing — prices and wage rates are determined by econometric equations. In the other industries prices are calculated as a constant mark-up on unit costs, while the growth rate of wages in the rest of the economy is related to that of industry 2. Total consumption is determined by an exogenous saving rate and real disposable income. Employment in industry 2 and 5 (private services) is obtained by a version of Okun's law. Finally, the balance of trade is determined primarily as a function of domestic and foreign income and relative prices.

The financial model, FIMO, is solved simultaneously with AMMA. It comprises seven institutional sectors: central and local government, social security funds, households, financial enterprises, non-financial enterprises and the foreign sector. There are no feedbacks from the financial part to the rest of the model apart from the household sector's determinations of private consumption.

3.   The labour market

Projections of the labour supply, specified as the number of persons in the labour force, N^s, and the average working-hours per employee, h, are supplied by *Statistics, Sweden* in a special study done for the Medium-Term Survey.

For the two main industries, mining and manufacturing (no. 2) and private services (no. 5), the rate of growth of labour demand in hours, L, is a function of the growth rate of value added, y, with a one year lag, i.e., Okun's law with a one year lag in production. Formally, we write this as

$$\dot{L}_i = \beta_i \big(\dot{y}_i(-1) - \alpha_i \big) \qquad i = 2, 5 \, , \tag{3.1}$$

where α_i is the growth rate needed to maintain employment at a constant level and b is the output elasticity of employment. The level of employment in mining and manufacturing is obtained as

$$L_2 = L_2(-1) + .37_i \big(\dot{y}_2(-1) - .45_i \big) L_2(-1) \, , \tag{3.2}$$

Specifications in AMMA

Industries:

1 Agriculture and forestry
2 Mining and manufacturing
3 Electricity, gas heating and water
4 Construction
5 Private services

Government sectors:

gc Central government
gl Local government

Investment categories:

Mining and manufacturing
Electricity, gas, heating and water (energy)
Housing
Other branches of industry
Central government
Local government
Inventory stocks

Export categories:

r Raw materials
g Manufactured goods (goods other than raw materials)
s Private services

Import categories:

g Goods (excluding crude oil and petroleum products)
o Crude oil and petroleum products
s Private services

and in private services as

$$L_5 = L_5(-1) + .39\ddot{y}_5(-1)L_5(-1).$$

(3.3)

An increase in production is thus followed by a simultaneous increase in labour productivity. Note also that the employment as given by (3.2) and (3.3) is predetermined by lagged production changes but not affected by the current growth rate.

Government labour demand is given exogenously. Industry demand for labour in sectors 1, 3 and 4 are functions of labour productivity and production, or alternatively, are exogenously given. Total labour demand (in number of workers) can now be written as

$$N = \left(L^g + \sum_{i}^{1,3,4} e_i Y_i + \sum_{i}^{2,5} L_i \right) \Big/ h,$$

(3.4)

where e_j is the exogenously determined labour requirement per unit of value-added, i.e., the inverse of labour productivity and L^g is (central and local) government employment in terms of the number of working-hours in a man-year. Finally, unemployment is by definition

$$U = N^s - N.$$

(3.5)

4. Private consumption

Total private consumption, c^d, is assumed to be a function of current real disposable income. The latter is defined in AMMA as the sum of labour income, pensions, net "interest" payments (on securities in a broad sense) and other transfers less taxes. Disposable nominal income, Y_D, is calculated by a sub-model in AMMA called FIMO. The main features of FIMO relevant to household incomes are described by the following equation.

$$Y_D = wL + \kappa B + r_A A - r_R R + T^r - (T^x_{-1} + t_m \Delta Y^t),$$

(4.1)

where w is the vector $(w_1, \ldots, w_5, w_{gl}, w_{gc})$ of average wage rates per hour (indices gl and gc refer to local and central government respectively), L is the vector $(L_1, \ldots, L_5, L_{gl}, L_{gc})$ of employment in hours, κ is pensions (exogenously given) measured in "basic units", B, r_A and r_R are interest rates on assets, A, and liabilities, R, respectively, T^r is other transfers, T^x is income taxes, t_m is the "macro" marginal tax rate, and Y^t is taxable income. Pension payments are calculated in inflation adjusted "basic units" (B). The stock of assets is calculated as a constant proportion of disposable income. The stock of liabilities is calculated as the previous year's stock plus the change in the stock of assets less financial savings, i.e., $R = R_{-1} + \Delta A - (Y_D - c^d - i^c)$, where i is households net real savings (investments). T^r includes imputed income from owner occupied housing (assumed constant in real terms, sickness benefits, unemployment benefits and other social benefits such as child allowances.

Total consumption, c^d, is determined as

$$c^d = (1 - s)Y_D/p_c, \qquad (4.2)$$

where s is the exogenous rate of savings (average propensity to save) and p_c is the consumer price.

Consumption demand by industry is found by constant shares.

$$c = \xi c^d, \qquad (4.3)$$

where the vector ξ is based on historical input-output data.

5.   Private investments

Investment projections in AMMA are all exogenous and broken down in seven categories. Investment forecasts for mining and manufacturing are based on a lagged accelerator principle and relative profitability.[2]

$$i_2 = \alpha + 1.35 \sum_{\tau=0}^{4} v_\tau \Delta y^f_{2,t-\tau} + 0.09K_2 + 0.002K_2(r_{2K} - r_F), \qquad (5.1)$$

where K_2 is the capital stock, r_{2k} is the rate of return on material capital (two-year average) and r_F is the rate of return on financial investments (two-year average). As a proxy for the latter, return on government long-term bonds has been used.

---

[2] A special study, by Hans Olsson, has been done for the MS 84 regarding profitability, investments and financing in the private sector with special emphasis on industrial development. In this study the capital stock included in (5.1) has also been calculated for the relevant period. See "Näringslivets lönsomhet, investeringar och finansering", Appendix 13 to *Långtidsutredningen 84*, SOU 1984:6.

The rate of return on capital is a function of gross profits, defined as value added valued at factor cost less wages, depreciation and the rate of inflation according to

$$r_{2K} = \left[y_2^f - W_2 L_2 + \Delta p_{iv} K_2(-1) - p_{iv} \delta_2 K_2(-1) \right] / p_{iv}(K_2 + S_2), \quad (5.2)$$

where δ_2 is the rate of physical depreciation of capital, S_2 is the stock of inventories and p_{iv} is the (implicit) price of investment goods.

This model has not produced very reliable forecasts, however, and the equation is only used as a basis for investment projections in AMMA.

The investment demand by industry

$$i = \phi \, i^d, \quad (5.3)$$

where i^d is the investment by seven categories.

6. Balance of trade

Exports are divided into three groups: raw-materials, x_r, manufactured goods x_g, and services, x_s. Export volumes and prices of raw materials are set exogenously in AMMA.

For the other two groups we assume that firms are facing a negatively sloped demand curve. Exports are a function of relative prices, world market demand and a time trend indicating changes in the world market due to, e.g., trade liberalization, the composition of exports and growing competition. In addition π_2, an endogenously determined profit variable with a two year lag, is included in the equation for the export of manufactured goods.

$$x_g = e^{-.007} t x_g^w \left[\frac{p_g^x}{p_g^w} \right]^{-1.01} \left[\frac{p_g^x}{p_g^w} \right]_{-1}^{-.76} \left[\frac{p_g^x}{p_g^w} \right]_{-2}^{-.18} (\pi_{2_{-2}})^{2.02} \quad (6.1)$$

$$x_s = e^{\alpha t} x_s^w \left[\frac{p_s^x}{p_s^w} \right]^{-.98} \left[\frac{p_s^x}{p_s^w} \right]_{-1}^{-.18} \quad (6.2)$$

where x_g^w and x_s^w are exogenous world market demand for domestic exports (depending primarily on world income), p^x and p^w are export prices and the world market prices, respectively.

The profit variable for sector 2 is defined as

$$\pi_2 = p_2^q q_2 / \left[p_2^q q_2 - (y_2^f - w_2 L_2) \right], \quad (6.3)$$

where p_2^q is the product price and y_2^f is the value added at factor cost in industry 2.

Imports are also divided into three groups: goods (manufactured and raw-materials, excluding crude oil and petroleum products), m_g, crude oil and petroleum products, m_0, and services, m_s. All three categories of imports depend upon domestic income and a time trend. The import of goods and services are also assumed to depend on relative prices. In the equation for the import of goods the profit variable defined above and exogenous capacity utilization, CU_2, are included as well. We have

$$m_g = e^{.025t} m_g^{y1.24} \left[\frac{p_g^h}{p_g^m}\right]^{.72} \left[\frac{p_g^h}{p_g^m}\right]_{-1}^{.53} \left[\frac{p_g^h}{p_g^m}\right]_{-2}^{.52} \pi_2^{-.75} CU_2^{.13}, \quad (6.4)$$

$$m_0 = e^{.035t} m_0^y \quad (6.5)$$

$$m_s = e^{\alpha t} m_s^y \left[\frac{p_s^h}{p_s^m}\right]^{.78} \left[\frac{p_s^h}{p_s^m}\right]_{-1}^{.39} \left[\frac{p_s^h}{p_s^m}\right]_{-2}^{.13} \quad (6.6)$$

where the m^y's are measures of domestic demand for imports, p^m is import prices and p^h is domestic import competing prices.

The balance of trade, BT, is defined as the difference between the values of export and import of goods and services.

$$BT = p_g^x x_g + p_r^x x_r + p_s^x x_s - (p_g^m m_g + p_0^m m_0 + p_s^m m_s), \quad (6.7)$$

Export and import demand by industry is

$$x = \Omega^x x^d \quad \text{and} \quad m = \Omega^m m^d, \quad (6.8)$$

where $x^d = (x_g, x_r, x_s)$ and $m^d = (m_g, m_0, m_s)$. The matrices Ω^x and Ω^m are based on input-output data.

7.   Prices and wages

To solve the model we need the price vectors introduced already: the consumer price p_{cm}, the price of investment goods, p_{iv}, and p_g^x, p_s^x, p_r^x, p_g^w, p_s^w, p_g^h, p_s^h, p_g^m, p_0^m and p_s^m in the balance-of-trade equations.

Product prices, p_2^q, and hourly wage rates w_2, in industry 2 are determined jointly by the following equations[3]:

$$w_2 = w_2(-1).059(\widehat{p_2^q})^{02}(\widehat{p_2^q}(-1))^{.56}(U(-1))^{.11}(\widehat{t^{px}})^{-.15}(\widehat{t^{dx}})^{-.28} \quad (7.1)$$

$$p_2^q = p_2^q(-1).012(\widehat{w_2^{px}})^{.18}(\widehat{y_2^f}(-1))^{.46}(\widehat{p_g^m})^{.54}, \quad (7.2)$$

where U is unemployment determined in section 3 above, t^{px} is $(1+$ the payroll tax rate), t^{dx} is $(1-$ direct tax rate for the mean wage), w_2^{px} is $w_2 \cdot t^{px}$, and p_g^m is the import price of goods. "$(\frown)$"denotes one plus the rate of change).

The price level is thus a function of cost factors, such as the wage rate and the import price. The latter variable also reflects a dependence of the world prices level. Demand factors are captured by the rate of growth of production in the price equation and by the level of unemployment in the wage equation which includes prices as a proxy for inflationary expectations or, by an alternative interpretation, profits.

The wage rate for each of the other sectors are proportional to w_2

$$w_i = \lambda_i w_2 \qquad i = 1, \ldots, 5, gc, gl, \quad (7.3)$$

where indices gc and gl denote central and local government sectors respectively. The implication of the assumption made in (7.3) is that the overall rate of wage increase is determined by the wage formation in the "wage-setting"industry.

Other industrial prices are determined by a simple mark-up procedure. Prices are set equal to the sum of costs of domestically produced and imported intermediate goods and labour costs per unit and a profit mark-up.

$$p_j^q = \sum_{i=1}^{5}\left[p_i^{qh}\omega_{ij}^h + \sum_k p_k^m \omega_{ijk}^m\right] + t_j^{px}w_j L_j/(\varrho_j q_j) \qquad j = 1, \ldots, 5, \quad (7.4)$$

where p_i^{qh} is the price of domestically produced goods, p_k^m is the import price, ω_{ij} is the share of intermediate goods delivered from sector i to sector j where the indices h and m denote domestic and imported products respectively, and k varies over g, o and s), L is employment and ϱ is the exogenous wage income share of (nominal) value added, i.e., $\varrho_j = (wL/y^f)_j$.

---

[3] For a derivation of these equations, see Holmlund, B. [1982], *Payroll Taxes and Wage Inflation: The Swedish Experience*, Working Paper No 68, Industrins Utrednings-institut, Stockholm.

In (7.4) above we introduced prices not yet defined, namely the domestic prices, p_i^{qh}. By definition, the value of total output of an industry must equal the sum of the value of domestically sold output— at domestic prices — and the value of exports, i.e.,

$$p_i^q q_i = p_i^{qh}(q_i - x_i) + p_i^x x i \qquad i = 1, \ldots, 5. \tag{7.5}$$

To solve for p_i^{qh} we need the export price of each industry. As pointed out above the price of raw materials, p_r^x, is exogenous. We assume that the export price of manufactured goods is in constant proportion to the industry's domestic price, p_i^{qh}, i.e.,

$$p_{gi}^x = \mu_i p_i^{qh} \qquad i = 1, \ldots, 3. \tag{7.6}$$

The export prices by industry, p^x, are then

$$p_i^x = (\mu_i p_{gi}^{qh} x_{gi} + p_r^w x_{ri})/x_i \qquad i = 1, \ldots, 3, \tag{7.7}$$

where x_i is the respective sector's total export. The export price of industry 5 (services) is given by $p_5^x = \mu_5 p_5^{qh}$. We also note in passing that industry 4 has no exports, so $p_4^{qh} = p_4^q$. The prices by export categories are

$$p_g^x = \sum_{i=1}^{3}\left[\mu_i p_i^{qh} x_{gi}/ \sum_{k=1}^{3} x_{gk}\right]. \tag{7.8}$$

The export price of services, p_s^x, will simply be $p_s^x = \mu_5 p_5^{qh}$, as industry 5 is identical to the service sector.

The import competing prices for goods are determined similarly.

$$p_g^h = \sum_{i=1}^{3}\left[p_i^{qh} m_{gi}/ \sum_{k=g}^{o,s} m_{gk}\right] \tag{7.9}$$

and for the service sector $p_s^h = p_5^{qh}$.

Finally the consumer prices, p_c, (and the prices for investment goods, p_{iv}, and products bought by local and central government, p_{gl} and p_{gc}, respectively) are obtained by weighing domestically produced and imported products by their respective shares in final consumptions, ω^h and ω^m:

$$p_j = \sum_{i=1}^{5}\left[p_j^{qh}\omega_{ij}^h + \sum_{k=g}^{o,s} p_k^m \omega_{ijk}^m\right] \qquad j = c, iv, gc, gl. \tag{7.10}$$

This completes the model presentation. As mentioned above private investments and government expenditures are not solved for in AMMA, but are determined outside the model. The main variables solved by the model are production in each of the industries as well as GDP, employment, unemployment, private consumption, the balance of trade, prices and wages by industry and hence the rate of inflation, and the development of export and import competing prices. The financial part of the model calculates profitability in the manufacturing sector and financial savings in each of the seven institutional sectors of the model.

It must be emphasized that AMMA is still only a preliminary framework for medium-term analysis, as many important economic relations are not included in the model. Labour supply and interest rates are, for example, not endogenized in the present formulation of the model and the savings ratio is exogenous. This implies that the interaction of the latter variables with the model must be subject to careful considerations if it is to produce reasonable values of the exogenous variables. At present efforts are being made to incorporate labour supply functions and the relationship of domestic interest rates to international rates.

In spite of the shortcomings of the model, it does provide a framework for making consistent analyses, calculations and tests of different projections of economic development. AMMA, including FIMO, also provides an opportunity for analysing the effects of specific economic scenarios on financial variables, such as the budget deficit and the profitability in the manufacturing sector.

8.   Simulations of devaluation and wage decreases

During the seventies Swedish producers lost their competitiveness on the international market. A contributing factor was the relative rise of costs and prices which caused a diminishing demand for domestically produced goods and services, squeezed profit margins and sharply reduced investments.

In order to adjust the internal cost situation the currency was devalued in 1976–1977. The inflation rate in Sweden remained above that of its main competitors and as a result, real growth stagnated in Sweden, particularly in manufacturing. The outcome of this devaluation is in accordance with the experiences of other countries: a devaluation not followed by a restrictive policy dampening inflation will at best have a minor and temporary positive effect in restoring competitiveness.

Another way to improve competitiveness is by decreasing the growth rate of nominal wages, either by an income policy or by a non-accommodating policy. Both measures have their drawbacks: An income policy implies intervention in free wage negotiations, while a non-accommodation policy may lead to depreciation of both human and material capital. Much is to be gained if a successful consensus policy can restrain the nominal wage growth.

As a basis for analysis of the effects of devaluations and decreases in wage costs, three simulations have been undertaken. One shows the results of a depreciation of the Swedish currency, the other two show a decrease in the wage rate both with and without an expansive fiscal policy. The results are presented as deviations from a baseline projection which covers the period 1984–1987.[4]

Table 1 and 2 present the effects of a 1% decrease in the exchange rate and the wage rate in 1984.

Wage reduction

The impact on GDP of a reduction in the wage rate is positive and increases over time. In 1987 the effect on GDP of the wage reduction is calculated 1.3 billion Skr. (1980-prices), which is the net result of counteracting effects from a decrease in private consumption of 0.2 billion Skr. and an increase of net exports and industry investments of 1.4 and 0.1 billion Skr., respectively.

Private consumption falls with a nominal decrease of the wage rate since wage income falls. In real terms, the effect is reduced since the inflation rate also diminishes and the negative effect is reduced over time mainly because employment increases.

The main impact on GDP comes from the improvement of net exports. The increased net exports are thus a result of reduced terms of trade and improved profit margins (see table 2). The positive effects are reduced by an increase in capacity utilization.

Employment in the private sector is determined by the employment functions described in section 3. The employment level depends on the production level in the previous year. The employment elasticity with respect to lagged production is approximately 0.4 for the manufacturing and approximately 0.5 for the private service sector. The elasticity with respect

---

[4] The baseline projection is the reference alternative presented in "The 1984 Medium-Term Survey of the Swedish Economy", Ministry of Finance, 1984.

Table 1: Real and price effects of a 1% decrease in the exchange rate and the nominal wage rate.

		Year			
		1984	1985	1986	1987
GDP	Wage 1	0.1	0.2	0.2	0.2
	Exchange rate	0.1	0.1	0.2	0.2
	Wage 2	0.1	0.4	0.5	0.6
Private	Wage 1	−0.1	−0.1	−0.1	−0.1
consumption	Exchange rate	−0.2	−0.2	−0.2	−0.1
	Wage 2	−0.1	−0.5	−0.7	−0.9
Export	Wage 1	0.2	0.3	0.3	0.3
volume	Exchange rate	0.3	0.5	0.5	0.4
	Wage 2	0.2	0.3	0.3	0.3
Import	Wage 1	−0.1	−0.3	−0.4	−0.5
volume	Exchange rate	−0.2	−0.3	−0.3	−0.3
	Wage 2	−0.1	−0.0	−0.0	−0.0
Employment	Wage 1	0.0	0.0	0.1	0.1
	Exchange rate	0.0	0.0	0.1	0.1
	Wage 2	0.0	0.0	0.2	0.3
Consumer	Wage 1	−0.5	−0.6	−0.5	−0.5
prices	Exchange rate	0.4	0.5	0.5	0.6
	Wage 2	−0.5	−0.7	−0.6	−0.6
Export	Wage 1	−0.3	−0.3	−0.3	−0.3
prices	Exchange rate	0.5	0.6	0.6	0.7
	Wage 2	−0.3	−0.3	−0.3	−0.3

Note: Exchange rate refers to a 1% decrease in the exchange rate. Wage 1 refers to a 1% decrease in the nominal wage rate *without* expansive fiscal policy and Wage 2 to the same decrease *with* expansive fiscal policy model.

to GDP, when public consumption remains unchanged, is approximately 0.5.

Manufacturing prices depend on a trend factor, hourly wage cost, last

Table 2: Financial effects of a 1% decrease in the exchange rate and the nominal wage rate.

		Year			
		1984	1985	1986	1987
Budget balance central government (billion Skr.)	Wage 1	−2.4	−2.3	−0.3	0.6
	Exchange rate	0.1	0.8	1.4	1.0
	Wage 2	−2.9	−5.5	−3.9	−6.9
Financial savings public sector (billion Skr.)	Wage 1	−1.4	−1.1	−0.8	−0.8
	Exchange rate	−0.2	0.3	0.7	0.9
	Wage 2	−2.0	−3.9	−3.5	−4.0
Balance on current account (billion Skr.)	Wage 1	0.2	1.0	1.3	1.6
	Exchange rate	0.2	1.5	1.5	1.4
	Wage 2	0.0	0.0	0.0	0.0
Gross profit share in manufacturing (percentage point)	Wage 1	1.1	1.3	1.3	1.4
	Exchange rate	0.4	0.5	0.3	0.3
	Wage 2	2.1	3.3	3.3	2.9

Note: Exchange rate refers to a 1% decrease in the exchange rate. Wage 1 refers to a 1% decrease in the nominal wage rate *without* expansive fiscal policy and Wage 2 to the same decrease *with* expansive fiscal policy model.

year's prices and import prices. The price elasticities of wage cost, lagged price and import price are 0.16, 0.07 and 0.54, respectively. In the other industries prices are determined from costs and exogenous gross profit margins. The reduction in the nominal wage rate will thus primarily reduce prices in the private sector, excluding manufacturing. In manufacturing the price reduction is smaller since the estimated elasticity of the hourly wage cost is about half of the wage cost share and a wage reduction will thus partly reduce prices and partly increase the profit margins. The export price of noncompetitive goods are exogenous and the export price of competitive goods follows closely the manufacturing price. This explains the relatively low elasticity of export prices with respect to the wage rate.

The effect on financial variables are presented in table 2. The lower level will initially have a negative effect on public sector income because the tax base deteriorates. The negative impact is further strengthened by the way the Swedish system for tax payments is constructed. The progressive income tax rates are not inflation adjusted. This results in the reduced ratio of taxes to wage income when the hourly wage decreases. The lower wage rate will, on the other hand, reduce public expenditures. The net effect is negative. Financial saving in the public sector gradually improves over time because of increased tax receipts from enterprises as higher profits and increased employment enlarge the tax base.

The central government budget balance falls by more than 2 billion Skr. the first two years and thereafter improves sharply. The balance of current account is almost unaffected at first, but improves over time as the lagged impact of the wage cost reduction on net export volume will dominate over the improved terms of trade.

Devaluation

As a result of devaluation the economy develops in real terms rather similar to the wage reduction case. The differing price development, however, implies different effects on the financial accounts. The higher inflation rate increases the central government tax ratio. Thus financial savings in the public sector improve in the medium term perspective.

The gross profit share in manufacturing shows just a small increase. The price in manufacturing rises initially by 0.5% due to the predicted effect of a 1% increase in the import price (national currency). But the increased costs of imports also raise the price of all intermediate goods from the private sector. The net effect is a considerably smaller improvement in the gross profit share than in the case of a reduced wage rate.

Contrary to past experiences, AMMA thus predicts a positive medium term effect on real growth, balance of current account and employment from a reduced exchange rate. This is so because the inflationary impulse from the devaluation is assumed to leave the rate of growth of domestic prices unaffected.

Wage reduction and expansive fiscal policy

To illustrate the combined impact of a slower wage increase and a less restrictive fiscal policy a simulation was made where again the wage rate level was reduced by 1% once and for all in 1984 and private consumption is stimulated by increased transfers from the central government until the balance of current accounts is the same as in the baseline projection.

Employment and GDP increases three times more than in the case with unchanged fiscal policy due to the extra expansion of domestic demand. Inflation increases to some extent due to higher capacity utilization. The small increase in the inflation rate has negligible effects, however.

Evaluation of the simulations

Model forecasts like those presented above can at best serve as a starting point for further assessment of likely responses to policy measures. The relations incorporated in a model can always be questioned since the functioning of the economy might change over time and even carefully estimated equations might be outdated.

The simulation results depend to a great extent on the modeling of price and cost formation. A severe shortcoming in AMMA when distinguishing between reactions of a devaluation and a wage decrease is the absence of price expectations as an influence on the rate of inflation. Deficits in financial savings in the public sector and in the balance of current account may have direct influence on prices via expectations. Such relations are not included in the model. The lagged influences between wages, unemployment and prices are not adequate to describe how prices adapt to costs and wages. The model predicts a sustained improvement of our relative prices in response to a reduced exchange rate and apart from an initial rise in the domestic price level the inflation rate is little affected thereafter. But the experience from the devaluations during the seventies in Sweden is that the inflationary impulses more or less permanently increased the domestic inflation rate above that of its main competitors. A change of the exchange rate not met by policy measures to restrain the ensuring price and cost development is likely to erode the competitive advantages gained. A reduction in the wage level on the other hand might influence price expectations in a reverse direction and more permanently bring the inflation rate down.

The interest rate is exogenous in AMMA which also makes the results less realistic. Even if the domestic interest rate is strongly influenced by the international rate of interest in a small open economy, its relative level should depend on such factors as public sector budget deficits, balance of payments and domestic inflation.

Import prices are exogenous in AMMA and follow world market prices. Experiences from the past decade, however, show a strong tendency among the importers to adjust their prices towards domestic producer prices. Therefore, the immediate inflationary impulse from a devaluation is probably overestimated. Whether the competitive advantage for domestic producers is overestimated is more difficult to say. The relative price effect is overstated but on the other hand the squeezed profits of the importers on the Swedish market will have a negative supply effect.

The calculations of income and expenditure in the financial block are quite detailed and the institutional bindings are modelled thoroughly. As far as possible income and expenditure entries are made dependent upon the development of volumes, prices and wages. The calculation of direct taxes does not differentiate, however, between the tax effect of an increase in average income, on the one hand, and an increase in the number of income earners, on the other. The macro marginal tax rate is, of course, higher in the former case. Available data does not allow separate tax functions for different income categories, e.g., pensioners and others.

Gross investments in manufacturing depend on expected growth of production, return on material capital relative to the return on financial investments and a constant depreciation rate. The link between investments and the change in production capacity goes via a homogeneous stock of capital and an exogenous capital-output ratio. No production function is incorporated which simultaneously relates the use of capital and labour to production. The simple approach taken in AMMA implies that a given growth of investments determines the capacity change irrespective of how the relative prices of capital and labour evolve. Moreover, the lack of a vintage structure makes productivity changes independent of the investment intensity. These shortcomings will cause an underestimation of the differences between a wage rate and an exchange rate reduction. But in a perspective as short as four years, the effects from vintage capital and capital-labour substitution should be minor. A more severe consequence is that, with such a simple capacity growth model, AMMA is less suitable for separating Keynesian unemployment from classical.

Labour supply in AMMA is exogenous and thus independent of wages, prices and labour demand. Such variables probably do affect the supply side but the influence is difficult to verify econometrically. Moreover the labour force is homogeneous in the model which makes it impossible to distinguish between demand and supply of skilled workers. This is a marked shortcoming, since expansion in several branches is often more restrained by lack of skilled workers than by lack of productive capital.

The trade-off between real wages and employment is studied under the assumptions of an unchanged and expansive fiscal policy, respectively. The latter experiment is carried out as an exogenous decrease in nominal wages positively affecting the external balance. The impact on employment is evaluated through the expansion of domestic demand (via an increase in private consumption) to restore the initial external balance. External balance thus being treated as a binding constraint.

The results are as follows. The short run elasticity of employment with respect to real wages are negligible for both unchanged and expansive fiscal policy. The medium-term elasticities are −.2 and −.8 with respect to unchanged and expansive fiscal policy respectively. The latter being considerably smaller than the long-run elasticity reported by Drèze and Modigliani [1981], whose estimates are in the neighbourhood of −2.

The small elasticity calculated by AMMA is basically explained by the small elasticity of employment with respect to production, due to the fact that the employment functions for the manufacturing and the private service sectors are designed to model employment output relations over business cycles rather than the long run, in combination with the balance of trade constraint being satisfied by an expansion of private consumption which is quite intensive in imports.

9.   Fiscal multipliers in AMMA

In this section the impacts of three policy instruments are evaluated by means of AMMAs

- Government investments
- Government consumption
- Transfers to households

Each of these expenditure items is assumed to increase by 1% of GDP in 1984. The increased level is sustained throughout the forecasting period. The calculations have been made under two assumptions about the way the expansive policy is financed. In the first alternative, the expansion is assumed to be financed by an increase in money supply. In the other alternative the expansive policy is financed by increased indirect taxes, i.e., by a higher VAT.

To improve the realism of the calculated results to some extent, the labour supply is assumed to be affected by an increased demand for labour. The labour supply has exogenously been increased by half of the increase in employment. The tax function has been corrected so that the increase of wages, which is due to increased employment, is taxed by the average tax ratio (about 40%). The increment of wages due to higher wage rates, on the other hand, is taxed by the marginal tax ratio (about 60%).

Table 3 presents the "medium-term" multipliers for the three policy measures and both financing alternatives. The "medium-term" multiplier refers to the effects in 1987 of a once and for all increase of the level of demand in 1984.

The real side of the economy is affected most strongly by an increase in public consumption.

The lower rise in employment when government investments and transfers increase compared to the government consumption case is partly explained by rising productivity in the business sector which reduces the multiplier effect via income and private consumption. The greater import shares of industry as compared to government will also reduce the GDP effect. In the transfer case the impact on the real side of the economy is further reduced since net transfers to the household sector are only about half the original gross transfers because of increased taxes.

When the expansive policy actions are financed by borrowing, the net effects on GDP, employment and private consumption are positive. When increased VAT is used to finance the expansion, increases in public consumption still have a positive effect on GDP and employment. Higher public investments, on the other hand, merely shift domestic resource utilization from private consumption to investments. Extra transfers to households have hardly any effect on the real variables since the resulting increase of private consumption in nominal terms is deflated by a higher consumer price index.

The level of the GDP price index falls initially in the money supply case since higher production in the private sector increases productivity. The lagged influence of an increased utilization of the labour force will, however, raise the percentage growth of hourly wage rates from 1985 and onwards. In the government consumption case the increase in wage costs dominates the productivity effect beginning in 1985. In the other two cases the price level for the term year is not much influenced. The GDP deflator exceeds the baseline projection for the whole time period in all tax financed cases. When the impact on real activity is small, as in the transfer case, the price level is shifted upwards by increased VAT. The slopes of the price curves in the other two cases depend on the changes in productivity and wage costs.

The financial savings in the public sector deteriorate substantially when public investments increase, but only half of the decrease is passed on to the foreign sector. As a consequence, financial savings improve in the other sectors, particularly so in nonfinancial enterprises. Also in the case of increased transfers, financial savings improve in the rest of the economy. In

Table 3: The "medium-term" effect of an increase of 1% of GDP in the level of public investments, level of government consumption and taxed transfers to households.

Percentage	Financing	Public	Public	Transfers
GDP[1]	money supply	0.8	1.1	0.4
	taxes	0.0	0.8	0.0
Private consumption[1]	money supply	0.4	1.2	1.1
	taxes	−2.1	0.3	−0.1
Employment[1]	money supply	0.5	1.1	0.2
	taxes	0.2	1.0	0.0
GDP deflator[1]	money supply	0.2	1.0	−0.0
	taxes	1.6	1.4	0.6
Budget balance for central government[2]	money supply	−0.1	0.3	−0.9
	taxes	0.9	0.6	−0.4
Financial saving for public sector[2]	money supply	−0.9	−0.3	−0.4
	taxes	0.0	0.0	0.0
Balance of current account[2]	money supply	−0.4	−0.4	−0.2
	taxes	0.2	−0.2	0.1

Note: The table shows the effect in 1987 of a once and for all increase in the level of expenditure in 1984. Taxes refer to the value-added tax.

[1] Percentage change relative to the baseline projection.
[2] Percentage change relative to GDP in the baseline projection.

the case of expanded government consumption, financial savings decrease also in the private sector. Therefore, the current accounts balance falls more than the financial deficit in the public sector.

The reduction in private sector savings as a result of increased government consumption is due to a smaller operating surplus and larger investment costs for nonfinancial enterprises. The decrease in operating surplus is the net effect of increased profits in enterprises outside industry where gross profit margins are exogenous, and of diminished profits within industry where gross profit margins are endogenous. Higher investment costs are mainly due to the rise in domestic prices.

In the transfer case the actual government deficit falls sharply. This is because all tax income is paid to and registered as income by the central government. Local government taxes are then transferred with a delay of two years. In the government consumption and investment cases, no such sharp reduction of the deficit occurs since direct tax incomes continue to grow faster during the forecast period. The faster growth of the direct taxes depends on a higher growth rate of nominal wages, which in turn is a consequence of both higher wage rates and increased employment.

10.   Concluding remarks

There are several features in AMMA that make the calculated effects of fiscal policy actions less realistic. For one, the interest rate is exogenous in the model. Thus, there are no negative effects on real activity from an increased budget deficit via e.g., increased capital costs. In the case of increased borrowing it is implicitly assumed that the money supply is adjusted so that the interest rate remains unaffected.

The nominal expansion of public spending results in both increased real activity and price changes. The inflationary effects depend on changes in unit labour costs because of higher wage rate growth due to increased demand for labour and higher productivity. Initially, the GDP deflator falls because the productivity gains of the increased activity dominate and unit labour costs are lowered.

AMMA probably underestimates the inflation effect in the case of increased money supply for several reasons. The price setting of enterprises is, apart from changes in costs, likely to be influenced by changes in capacity utilization. This effect is not included in the calculations. Thus the demand effect on inflation is disregarded.

References

Drèze, J.H. and F. Modigliani [1981], "The trade off between real wages and employment in an open economy (Belgium)", *European Economic Review, 15*, 1–40.

Holmlund, B. [1982], "Payroll taxes and wage inflation: The Swedish experience", Working paper no. 68, Industrins Utredningsinstitutt, Stockholm.

Ministry of Finance [1984], "The 1984 medium term survey of the Swedish economy", Stockholm.

Olofsson, T. [1987], "An econometric model for medium-term analysis (EMMA)", in this volume.

SOU [1984], "Näringslivets lönsomhet, investeringar och finansiering", Appendix 13 til Långtidsutredningen, 84, SOU 1984: 6, Stockholm.

Subject index

Author index